Time Series Clustering and Classification

Chapman & Hall/CRC
Computer Science & Data Analysis Series

SERIES EDITORS
David Blei, Princeton University
David Madigan, Rutgers University
Marina Meila, University of Washington
Fionn Murtagh, Royal Holloway, University of London

Recently Published Titles
Time Series Clustering and Classification
Elizabeth Ann Maharaj, Pierpaolo D'Urso, Jorge Caiado

Bayesian Regression Modeling with INLA
Xiaofeng Wang, Yu Yue Ryan, Julian J. Faraway

Chain Event Graphs
Rodrigo A. Collazo, Christiane Goergen, Jim Q. Smith

Data Science Foundations
Geometry and Topology of Complex Hierarchic Systems and Big Data Analytics
Fionn Murtagh

Exploratory Data Analysis with MATLAB
Wendy L. Martinez, Angel R. Martinez, Jeffrey Solka

Microarray Image Analysis: An Algorithmic Approach
Karl Fraser, Zidong Wang, Xiaohui Liu

Introduction to Data Technologies
Paul Murrell

Exploratory Multivariate Analysis by Example Using R
Francois Husson, Sebastien Le, Jérôme Pagès

Music Data Analysis: Foundations and Applications
Claus Weihs, Dietmar Jannach, Igor Vatolkin, Guenter Rudolph

Computational Statistics Handbook with MATLAB
Wendy L. Martinez, Angel R. Martinez

Statistics in MATLAB: A Primer
MoonJung Cho, Wendy L. Martinez

Visualization and Verbalization of Data
Jorg Blasius, Michael Greenacre

For more information about this series, please visit:
https://www.crcpress.com/Chapman--HallCRC-Computer-Science--Data-Analysis/book-series/CHCOSCDAANA

Time Series Clustering and Classification

Elizabeth Ann Maharaj
Department of Econometrics and Business Statistics, Monash
University, Australia

Pierpaolo D'Urso
Department of Social and Economic Sciences, Sapienza –
University of Rome, Italy

Jorge Caiado
Department of Mathematics, ISEG, Lisbon School of Economics
& Management, University of Lisbon, Portugal

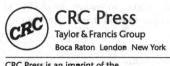

CRC Press
Taylor & Francis Group
Boca Raton London New York

CRC Press is an imprint of the
Taylor & Francis Group, an **informa** business
A CHAPMAN & HALL BOOK

CRC Press
Taylor & Francis Group
6000 Broken Sound Parkway NW, Suite 300
Boca Raton, FL 33487-2742

First issued in paperback 2021

© 2019 by Taylor & Francis Group, LLC
CRC Press is an imprint of Taylor & Francis Group, an Informa business

No claim to original U.S. Government works

ISBN-13: 978-1-03-209349-9 (pbk)
ISBN-13: 978-1-4987-7321-8 (hbk)

We dedicate this book to:

Paul and Claudia

Giordana

Dina, Maria, and Martim

Contents

Preface

The beginning of the age of artificial intelligence and machine learning has created new challenges and opportunities for data analysts, statisticians, mathematicians, econometricians, computer scientists and many others. At the root of these techniques, we find algorithms and methods for clustering and classifying different types of large datasets, including time series data, spatial data, panel data, categorical data, functional data and digital data. The emphasis of this book is on the clustering and classification of time series data, and it can be regarded as a reference manual on this topic.

The subject of clustering and classification of time series with applications in fields such as geology, medicine, environmental science, astronomy, finance and economics, has attracted substantial attention over the last two to three decades. Our goal in publishing this book is to provide research students and other researchers with a broad spectrum of techniques, all of which are located in one place. It provides the relevant developments in observation-based, feature-based and model-based traditional and fuzzy clustering methods, feature-based and model-based classification methods, and machine learning methods, in a concise manner using applied and simulated studies. Presently, these techniques can be found scattered in articles in many different journals and book chapters.

In truth, we have been researching these topics for more than 20 years. Our research has led to numerous publications in scientific journals in several fields, such as economics, business, management, finance, statistics, data analysis, marketing, medicine, physics, biology, hydrology and many others. We have included our work as well as works of several other authors, thus collecting as many methods on the clustering and classifying time series as we could. However, it should be noted that the book contains as many methods as we were aware of at the time of writing, and clearly new methods have since been proposed and published in journals.

We have divided the book into three parts and eleven chapters. Chapter 1 begins with a very brief overview of the contents of the book. Chapter 2 introduces some fundamental concepts in time series, spectral and wavelet analyses that are necessary for understanding the classification and clustering methods discussed in the book. Part I is about unsupervised clustering techniques for time series and consists of five chapters. Chapter 3 outlines the basic concepts of traditional cluster analysis. Chapter 4 discusses fuzzy clustering methods. Chapter 5 considers observation-based clustering methods. Chapter 6 deals with feature-based methods in the time, frequency and wavelet domains. Chapter 7 discusses model-based clustering methods, while Chapter 8 discusses other time series clustering approaches. Part II, which deals with supervised classification techniques for time series, consists of two chapters. Chapter 9 discusses discriminant analysis and classification methods based on time series features and models. Chapter 10 explores machine learning methods, such as classification trees, support vector machines and nearest neighbour algorithms. Finally, Part III, which consists of Chapter 11, presents links to computer programs in Matlab and R, data sets and real examples through demonstration.

It would not have been possible to complete this project successfully without the unconditional support of several people. Firstly, we are greatly indebted to our families for their constant support and patience. Secondly, we would like to thank Nuno Crato, Daniel Peña, João Bastos, Andrés Alonso, Livia De Giovanni, José Vilar and the Taylor & Francis's team for their helpful suggestions and contributions. Finally, we would like to thank some of our colleagues in our departments at Monash University, Sapienza - University of Rome and University of Lisbon for their support and encouragement.

A comprehensive webpage providing additional material to support this book can be found at http://www.tsclustering.homepage.pt/

Elizabeth Ann Maharaj, Melbourne, Australia
Pierpaolo D'Urso, Rome, Italy
Jorge Caiado, Lisbon, Portugal
February 2019

Authors

Elizabeth Ann Maharaj is an Associate Professor in the Department of Econometrics and Business Statistics at Monash University, Australia. She has a Ph.D. from Monash University on the Pattern Recognition of Time Series. Ann is an elected member of the International Statistical Institute (ISI), a member of the International Association of Statistical Computing (IASC) and of the Statistical Society of Australia (SSA). She is also an accredited statistician with the SSA. Ann's main research interests are in time series classification, wavelets analysis, fuzzy classification and interval time series analysis. She has also worked on research projects in climatology, environmental science, labour markets, human mobility and finance.

Pierpaolo D'Urso is a full professor of Statistics at Sapienza - University of Rome. He is the chair of the Department of Social and Economic Sciences, Sapienza - University of Rome. He received his Ph.D. in Statistics and his bachelor's degree in Statistics both from Sapienza. He is associate editor and member of the editorial board of several journals. He has been member of several program committees of international conferences and guest editor of special issues. His recent research activity is focussed on fuzzy clustering, clustering and classification of time series, clustering of complex structures of data, and statistical methods for marketing, local labour systems, electoral studies and environmental monitoring.

Jorge Caiado has a Ph.D. in Applied Mathematics to Economics and Management. He is a Professor of Econometrics and Forecasting Methods at the Lisbon School of Economics and Management (ISEG) and Researcher at the Centre for Applied Mathematics and Economics. His research in econometrics, finance, time series analysis, forecasting methods and statistical software has led to numerous publications in scientific journals and books. He is serving as econometric and statistical consultant and trainer for numerous companies and organizations including central banks, commercial and investment banks, bureau of statistics, bureau of economic analysis, transportation and logistics companies, health companies and insurance companies. He is also a co-founder and partner of GlobalSolver.

1

Introduction

CONTENTS

1.1 Overview

Time series clustering and classification has relevance in a diverse range of fields which include geology, medicine, environmental science, finance and economics. Clustering is an unsupervised approach to grouping together similar items of interest and was initially applied to cross-sectional data. However, clustering time series data has become a popular research topic over the past three to four decades and a rich literature exists on this topic. A set of time series can be clustered using conventional hierarchical and non-hierarchical methods, fuzzy clustering methods, machine learning methods and model-based methods.

Actual time series observations can be clustered (e.g., D'Urso, 2000; Coppi and D'Urso, 2001, D'Urso, 2005), or features extracted from the time series can be clustered. Features are extracted in the time, frequency and wavelets domains. Clustering using time domain features such as autocorrelations, partial autocorrelations, and cross-correlations have been proposed by several authors including Goutte et al. (1999), Galeano and Peña (2000), Dose and Cincotti (2005), Singhal and Seborg (2005), Caiado et al. (2006), Basalto et al. (2007), Wang et al. (2007), Takayuki et al. (2006), Ausloos and Lambiotte (2007), Miskiewicz and Ausloos (2008), and D'Urso and Maharaj (2009).

In the frequency domain, features such as the periodogram and spectral and cepstral ordinates are extracted; included in the literature are studies by Kakizawa et al. (1998), Shumway (2003), Caiado et al. (2006), Maharaj and D'Urso (2010, 2011).

The features extracted in the wavelets domain are discreet wavelet transforms (DWT), wavelet variances and wavelet correlations and methods have been proposed by authors such as Zhang et al. (2005), Maharaj et al. (2010), D'Urso and Maharaj (2012) and D'Urso et al. (2014). As well, time series

1

can be modelled and the parameters estimates used as the clustering variables. Studies on the model-based clustering method include those by Piccolo (1990), Tong and Dabas (1990), Maharaj (1996, 2000), Kalpakis et al. (2001), Ramoni et al.(2002), Xiong and Yeung (2002), Boets (2005), Singhal and Seborg (2005), Savvides et al. (2008), Otranto (2008), Caiado and Crato (2010), D'Urso et al. (2013), Maharaj et al. (2016) and D'Urso et al. (2016).

Classification is a supervised approach to grouping together items of interest and discriminant analysis and machine learning methods are amongst the approaches that have been used. Initially classification was applied to cross-sectional data but a large literature now exists on the classification of time series which includes many very useful applications. These time series classification methods include the use of feature-based, model-based and machine learning techniques. The features are extracted in the time domain (Chandler and Polonok, 2006; Maharaj, 2014), the frequency domain (Kakizawa et al., 1998; Maharaj, 2002; Shumway, 2003) and the wavelets domain (Maharaj, 2005; Maharaj and Alonso, 2007, 2014; Fryzlewicz and Omboa, 2012). Model-based approaches for time series classification include ARIMA models, Gaussian mixture models and Bayesian approaches (Maharaj, 1999, 2000; Sykacek and Roberts, 2002; Liu and Maharaj, 2013; Liu et al., 2014; Kotsifakos and Panagiotis, 2014), while machine learning approaches include classification trees, nearest neighbour methods and support vector machines (Douzal-Chouakria and Amblard, 2000; Do et al., 2017; Gudmundsson et al., 2008; Zhang et al., 2010).

It should be noted that clustering and classifying data evolving in time is substantially different from classifying static data. Hence, the volume of work on these topics focuses on extracting time series features or considering specific time series models and also understanding the risks of directly extending the common-use metric for static data to time series data.

1.2 Examples

We discuss three examples to illustrate time series clustering and classification before going into detail about these and other approaches in subsequent chapters. The first example illustrates clustering using time domain features, the second is observation-based and the third illustrates classification using wavelet features.

Example 1.1 D'Urso and Maharaj (2009) illustrate through simulated data, crisp clustering (traditional hierarchical and non-hierarchical) and fuzzy clustering of time series using the time domain features of autocorrelations. The aim here is to bring together series generated from the same process in order to understand the classification success. Fig. 1.1 shows the autocorrelation

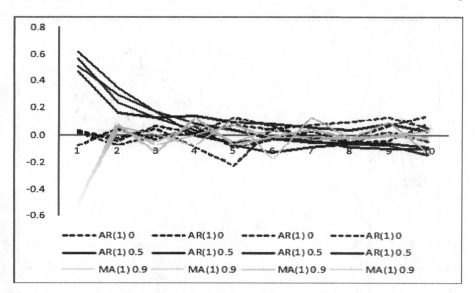

FIGURE 1.1: Autocorrelation function of series generated from three processes.

TABLE 1.1: Percentage of correct classifications using autocorrelation.

	Percentage of correct classifications
k-means	83.5
Single Linkage	85.5
Complete Linkage	93.0
Average Linkage	92.5
Ward's Method	97.8
Fuzzy c-means	87.9 - 99.5

functions (ACFs) over 10 lags for 12 simulated series, 4 of each generated from an AR(1) process with $\phi = 0$ (a white noise process), an AR(1) process with $\phi = 0.5$ and an MA(1) process with $\theta = 0.9$. The patterns of the ACFs associated with each process are clearly distinguishable at the early lags. Table 1.1 show a summary of results of clustering the 12 series, 4 from each process over 1000 simulations. The fuzzy c-means results are subject to specific choices of parameter values. It is clear from the results in Table 1.1 that the autocorrelations provide good separation features.

Example 1.2 D'Urso (2005) illustrates the application of a fuzzy clustering model to a set of short synthetic series consisting of three well-separated clusters of time series with 4, 2, and 2 time series each, respectively, and one switching time series (the 7th time series). This illustration is presented in

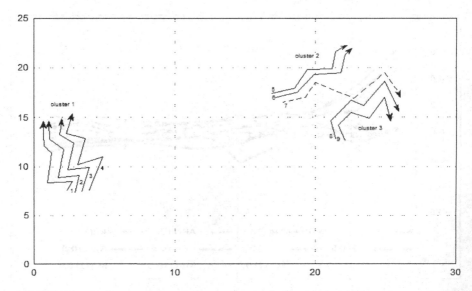

FIGURE 1.2: A set of short time series including a switching time series.

Fig.1.2 from where it can be observed that the switching time series, for the initial time period, presents an instantaneous position and slope similar to the time series belonging to Cluster 2 (series 5 and 6), while at a later time, it has an instantaneous position and slope similar to the time series belonging to Cluster 3 (series 8 and 9). Table 1.2 shows the membership degrees of each time series in each cluster and it is clear that series 1-4, 5-6 and 8-9 have crisp memberships in Clusters 1, 2 and 3 respectively, while series 7 has fuzzy membership in Clusters 2 and 3.

TABLE 1.2: Membership degrees of each time series in each cluster.

	Cluster 1	Cluster 2	Cluster 3
1	0.973	0.013	0.014
2	0.991	0.005	0.004
3	0.995	0.003	0.002
4	0.961	0.024	0.015
5	0.003	0.977	0.002
6	0.001	0.997	0.002
7	0.084	0.497	0.419
8	0.004	0.027	0.969
9	0.001	0.002	0.997

Example 1.3 Maharaj and Alonso (2014) illustrate the classification of multivariate synthetic time series using the wavelet features of variances and correlations with both linear and quadratic discriminant functions. Fig. 1.3 shows

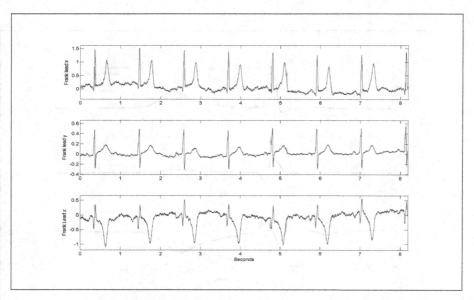

FIGURE 1.3: Synthetic ECG signals.

synthetic electrocardiogram (ECG) signals for three leads based on a three-dimensional formulation of a single dipole of the heart. Refer to Sameni et al. (2007) and Clifford et al. (2010) for more details on the development of these synthetic signals. The signals shown in Fig. 1.3 could represent those of an individual with normal heart beats. One of the parameters, λ, can be varied to simulate signals of an individual with the heart condition, acute myocardial infarction (AMI). This is done by setting $\lambda > 1$. Fig. 1.4 shows a single beat of a synthetic ECG that is normal with four scenarios of AMI when λ is varied.

For each population (Normal and AMI), 100 ECGs, each of length T=4096 were simulated and linear and quadratic discriminant analysis applied to the wavelet variances and wavelet correlations extracted from the signals. Fig. 1.5 and 1.6 show the classification rates (from hold-out-one cross-validation) using several wavelet filters with linear and quadratic discriminant functions, respectively. The results reveal with the exception of the scenario where λ was set to the smallest value greater than one, the wavelet variances and the combination of wavelet variance and correlations appear to be reasonably good features for discriminating between normal beats and those associated with AMI.

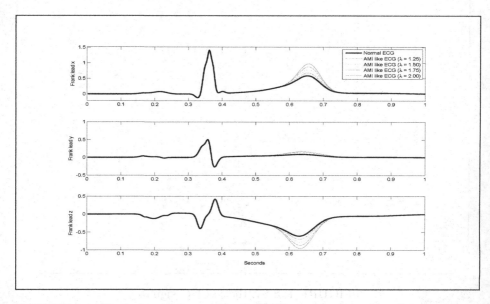

FIGURE 1.4: Single beat of a synthetic ECG signal: normal and acute myocardial infarction.

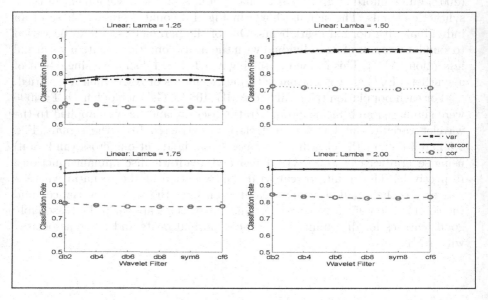

FIGURE 1.5: Classification rates for synthetic ECGs using linear discriminant functions.

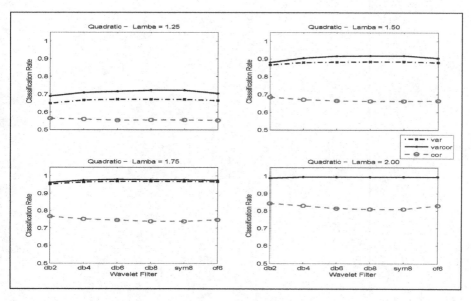

FIGURE 1.6: Classification rates for synthetic ECGs using quadratic discriminant functions.

1.3 Structure of the book

After this chapter, time series concepts essential for what is to follow are discussed in Chapter 2. The rest of the book is divided into three parts. Part 1 consisting of Chapters 3 to 8 is on unsupervised approaches to classifying time series, namely, clustering techniques. Traditional cluster analysis and fuzzy clustering are discussed in Chapters 3 and 4, respectively, and this is followed by observation-based, feature-based, model-based clustering, and other time series clustering approaches in Chapters 5 to 8.

Part 2 is on supervised classification approaches. This includes feature-based approaches in Chapter 9 and other time series classification approaches in Chapter 10. Throughout the book, many examples of simulated scenarios and real-world applications are provided, and these are mostly drawn from the research of the three authors. Part 3 provides links to software packages, some specific programming scripts used in these applications and simulated scenarios, as well as links to relevant data sets.

2

Time series features and models

CONTENTS

2.1 Introduction

The topic of time series analysis is the subject of a large number of books and journal articles. In this chapter, we highlight fundamental time series concepts, as well as features and models that are relevant to the clustering and classification of time series in subsequent chapters. Much of this material on time series analysis, in much greater detail, is available in books by authors such as Box et al. (1994), Chatfield (2004), Shumway and Stoffer (2016), Percival and Walden (2016) and Ord and Fildes (2013).

2.2   Stochastic processes

A stochastic process is defined as a collection of random variables that are ordered in time and defined as a set of points which may be discrete or continuous. We denote the random variable at time t by $X(t)$ if time is continuous or by X_t if time is discrete. A continuous stochastic process is described as $\{X(t), -\infty < t < \infty\}$ while a discrete stochastic process is described as $\{X_t, t = ..., -2, -1, 0, 1, 2, ...\}$.

Most statistical problems are concerned with estimating the properties of a population from a sample. The properties of the sample are typically determined by the researcher, including the sample size and whether randomness is incorporated into the selection process. In time series analysis there is a different situation in that the order of observations is determined by time. Although it may be possible to increase the sample size by varying the length of the observed time series, there will be a single outcome of the process and a single observation on the random variable at time t. Nevertheless, we may regard the observed time series as just one example of an infinite set of time series that might be observed. The infinite set of time series is called an ensemble. Every member of the ensemble is a possible realization of the stochastic process. The observed time series can be thought of as one possible realization of the stochastic process and is denoted by $\{x(t), -\infty < t < \infty\}$ if time is continuous or $\{x_t, t = 0, 1, 2, ..T\}$ if time is discrete. Time series analysis is essentially concerned with evaluating the properties of the underlying probability model from this observed time series. In what follows, we will be working with mainly discrete time series which are realizations of discrete stochastic processes.

Many models for stochastic processes are expressed by means of algebraic expressions relating the random variable at time t to past values of the process, together with values of an unobservable error process. From one such model we may be able to specify the joint distribution of $X_{t_1}, X_{t_2}, ..., X_{t_k}$, for any set of times $t_1, t_2, ..., t_k$ and any value of k. A simple way to describe a stochastic process is to examine the moments of the process, particularly the first and second moments, namely, the mean and autocovariance function.

$$\mu_t = E(X_t)$$

$$\gamma_{t_1, t_2} = E[(X_{t_1} - \mu_t)(X_{t_2} - \mu_t)]$$

The variance is a special case of the autocovariance function when $t_1 = t_2$, that is,

$$\sigma_t^2 = E[(X_t - \mu_t)^2].$$

An important class of stochastic processes is that which is stationary. A time series is said to be stationary if the joint distribution of $X_{t_1}, X_{t_2}, ..., X_{t_k}$

is the same as that of $X_{t_1+\tau}, X_{t_2+\tau}, ..., X_{t_k+\tau}$, for all $t_1, t_2, ..., t_k, \tau$. In other words, shifting the time origin by the amount τ has no effect on the joint distribution which must therefore depend only on the intervals between $t_1, t_2, ..., t_k$.

This definition holds for any value of k. In particular, if $k = 1$, strict stationarity implies that the distribution of X_t is the same for all t, provided the first two moments are finite and are both constant, that is, $\mu_t = \mu$ and $\sigma_t^2 = \sigma^2$. If $k = 2$, the joint distribution of X_{t_1} and X_{t_2} depends only on the time difference $t_1 - t_2 = \tau$ which is called a lag. Thus the autocovariance function which depends only on $t_1 - t_2$ may be written as

$$\gamma_\tau = COV(X_t, X_{t+\tau}) = E[(X_t - \mu)(X_{t+\tau} - \mu)].$$

In practice it is often useful to define stationarity in a less restricted way than that described above. A process is called second order stationary or weakly stationary if its mean is constant and its autocovariance function depends only on the lag. No requirements are placed on moments higher than that of second order. This weaker definition will generally be used as many of the properties of stationary processes depend only on the structure of the process as specified by its first and second moments. One important class of processes where this is particularly true is the class of normal processes where the joint distribution of $X_{t_1}, X_{t_2}, ..., X_{t_k}$ is multivariate normal for all $t_1, t_2, ..., t_k$. The multivariate normal distribution is completely characterized by it first and second moments, and so it follows that second order stationarity implies strict stationarity for normal process. However, μ and γ_τ may not adequately describe stationary processes which depart considerably from normality.

The size of an autocovariance coefficient depends on the units in which X_t is measured. Thus for interpretative purposes, it is helpful to standardize the autocovariance function to produce the autocorrelation function which is defined by

$$\rho_\tau = \frac{\gamma_\tau}{\gamma_0}$$

where

$$\gamma_0 = \sigma^2 = E[(X_t - \mu)^2]$$

is the variance of the process. ρ_τ measures the correlation between X_t and $X_{t+\tau}$. The autocovariance and autocorrelation function are even functions, that is,

$$\gamma_\tau = \gamma_{-\tau}$$

and

$$\rho_\tau = \rho_{-\tau}.$$

The sample counterparts, that is, for the observed time series, of the autoco-variance and autocorrelation coefficients are, respectively

$$\widehat{\gamma}_\tau = c_k = \frac{1}{T} \sum_{k=1}^{T-k} (x_t - \overline{x})(x_{t+k} - \overline{x})$$

and

$$\widehat{\rho}_\tau = r_k = \frac{c_k}{c_o},$$

where

$$c_o = \frac{1}{T} \sum_{t=1}^{T-1} (x_t - \overline{x}^2)$$

is the variance of the time series. It has been shown that the autocovariance estimator c_k is biased, that is,

$$E(c_k) \neq \gamma_k,$$

but the bias is of order $1/T$. However, it is asymptotically unbiased, that is,

$$\lim_{T \to \infty} E(c_k) = \gamma_k.$$

2.3   Autocorrelation and partial autocorrelation functions

Autocovariance and autocorrelation measure the linear relationship between various values of an observed time series that are lagged k periods apart, that is, given an observed time series $\{x_t, t = 0, 1, 2, ..T\}$, we measure the relationship between x_t and x_{t-1}, x_t and x_{t-2}, x_t and x_{t-3}, etc.. Thus, the autocorrelation function is an important tool for assessing the degree of de-pendence in observed time series. It is useful in determining whether or not a time series is stationary. It can suggest possible models that can be fitted to the observed time series and it can detect repeated patterns in a time series such as the presence of a periodic signal which has been buried by noise. The sample autocorrelation function (ACF), r_k, $k = 1,2, \ldots$ is typically plotted for at least a quarter of the number of lags or thereabouts. The plot is sup-plemented with 5% significance limits to enable a graphical check of whether of not dependence is statistically significant at a particular lag.

Partial autocorrelations are used to measure the relationship between x_t and x_{t-k}, with the effect of the other time lags, 1, 2, . . . , k-1 removed. It is also useful to plot the partial autocorrelation function (PACF) because it, together with the plot of the ACF, can help inform one on a possible

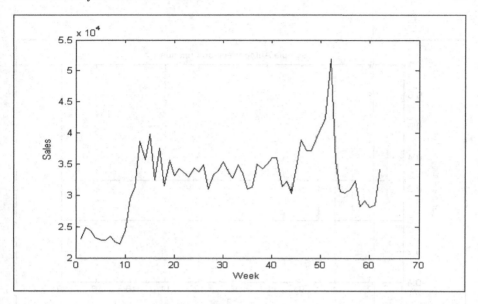

FIGURE 2.1: Time series plot of weekly sales.

appropriate model that can be fitted to the time series. Refer to any of the references mentioned in Section 2.1 for more details on the ACF and PACF including their sampling distributions which enable the determination of the significance limits.

Example 2.1 Fig. 2.1 shows a time series of weekly sales of a consumer product in a certain market area over 62 months, with the first week being that of January. Refer to Ord and Fildes (2013) for more details about this data set. Features apparent in this time series are that sales are low for the first twelve months and then remain stable until the 46th week, then increase over a few months peaking in the 52nd week and then more or less returning to the previous level.

Fig. 2.2 and Fig. 2.3 show the ACF and PACF of this time series. We observe from the ACF that the first few autocorrelations are positive indicating a carry over in sales level from one week to the next and the autocorrelations are significant up to lag 5. As the lag increases, the autocorrelation dies away. The PACF is highly significant at the first lag indicating that there is a significant and linear relationship between x_t and x_{t-1}. The relationship between x_t and x_{t-2} with the effect of the first lag removed is not significant. Likewise, the PACF can be explained at the other lags. The patterns of the ACF and PACF can inform us of the possibility of fitting a particular stationary model to this time series.

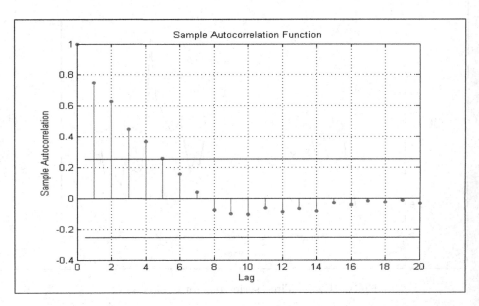

FIGURE 2.2: Autocorrelation function of weekly sales.

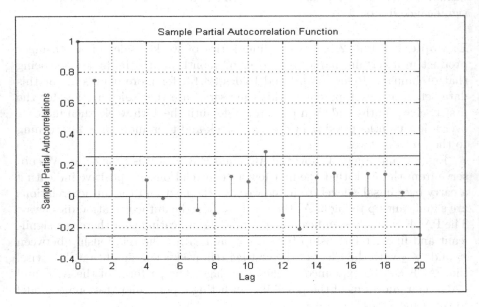

FIGURE 2.3: Partial autocorrelation function of weekly sales.

2.4 Time series models

2.4.1 Stationary models

An autoregressive (AR) model is one for which the current value of the deviation of the process from the mean is expressed as a finite, linear combination of previous values of the process and a shock or error term. Given a stochastic process $\{X_t\}$, the AR model is expressed as:

$$\phi(B)Z_t = \varepsilon_t$$

where $Z_t = X_t - \mu$, is the deviation from the mean, ε_t is a white noise or random process with mean 0 and variance σ_t^2,

$$\phi(B) = 1 - \phi_1 B - \phi_2 B^2 - ... - \phi_p B^p,$$

is the autoregressive operator, p is the order of the AR model and B is the backshift operator. In particular, we refer to it as an AR(p) model. This model is stationary and a necessary requirement for stationarity is that all roots of $\Phi(B) = 0$ must lie outside the unit circle.

A moving average (MA) model is one where the current value of the deviation of the process from the mean is expressed as a linear combination of a finite number of previous error terms. The MA model is expressed as:

$$Z_t = \theta(B)\varepsilon_t$$

where

$$\theta(B) = 1 - \theta_1 B - \theta_2 B^2 - ... - \theta_q B^q,$$

and q is the order of the MA model. In particular, we refer to it as an MA(q) model. This model is also stationary with a similar stationarity condition as that of the AR model applying. While the AR and MA are useful representations of observed time series, it is sometimes useful to include both AR and MA terms in a model, resulting in an autoregressive, moving average (ARMA) model or an ARMA(p, q) model which is expressed as:

$$\phi(B)Z_t = \theta(B)\varepsilon_t. \tag{2.1}$$

In order for the AR(p), MA(q) and ARMA(p, q) models to be fitted to an observed time series, it is assumed that the series is stationary, that is, it fluctuates about a fixed mean and its variance is constant.

In order to identify a suitable model that may be fitted to an observed stationary time series, we examine the ACF and PACF of this series to determine if it to some extent emulates the theoretical ACF and PACF associated with the model. For an AR(1) model, the ACF shows exponential decay while the PACF is zero beyond lag 1. Hence, we can infer that an AR(1) model would be an appropriate fit to an observed time series, when the ACF decays exponentially and when the PACF has a single significant spike at lag 1. Given that this is the behaviour displayed by the ACF and PACF of the observed series in Example 2.1, we could infer that an AR(1) model is possibly an appropriate model to fit to this series. In general, for an AR(p) model, with $p \geq 2$, the ACF can show exponential decay or a damped sin wave pattern, whereas the PACF is zero beyond lag q.

For an MA(1) model, the PACF shows exponential decay while the ACF is zero beyond lag 1 . Hence, if the ACF of an observed stationary time series has a single significant spike at lag 1, and the PACF decays exponentially, we can infer that an MA(1) model would be an appropriate fit to this series. In general, for an MA(q) model, with $q \geq 2$, the ACF is zero beyond lag p, while the PACF can show exponential decay or a damped sin wave pattern. Refer to books such as Chatfield (2004), Makridakis et al. (1998) and Ord and Fildes (2013) for more details about the theoretical behaviour of ARMA models in general.

2.4.2   Non-stationary models

Many time series encountered in various fields exhibit non-stationary behaviour and in particular they do not fluctuate about a fixed level. Although the level about which the series fluctuates may be different at different times, when differences in levels are taken, they may be similar. This is referred to as homogeneous non-stationary behaviour (Box et al., 1994) and the series can be represented by a model that requires the d-th difference of the process to be stationary. In practice, d is usually no more than 2. Hence, an ARMA model can be extended to what is known as an autoregressive, integrated moving average (ARIMA) model, or ARIMA(p, d, q) to represent a homogeneous non-stationary time series. This model is expressed as

$$\phi(B)(1 - B)^d Z_t = \theta(B)\varepsilon_t.$$

In practice, time series may also have a seasonal component. Just as the consecutive data points of an observed time series may exhibit AR, MA or ARMA properties, so data separated by a whole season (for example, a year or a quarter) may exhibit similar properties. The ARIMA notation can be extended to incorporate seasonal aspects and in general we have an ARIMA(p, d, q)(P, D, Q)$_s$ model which can be expressed as

$$\phi(B)\Phi(B)(1 - B)^d(1 - B^s)^D Z_t = \theta(B)\Theta(B)\varepsilon_t$$

where

$$\Phi(B) = 1 - \Phi_1 B^s - \Phi_2 B^{2s} - ... - \Phi_P B^{Ps},$$

$$\Theta(B) = 1 - \Theta_1 B^s - \Theta_2 B^{2s} - ... - \Theta_Q B^{Qs},$$

D is the degree of seasonal differencing and s is the number of periods per season. For example, $s = 12$ for monthly time series and $s = 4$ for quarterly time series. Refer to books such as Makridakis et al. (1994) and Ord and Fildes (2013) for more details about fitting non-stationary models that may be seasonal or not.

2.4.3 Some other models

All these models discussed thus far are linear and are applicable to univariate time series. A popular extension to fitting models to stationary multivariate time series are vector autoregressive moving average models (VARMA). One of the large number of books in which details of these models can be found is Lutkepohl (1991). There are also several classes of non-linear models. A particular class is one that is concerned with modeling changes in variance or the volatility of a time series. These include autoregressive conditionally heteroscedastic (ARCH) and generalized autoregressive conditionally heteroscedastic (GARCH) models. One of the large number of books in which details of these models can be found is Tsay (2010).

2.5 Spectral representation of time series

Associated with every stationary stochastic process $\{X_t\}$ is the spectral density function which is a tool for considering the frequency properties of a stationary time series. The spectral density function, also referred to as the power spectral density function or the spectrum, is the derivative of the spectral distribution function $F(\omega)$, where ω is the frequency, which is defined as the number of radians per unit time. This is a continuous function that is monotone and bounded in the interval $[0, \pi]$. This derivative is denoted by $f(\omega)$, so that

$$f(\omega) = \frac{dF(\omega)}{d\omega}. \tag{2.2}$$

When $f(\omega)$ exists, Eq. 2.2 can be expressed as

$$\gamma_k = \int_0^\pi \cos \omega k f(\omega) d\omega. \tag{2.3}$$

When $k = 0$, Eq. 2.3 becomes

$$\gamma_0 = \sigma_X^2 = \int_0^\pi f(\omega) d\omega = F(\pi). \tag{2.4}$$

The interpretation of the spectrum is that $f(\omega)d\omega$ represents the contribution to variance of components of frequencies in the range $(\omega, \omega + d\omega)$. Eq. 2.4 indicates that the total area under the curve of the spectrum is equal to the variance of the process. A peak in the spectrum indicates an important contribution of variance at frequencies near the values that correspond to the peak.

It should be noted that the autocovariance function and the spectral density function are equivalent ways of describing a stationary stochastic process.

From Eq. 2.3, the corresponding inverse can be obtained, namely

$$f(\omega) = \frac{1}{\pi} \sum_{k=-\infty}^{\infty} \gamma_k e^{-i\omega k}. \tag{2.5}$$

This implies that the spectral density function is the Fourier transform of the autocovariance function. Refer to Chatfield (2004) for details on the Fourier transform. Since γ_k is an even function of k, Eq. 2.5 can be expressed as

$$f(\omega) = \frac{1}{\pi} \left[\gamma_0 + 2 \sum_{k=1}^{\infty} \gamma_k \cos \omega k \right]. \tag{2.6}$$

The normalized form of the spectral density function is given by

$$f^*(\omega) = \frac{f(\omega)}{\sigma_{X_t}^2} = \frac{dF^*(\omega)}{d\omega}.$$

This is the derivative of the normalized spectral distribution function. Hence, $f^*(\omega)$ is the Fourier transform of the autocorrelation function, namely,

$$f^*(\omega) = \frac{1}{\pi} \left[1 + 2 \sum_{k=1}^{\infty} \rho_k \cos \omega k \right].$$

This implies that $f^*(\omega)d\omega$ is the proportion of variance in the interval $(\omega, \omega + d\omega)$.

2.5.1 Periodogram

An estimator of the spectral density function is the periodogram $I(\omega)$ where at an ordinate p it is expressed as:

$$I(\omega_p) = \frac{1}{\pi} \left(c_0 + 2 \sum_{k=1}^{T-1} c_k \cos(\omega_p k) \right),$$

where c_k is the sample autocovariance coefficient at lag k, T is the length of the observed time series, and $p = 1, 2, \ldots, (T/2)$-1. The periodogram is asymptotically unbiased, that is,

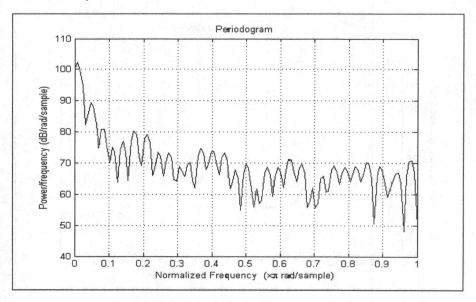

FIGURE 2.4: Periodogram of weekly sales.

$$\lim_{T \to \infty} E[I(\omega)] = f(\omega).$$

However, $I(\omega)$ is not a consistent estimator of $f(\omega)$. It can be shown that neighbouring periodogram ordinates are asymptotically independent. Refer to Chatfield (2004) for more details on periodogram analysis including the distribution associated with the periodogram ordinates.

Example 2.2 Consider the observed time series of weekly sales of a consumer product from Example 2.1. Fig. 2.4 shows the periodogram of this series. The peak occurs around a normalized frequency between 0 and 0.05, indicating that most of the largest contribution to the variance of the series is within this frequency range. The frequency range around which a peak occurs gives an indication of the frequency at which that cyclic component may exist.

Note that just as the spectral density function can be normalized, the periodogram can be normalized. In particular, the normalized periodogram is

$$I^*(\omega) = \frac{I(\omega)}{Var(x_t)}.$$

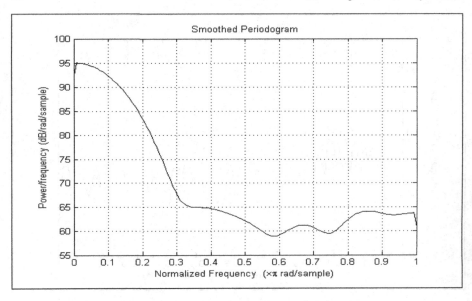

FIGURE 2.5: Smoothed periodogram of weekly sales.

2.5.2 Smoothed periodogram

While the periodogram is useful in assessing whether there are one or more strong cyclic components in a time series, the sampling error associated with its ordinates is quite large and confidence intervals set up around the ordinates would therefore be very wide. Therefore, the periodogram is not a very good estimator of the spectral density function especially when the signal to noise ratio of time series is low, that is, when the time series is very noisy. The periodogram can be smoothed to overcome these problems and there is a vast literature on windows that are used to smooth the periodogram. Refer to Chatfield (2004) for details about smoothing the periodogram.

Fig. 2.5 shows a smoothed periodogram, from which it is clear that the fluctuations in the periodogram have been smoothed out to better assess which frequency bands account for most of the variance in the time series.

2.6   Wavelet representation of time series

Time series features such as autocorrelations and partial autocorrelations describe the dynamics of a stationary time series in the time domain, whereas spectral ordinates describe the dynamics of a stationary time series in the frequency domain. When an observed time series is nonstationary in the mean, it first has to be differenced to be made stationary before analyzing its dynamics using autocorrelations, partial autocorrelations and spectral ordinates. When a time series is decomposed into wavelet series, the wavelet coefficients describe the dynamics of a time series in both the time and frequency domains. Furthermore, wavelet analysis is applicable to both stationary and non-stationary time series without the need for differencing a non-stationary time series. While we present just a brief description of relevant aspects of wavelet analysis as applicable to discrete times here, more specific and general details can be found in several books on the topic, one of which is by Percival and Walden (2000). Our descriptions that follow mostly use their notations.

2.6.1 Discrete wavelet transform (DWT)

The Discrete Wavelet Transform (DWT), which is an orthonormal transform, re-expresses a time series of length T in terms of coefficients that are associated with a particular time and with a particular dyadic scale as well as one or more scaling coefficients. The j-th dyadic scale is of the form 2^{j-1} where $j = 1, 2, \ldots, J$, and J is the maximum allowable number of scales.

The number of coefficients at the j-th scale is $T/2^j$, provided $T = 2^J$. In general the wavelet coefficients at scale 2^{j-1} are associated with frequencies in the interval $[1/2^{j+1}, 1/2^j]$. Large time scales give more low frequency information, while small time scales give more high frequency information about the time series. The coefficients are obtained from projecting the time series with translated and dilated versions of a wavelet filter. The DWT is computed using what is known as the pyramid algorithm.

In general, the wavelet coefficients are proportional to the differences of averages of the time series observations at each scale, whereas the scaling coefficients are proportional to the averages of the original series over the largest scale. The scaling coefficients reflect long-term variations, which would exhibit a similar trend to the original series. The DWT re-expresses a time series in terms of coefficients that are associated with a particular time and a particular dyadic scale. These coefficients are fully equivalent to the information contained in the original series in that a time series can be perfectly reconstructed from its DWT coefficients. An important aspect of the DWT is that it de-correlates even highly correlated series; that is, the wavelet coefficients at each scale are approximately uncorrelated.

It is possible to recover the time series $\{x_t, t = 1, 2, \ldots, T\}$ from its DWT by synthesis, that is, the multi-resolution analysis (MRA) of a time series which is expressed as

$$x_t = \sum_{j=1}^{J} d_j + s_J,$$

where d_j is the wavelet detail (series of inverse wavelet coefficients at scale j) and s_J is the smooth series which is the inverse of the series of scaling coefficients. Hence a time series and its DWT are actually two representations of the same mathematical entity.

2.6.2   Modified discrete wavelet transform (MODWT)

The maximum overlap discrete wavelet transform (MODWT) is a modification of the DWT. Under the MODWT, the number of wavelet coefficients created will be the same as the number of observations in the original time series. Because the MODWT decomposition retains all possible times at each time scale, the MODWT has the advantage of retaining the time invariant property of the original time series. The MODWT can be used in a similar manner to the DWT in defining a multi-resolution analysis of a given time series. In contrast to the DWT, the MODWT details and smooths are associated with zero phase filters making it easy to line up features in a MRA with the original time series more meaningfully.

Many families of wavelet filters, whose qualities vary according to a number of criteria, are available. Some commonly used filters of width N (where N is an integer) are from the Daubechies family abbreviated as DB(N). These filters are asymmetric. The Haar filter which is the simplest wavelet filter is a DB(2) filter. Another family of filters which is a modification of the Daubechies family is the least asymmetric family LA(N) (also referred to as the symmletts family SYM(N)). These filters are nearly symmetric and have the property of aligning the wavelet coefficients very well with the given time series. The coiflets family of filters, CF(N) also possess this property and are symmetric filters. Filters from the least symmetric and coiflets families are usually recommended for use with time series because of their good alignment properties.

Example 2.3 Fig. 2.6 shows the total seasonally adjusted retail turnover in Australia from January 2005 to August 2015 (128 months) from the website of the Australian Bureau of Statistics, while Fig. 2.7 shows the MODWT decomposition of this series over 5 scales using the LA(8) filter. $d1$ to $d6$ represent the series of wavelet coefficients at five scales and $s6$ the series of scaling coefficients at the 5th scale. It can be observed while the series is non-stationary in mean, the wavelet series are stationary in the mean. The $d1$ series describes the series dynamics over 2-4 months, $d2$, over 4-8 months, $d3$, over 8-16 months, $d4$, over 15-32 months and $d5$, over 32-64 months. The $s6$ series describes the variation over the 128-month period.

2.6.3   Wavelet variance

If $\{\tilde{h}_{j,l}, l = 0, 1, \ldots, L_j\}$ is the j-level MODWT wavelet filter of length L_j, associated with scale $\tau_j \equiv 2^{j-1}$ then if $\{X_t\}$ is a discrete parameter stochastic process and

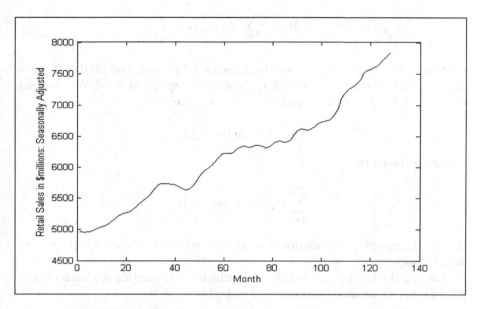

FIGURE 2.6: Retail turnover: January 2005 - August 2015.

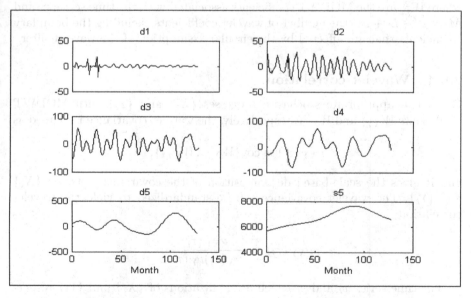

FIGURE 2.7: MODWT decomposition of retail turnover.

$$W_{j,t} \equiv \sum_{l=0}^{L_j} \tilde{h}_{j,l} X_{t-l}$$

represents the stochastic process by filtering $\{X_t\}$ with the MODWT filter $\{\tilde{h}_{j,l}\}$, and if it exists and is finite, the time independent MODWT wavelet variance at the j-th dyadic scale $\tau_j \equiv 2^{j-1}$ is defined as

$$\nu_X^2(\tau_j) \equiv \text{var}\{W_{X,j,t}\}.$$

It can be shown that

$$\sum_{j=1}^{\infty} \nu_X^2(\tau_j) = \text{var}\{X_t\},$$

that is, the wavelet variance decomposes the variance of the stochastic process across scales.

Given a time series $x_t, t = 1, 2 \ldots, T$, which is a realization of the stochastic process X_t, an unbiased estimator of $\nu_X^2(\tau_j)$ is

$$\hat{\nu}_X^2(\tau_j) \equiv \frac{1}{M_j} \sum_{t=L_j-1}^{T-1} \widehat{W}_{X,j,t}^2,$$

where $\widehat{W}_{j,t}^2$ are the MODWT coefficients associated with the time series x_t and $M_j = N - L_j + 1$ is the number of wavelet coefficients excluding the boundary coefficients that are affected by the circular assumption of the wavelet filter.

2.6.4 Wavelet correlation

Given two appropriate stochastic processes $\{X_t\}$ and $\{Y_t\}$ with MODWT coefficients $W_{Xj,t}$ and $W_{Yj,t}$, respectively, the wavelet covariance is defined as

$$\nu_{XY}(\tau_j) \equiv \text{cov}\{W_{Xj,t}, W_{Yj,t}\},$$

and it gives the scale-based decomposition of the covariance between $\{X_t\}$ and $\{Y_t\}$. The wavelet covariance can be standardized to yield the wavelet correlation

$$\rho_{XY}(\tau_j) \equiv \frac{\nu_{XY}(\tau_j)}{\nu_X(\tau_j)\nu_Y(\tau_j)}.$$

For time series x_t and y_t which are realizations of $\{X_t\}$ and $\{Y_t\}$ respectively, replacing the wavelet variances and covariance by their unbiased estimators, we get the estimated wavelet correlation

$$\widehat{\rho}_{XY}(\tau_j) \equiv \frac{\widehat{\nu}_{XY}(\tau_j)}{\widehat{\nu}_X(\tau_j)\widehat{\nu}_Y(\tau_j)}.$$

2.7   Conclusion

In subsequent chapters, we will describe in detail how the time series features and model estimates are used to cluster and classify time series. In some cases, we will be using modifications of and extensions to the concepts, features and models discussed above.

Part I

Unsupervised Approaches: Clustering Techniques for Time Series

3

Traditional cluster analysis

CONTENTS

3.1   Introduction

In many cases, traditional cluster analysis, that is, hierarchical clustering, is used for clustering time series. In this case, first a suitable distance measure inheriting the dynamic features of the time series is defined for comparing time series and, successively, a standard hierarchical (e.g., agglomerative) cluster analysis is applied using the defined distance. For this reason, in this chapter, we briefly describe the traditional clustering methods.

The aim of cluster analysis is to assign units (objects) to clusters so that units within each cluster are similar to one another with respect to observed variables, and the clusters themselves stand apart from one another. In other words, the goal is to divide the units into homogeneous and distinct (well separated) clusters. Generally clustering methods are classified as hierarchical clustering and non-hierarchical clustering (or partitional clustering) methods, based on the properties of the generated clusters (Everitt et al., 2011; Xu and Wunsch, 2009). Hierarchical clustering (see Section 3.3) groups data with a sequence of nested partitions, either from singleton clusters to a cluster including all individuals or vice versa. The former is known as agglomerative clustering, and the latter is called divisive clustering. Both agglomerative and divisive clustering methods organize data into the hierarchical structure based on suitable proximity measures (that is, distance measures (see Section 3.2), dissimilarity measures, similarity indices). In Section 3.3, we focus our attention only on the agglomerative approach. Non-hierarchical clustering (see Section 3.4) directly divides data points into some pre-specified number of clusters without the hierarchical structure. For more details, see Everitt et al. (2011) and Xu and Wunsch (2009).

3.2   Distance measures

Let $\mathbf{X} = \{x_{ij} : 1,\ldots,I; j = 1,\ldots J\} = \{\mathbf{x}_i = (x_{i1},\ldots,x_{ij},\ldots x_{iJ})' : i = 1,\ldots,I\}$ be the data matrix where x_{ij} represents the j-th variable observed on the i-th object and $\mathbf{x}_i$ represents the vector of the i-th observation. The most common class of distance measure used in cluster analysis is the distance class of Minkowski (Everitt et al., 2011):

$$_r d_{il} = \left[\sum_{j=1}^{J} |x_{ij} - x_{lj}|^r \right]^{\frac{1}{r}}, \quad r \geq 1.$$

For $r = 1$, we have the city-block distance (or Manhattan distance):

$$_1 d_{il} = \sum_{j=1}^{J} |x_{ij} - x_{lj}|$$

and for $r = 2$, we have the Euclidean distance, probably the most commonly used distance measure in cluster analysis:

$$_2 d_{il} = \left[\sum_{j=1}^{J} (x_{ij} - x_{lj})^2 \right]^{\frac{1}{2}}.$$

An interesting weighted version of the previous distance class of Minkowski is (Everitt et al., 2011):

$$_r \tilde{d}_{il} = \left[\sum_{j=1}^{J} w_j^r |x_{ij} - x_{lj}|^r \right]^{\frac{1}{r}}, \quad r \geq 1$$

and then,

$$_1 \tilde{d}_{il} = \sum_{j=1}^{J} w_j^1 |x_{jl} - x_{lj}| \qquad (r = 1) \quad \text{(weighted city-block distance)}$$

$$_2 \tilde{d}_{il} = \left[\sum_{j=1}^{J} w_j^2 (x_{jl} - x_{lj})^2 \right]^{\frac{1}{2}} \quad (r = 2) \quad \text{(weighted Euclidean distance)}$$

where w_j $(j = 1,\ldots,J)$ represents a suitable weight for j-th variable.

For using the distance measures in the clustering techniques (that is, in hierarchical clustering) it is useful to collect all the distances for each pair of units in a (squared) matrix form; e.g., the Minkowski distance matrix can be represented as follows:

$$_r\mathbf{D} = \left\{ _rd_{il} = \left[\sum_{j=1}^{J} |x_{ij} - x_{lj}|^r \right]^{\frac{1}{r}} \; : \; i,l = 1,\ldots,I \right\}, \; r \geq 1.$$

See Everitt et al. (2011) for more details on the distance measures and their use in cluster analysis.

3.3 Hierarchical clustering

In this section, we focus our attention only on agglomerative methods which are probably the most widely used of the hierarchical methods. They produce a series of partitions of the data: the first consists of I single-member clusters; the last consists of a single cluster containing all I units (Everitt et al., 2011). Agglomerative clustering starts with I clusters, each of which includes exactly one data point. A series of merge operations is then followed that eventually forces all objects into the same group. The general agglomerative clustering can be summarized by the following procedure (Xu and Wunsch, 2009):

1. Start with I singleton clusters. Calculate the proximity matrix, e.g. distance matrix, for the I clusters;
2. In the distance matrix, search the minimal distance $d(C_c, C_{c'}) = \min_{\substack{1 \leq p,q \leq I \\ p \neq q}} d(C_p, C_q)$, where $d(\cdot, \cdot)$ is the distance function discussed later in the following, and combine cluster C_c and $C_{c'}$ to form a new cluster $C_{cc'}$;
3. Update the distance matrix by computing the distances between the cluster $C_{cc'}$ and the other clusters;
4. Repeat steps 2 and 3 until only one cluster remains.

The merging of a pair of clusters or the formation of a new cluster is dependent on the definition of the distance function between two clusters. There exist a large number of distance function definitions between a cluster C_q and a new cluster $C_{cc'}$ formed by the merge of two clusters C_c and $C_{c'}$. In the following we show briefly some methods for defining distance functions:

- *Single linkage method* (nearest neighbor method): the distance between a pair of clusters is determined by the two closest units to the different clusters. Single linkage clustering tends to generate elongated clusters, which causes the chaining effect (Everitt et al., 2011). As a result, two clusters with quite different properties may be connected due to the existence of noise. However, if the clusters are separated far from each other, the single linkage method works well.

- *Complete linkage method*: in contrast to single linkage clustering, the complete linkage method uses the farthest distance of a pair of objects to define inter-cluster distance.
- *Group average linkage method* (unweighted pair group method average, that is, UPGMA): the distance between two clusters is defined as the average of the distances between all pairs of data points, each of which comes from a different cluster.
- *Weighted average linkage method* (weighted pair group method average, that is, WPGMA): similar to UPGMA, the average linkage is also used to calculate the distance between two clusters. The difference is that the distances between the newly formed cluster and the rest are weighted based on the number of data points in each cluster.
- *Centroid linkage method* (unweighted pair group method centroid, that is, UPGMC): two clusters are merged based on the distance of their centroids (means).
- *Ward's method* (minimum variance method): the aim of Ward's method is to minimize the increase of the so-called within-class sum of the squared errors.

Single linkage, complete linkage, and average linkage consider all points of a pair of clusters when calculating their inter-cluster distance, and they are also called graph methods. The others are called geometric methods because they use geometric centres to represent clusters and determine their distances (Xu and Wunsch, 2009). See Everitt et al. (2011) for the features and properties of these methods and experimental comparative studies. The results of hierarchical clustering are usually depicted by a particular graphic called *dendrogram*. The root node of the dendrogram represents the whole data set, and each leaf node is regarded as a data point. The intermediate nodes thus describe the extent to which the objects are proximal to each other; and the height of the dendrogram usually expresses the distance between each pair of data points or clusters, or a data point and a cluster. The ultimate clustering results can be obtained by cutting the dendrogram at different levels. This representation provides very informative descriptions and a visualization of the potential data clustering structures, especially when real hierarchical relations exist in the data (Everitt et al., 2011; Xu and Wunsch, 2009).

Examples of dendrograms are shown in the subsequent chapters. In particular, with respect to the choice of the optimal partition (optimal number of clusters) we have different cluster validity criteria for hierarchical and partitioning methods. For hierarchical clustering methods the optimal partition is achieved by selecting one of the solutions in the nested sequence of clusterings that the hierarchy comprises, equivalent to cutting a dendrogram at a particular height (sometimes termed the best cut). This defines a partition such that clusters below that height are distant from each other by at least that amount, and the appearance of the dendrogram can thus informally suggest the number of clusters. Large changes in fusion levels are taken to indicate the best cut. For other criteria based on the investigation of the dendrogram see Everitt et al. (2011). More formal approaches to the problem of determining the number of clusters have been reviewed by Milligan and Cooper (1985) (Everitt et al., 2011). Some of these methods are briefly described in Section 3.4.

3.4 Non-hierarchical clustering (partitioning clustering)

In contrast to hierarchical clustering, which yields a successive level of clusters by iterative fusions or divisions, non-hierarchical or partitioning clustering assigns a set of data points into c clusters without any hierarchical structure. This process usually accompanies the optimization of a criterion function, usually the minimization of a objective function representing the within variability of the clusters (Xu and Wunsch, 2009). One of the best-known and most popular non-hierarchical clustering methods is c-means clustering. Another interesting partitioning method is c-medoids clustering. In the following sections, we briefly present these methods and the cluster validity criteria for determining the optimal number of clusters that have to be pre-specified in these methods.

3.4.1 c-Means clustering method

The c-means clustering method (MacQueen, 1967) which is also known as k-means clustering is one of the best-known and most popular clustering methods. It is also commonly known as k-means clustering. The c-means clustering methods seeks an optimal partition of the data by minimizing the sum-of-squared-error criterion shown in Eq. (3.1) with an iterative optimization procedure, which belongs to the category of hill-climbing algorithms (Xu and Wunsch, 2009). The basic clustering procedure of c-means clustering is summarized as follows (Everitt et al., 2011; Xu and Wunsch, 2009):

1. Initialize a c-partition randomly or based on some prior knowledge. Calculate the cluster prototypes (centroids or means) (that is, calculate the mean in each cluster considering only the observations belonging to each cluster).
2. Assign each unit in the data set to the nearest cluster by using a suitable distance measure between each pair of units and centroids.
3. Recalculate the cluster prototypes (centroids or means) based on the current partition.
4. Repeat steps 2 and 3 until there is no change for each cluster.

Mathematically, the c-means clustering method is formalized as follows:

$$\min : \sum_{i=1}^{I} \sum_{c=1}^{C} u_{ic} \, d_{ic}^2 = \sum_{i=1}^{I} \sum_{c=1}^{C} u_{ic} \, \|\mathbf{x}_i - \mathbf{h}_c\|^2, \tag{3.1}$$

$$\sum_{c=1}^{C} u_{ic} = 1, \; u_{ic} \geq 0, u_{ic} = \{0, 1\} \tag{3.2}$$

where u_{ic} indicates the membership degree of the i-th unit to the c-th cluster; $u_{ic} = \{0, 1\}$, that is, $u_{ic} = 1$ when the i-th unit belongs to the c-th cluster; $u_{ic} = 0$ otherwise; $d_{ic}^2 = \|\mathbf{x}_i - \mathbf{h}_c\|^2$ indicates the squared Euclidean distance between the i-th object and the centroid of the c-th cluster.

3.4.2   c-Medoids clustering method

By considering the c-medoids clustering method or *partitioning around medoids (PAM)* method (Kaufman and Rousseeuw, 1987, 1990), units are classified into clusters represented by one of the data points in the cluster (this method is also often referred to as k-medoids). These data points are the prototypes, the so-called medoids. Each medoid synthesizes the cluster information and represents the prototypal features of the clusters and then synthesizes the characteristics of the units belonging to each cluster. Following the c-medoids clustering method, we minimize the objective function represented by the sum (or mathematically equivalent, average) of the dissimilarity of units to their closest representative units. The c-medoids clustering method first computes a set of representative units, the *medoids*. After finding the set of medoids, each unit of the data set is assigned to the nearest medoid units. The algorithm suggested by Kaufman and Rousseeuw (1990) for the c-medoids clustering method proceeds in two phases:

Phase 1 (*BUILD*): This phase sequentially selects c "centrally located" units to be used as initial medoids.

Phase 2 (*SWAP*): If the objective function can be reduced by interchanging (swapping) a selected unit with an unselected unit, then the swap is carried out. This is continued until the objective function can no longer be decreased. Then, by considering a set of I units by $\mathbf{X}$ (set of the observations) and a subset of $\mathbf{X}$ with C units by $\tilde{\mathbf{X}}$ (set of the medoids) (where $C << I$), we could formalize the model as follows:

$$\min : \sum_{i=1}^{I} \sum_{c=1}^{C} u_{ic} \, \tilde{d}_{ic}^2 = \sum_{i=1}^{I} \sum_{c=1}^{C} u_{ic} \, \|\mathbf{x}_i - \tilde{\mathbf{x}}_c\|^2, \tag{3.3}$$

$$\sum_{c=1}^{C} u_{ic} = 1, \; u_{ic} \geq 0, u_{ic} = \{0, 1\} \tag{3.4}$$

where u_{ic} indicates the membership degree of the i-th unit to the c-th cluster; $u_{ic} = \{0, 1\}$, that is, $u_{ic} = 1$ when the i-th unit belongs to the c-th cluster; $u_{ic} = 0$ otherwise; $\tilde{d}_{ic}^2 = \|\mathbf{x}_i - \tilde{\mathbf{x}}_c\|^2$ indicates the squared Euclidean distance between the i-th object and the medoid of the c-th cluster.

3.5 Some cluster validity criteria

Useful cluster validity criteria for determining the number of clusters are the following.

3.5.1 Calinski and Harabasz criterion

Calinski and Harabasz (1974) suggest taking the value of g, the number of clusters, which corresponds to the maximum value of CH_C:

$$CH_C = \frac{\text{trace}\,(\mathbf{B})}{(C-1)} : \frac{\text{trace}\,(\mathbf{W})}{(I-C)}.$$

where $\mathbf{B}$ is the between-groups dispersion matrix and $\mathbf{W}$ is the within-group dispersion matrix. As with all techniques for determining the number of groups, the evaluation of this criterion at a given number of groups, C, requires knowledge of the group membership to determine the matrices $\mathbf{B}$ and $\mathbf{W}$. Notice that $\mathbf{T} = \mathbf{W} + \mathbf{B}$, where $\mathbf{T}$ indicates the total dispersion matrix. See, Everitt et al. (2011) for more details. In general, the number of groups chosen depends on the cluster method (and implementation) used (Everitt et al., 2011).

3.5.2 Silhouette criterion

This criterion was proposed by Rousseeuw (1987). Consider a unit $i \in (1, \ldots, I)$ belonging to cluster $p \in (1, \ldots, C)$. E.g., by a c-means clustering algorithm, this means that i-th unit is closer to the centroid of the p-th cluster than to any other centroid. Let the average (squared Euclidean) distance of i-th unit to all other units belonging to cluster p be denoted by a_{ip}. Also, let the average distance of this unit to all units belonging to another cluster q, $q \neq p$, be called d_{iq}. Finally, let b_{ip} be the minimum d_{iq} computed over $q = 1, \ldots, c, q \neq p$, which represents the dissimilarity of the i-th unit to its closest neighboring cluster. Then, the silhouette of the i-th object is defined as follows:

$$S_i = \frac{b_{ip} - a_{ip}}{\max\{a_{ip}, b_{ip}\}} \tag{3.5}$$

where the denominator is a normalization term. Evidently, the higher the S_i value is, the better the assignment of the i-th unit to the c-th cluster. The silhouette defined as the average of S_i over $i = 1, \ldots, I$ is:

$$SIL = \frac{1}{I} \sum_{i=1}^{I} S_i. \tag{3.6}$$

The best partition is achieved when the silhouette is maximized, which implies minimizing the intra-cluster distance (a_{ip}) while maximizing the inter-cluster distance (b_{ip}).

4

Fuzzy clustering

CONTENTS

4.1 Introduction

In this chapter[1], we illustrate some relevant clustering methods in a fuzzy framework useful for clustering time series. As we can see in the following chapters, different observation, feature and model-based fuzzy clustering methods have been proposed for classifying time series from an unsupervised point of view. As we saw in Chapter 3, in traditional clustering, each object is exactly assigned to only one cluster obtaining exhaustive partitions characterized by nonempty and pairwise disjoint subsets. Such hard assignment of objects to clusters can be inadequate in the presence of objects that are almost equally distant from two or more clusters. Such special objects can represent hybrid-types which are more or less equally similar to two or more types. Traditional clustering arbitrarily forces the full assignment of such an object to one of the clusters, although they should almost equally belong to all of them. Fuzzy clustering relaxes the requirement that objects have to be assigned to only one

---

[1]This chapter represents a synthesis of the chapter "Fuzzy Clustering" by D'Urso (2015) in the Handbook of Cluster Analysis, Henning C., Meila M., Murtagh F. and Rocci R. (eds.), Chapman and Hall.

cluster. Objects can belong to more than one cluster and even with different degrees of membership to the different clusters. This gradual cluster assignment can reflect cluster structure in a more natural way, especially when clusters overlap (D'Urso, 2015; Kruse et al., 2007). The fundamental justification concerning the adoption of a fuzzy approach in a clustering framework lies in the recognition of the vague (fuzzy) nature of the cluster assignment task. In this case, the fuzziness is embodied in the clustering model in the assignment process of time series to clusters. In particular, in order to incorporate the fuzziness in the clustering procedure, the so called membership degree of each time series to different groups is considered as a means of evaluating the fuzziness in the assignment procedure. Fuzzy methods are suitable for clustering time series for the following motivations:

1. The fuzzy clustering algorithm is attractive because it is a distribution-free procedure.

2. Due to the difficulty of identifying a clear boundary between clusters in real world problems, the partial classification of fuzzy clustering appears more attractive than the deterministic classification of non-overlapping clustering methods such as c-means (McBratney and Moore, 1985; Wedel and Kamakura, 2012).

3. The fuzzy clustering is computationally more efficient because dramatic changes in the value of cluster membership are less likely to occur in estimation procedures (McBratney and Moore, 1985) and it has been shown to be less afflicted by local optima problems (Heiser and Groenen, 1997).

4. The memberships for any given set of respondents indicate whether there is a second-best cluster almost as good as the best cluster, a result which traditional clustering methods cannot uncover (Everitt et al., 2011).

5. Greater sensitivity in capturing the details characterizing the time series. In many cases, since the dynamics of the time series are drifting or switching, the standard (non-fuzzy) clustering approaches are likely to miss this underlying structure. The switches, which are usually vague, can be naturally treated by means of fuzzy clustering (D'Urso, 2005).

6. Greater adaptivity in defining the prototype time series. This can be better appreciated when the observed time patterns do not differ too much from each other. In this case, the fuzzy definition of the clusters allows us to single out underlying structures, if these are likely to exist in the given set of time series (D'Urso, 2005).

4.2   Fuzzy c-Means (FcM) clustering

Let $\mathbf{X} = \{x_{ij} : i = 1, \ldots, I; j = 1, \ldots, J\} = \{\mathbf{x}_i = (x_{i1}, \ldots, x_{ij}, \ldots, x_{iJ})' : i = 1, \ldots, I\}$ be a data matrix, where x_{ij} represents the j-th quantitative variable observed on the i-th object and $\mathbf{x}_i$ represents the vector of the i-th observation. The FcM clustering method proposed by Bezdek (1981) is formalized in the following way:

$$\min : \sum_{i=1}^{I} \sum_{c=1}^{C} u_{ic}^m d_{ic}^2 = \sum_{i=1}^{I} \sum_{c=1}^{C} u_{ic}^m \|\mathbf{x}_i - \mathbf{h}_c\|^2; \qquad \sum_{c=1}^{C} u_{ic} = 1, \, u_{ic} \geq 0 \quad (4.1)$$

where u_{ic} denotes the membership degree of the i-th object to the c-th cluster; $d_{ic}^2 = \|\mathbf{x}_i - \mathbf{h}_c\|^2$ is the squared Euclidean distance between the i-th unit and the centroid of the c-th cluster; $\mathbf{h}_c = (h_{c1}, \ldots, h_{cj}, \ldots, h_{cJ})'$ represents the c-th centroid, where h_{cj} indicates the j-th component (j-th variable) of the c-th centroid vector; $m > 1$ is a parameter that controls the fuzziness of the partition (for the selection of m, see D'Urso, 2015). By putting $m = 1$ in Eq. (4.1), we obtain the standard c-means (cM) clustering method (MacQueen, 1967) (see Chapter 3). Solving the constrained optimization problem Eq. (4.1) with the Lagrangian multipliers method, the conditional optimal iterative solutions are (see Bezdek, 1981):

$$u_{ic} = \frac{1}{\sum_{c'=1}^{C} \left[\frac{\|\mathbf{x}_i - \mathbf{h}_c\|}{\|\mathbf{x}_i - \mathbf{h}_{c'}\|} \right]^{\frac{2}{m-1}}}, \qquad \mathbf{h}_c = \frac{\sum_{i=1}^{I} u_{ic}^m \mathbf{x}_i}{\sum_{i=1}^{I} u_{ic}^m}. \quad (4.2)$$

4.3 Cluster validity criteria

In the FcM clustering method Eq. (4.1), before computing the membership degrees and the centroids iteratively, by means of Eq. (4.2), we have to set a suitable number of clusters c. Many cluster-validity criteria have been suggested. For a review on fuzzy cluster validity criteria see, among others, Xu and Brereton (2005) and Wang and Zhang (2007).

4.3.1 Criteria based on partition coefficient and partition entropy

The first cluster validity criteria are based on the partition coefficient (PC) (Dunn, 1974), partition entropy (PE) (Bezdek, 2001) and modified partition coefficient (MPC) (Dunn, 1977). In particular:

$$\mathrm{PC} = \frac{1}{I} \sum_{i=1}^{I} \sum_{c=1}^{C} u_{ic}^2, \quad (4.3)$$

$\frac{1}{c} \leq$ PC ≤ 1: if PC=1 / C we have maximum fuzziness; if PC=1 we have a hard partition;

$$\text{PE} = -\frac{1}{I} \sum_{i=1}^{I} \left(\sum_{c=1}^{C} u_{ic} \log u_{ic} \right), \tag{4.4}$$

$0 \leq \log C$: if PE=0 we have a hard partition; if PE= $\log C$ we have maximum fuzziness;

$$\text{MPC} = 1 - \frac{C}{C-1}(1 - \text{PC}) \tag{4.5}$$

$0 \leq$ MPC ≤ 1: if MPC $= 0$ we have maximum fuzziness; if MPC $= 1$ we have a hard partition.

4.3.2 The Xie-Beni criterion

A widely used cluster validity criterion for selecting C is the *Xie-Beni criterion* (Xie and Beni, 1991):

$$\min_{C \in \Omega_C} : XB = \frac{\sum_{i=1}^{I} \sum_{c=1}^{C} u_{ic}^{m} \|\mathbf{x}_i - \mathbf{h}_c\|^2}{I \min_{c,c'} \|\mathbf{h}_c - \mathbf{h}_{c'}\|^2}, \tag{4.6}$$

where Ω_C represents the set of possible values of C $(C < I)$.

The numerator of XB represents the *total within-cluster distance*, which is equal to the objective function called J, of FcM clustering method. The ratio J/I is called the *compactness* of the fuzzy partition. The smaller this ratio, the more compact a partition with a fixed number of clusters (despite the number of data objects in a given data set). The minimum squared distance between centroids in the denominator of XB is called *separation*. The greater this distance, the more separate a data partition with a fixed number of clusters. Therefore, for a fixed number of clusters, the smaller the XB value is, the better the partition.

4.3.3 The Silhouette criterion

Another interesting cluster validity procedure is the fuzzy extension of the *Silhouette criterion* (Campello and Hruschka, 2006) (see Chapter 3).

The fuzzy silhouette makes explicit use of the fuzzy partition matrix $\mathbf{U} = \{u_{ic} : i = 1, \ldots, I; c = 1, \ldots, C\}$. It may be able to discriminate between overlapped data clusters even if these clusters have their own distinct regions with higher data densities, since it considers the information contained in the fuzzy partition matrix $\mathbf{U}$ based on the degrees to which clusters overlap one another. This information can be used to reveal those regions with high data densities by stressing the importance of time series data concentrated in the vicinity of the cluster prototypes while reducing the importance of objects lying in overlapping areas. The fuzzy silhouette $(SIL.F)$ is defined as follows:

$$SIL.F = \frac{\sum_{i=1}^{I}(u_{ic} - u_{ic'})^\gamma S_i}{\sum_{i=1}^{I}(u_{ic} - u_{ic'})^\gamma}. \tag{4.7}$$

where S_i is represented by Eq. (3.5), u_{ic} and $u_{ic'}$ are the first and second largest elements of the i-th row of the fuzzy partition matrix, respectively, and $\gamma \geq 0$ is a weighting coefficient. The effect of varying this parameter on the weighting terms in Eq. (4.7) is investigated in Campello and Hruschka (2006).

As remarked by Campello and Hruschka (2006), the fuzzy silhouette Eq. (4.7) differs from SIL "for being a weighted average (instead of an arithmetic mean) of the individual silhouettes S_i. The weight of each term is determined by the difference between the membership degrees of the corresponding object to its first and second best matching fuzzy clusters, respectively. In this way, an object in the near vicinity of a cluster prototype is given more importance than another object located in an overlapping area (where the membership degrees of the objects of two or more fuzzy clusters are similar)".

With respect to other well known validity criteria based uniquely upon the fuzzy partition matrix (such as the Partition Coefficient), the fuzzy silhouette Eq. (4.7) takes into account the geometrical information related to the data distribution through the term S_i.

4.4   Fuzzy c-Medoids (FcMd) clustering

In a fuzzy framework, Krishnapuram et al. (1999) and Krishnapuram et al. (2001) suggested the so-called Fuzzy c-Medoids (FcMd) clustering method.

Let $\mathbf{X} = \{\mathbf{x}_1, \ldots, \mathbf{x}_i, \ldots, \mathbf{x}_I\}$ be a set of I objects (data matrix) and let us indicate with $\tilde{\mathbf{X}} = \{\tilde{\mathbf{x}}_1, \ldots, \tilde{\mathbf{x}}_i, \ldots, \tilde{\mathbf{x}}_C\}$ a sub-set of $\mathbf{X} = \{\mathbf{x}_1, \ldots, \mathbf{x}_i, \ldots, \mathbf{x}_I\}$ with cardinality C.

The FcMd clustering method is formalized as follows:

$$\min : \sum_{i=1}^{I}\sum_{c=1}^{C} u_{ic}^m \tilde{d}_{ic}^2 = \sum_{i=1}^{I}\sum_{c=1}^{C} u_{ic}^m \|\mathbf{x}_i - \tilde{\mathbf{x}}_c\|^2; \qquad \sum_{c=1}^{C} u_{ic} = 1, \, u_{ic} \geq 0 \tag{4.8}$$

where $\tilde{d}_{ic}^2 = \|\mathbf{x}_i - \tilde{\mathbf{x}}_c\|^2$ indicates the squared Euclidean distance between the i-th object and the medoid of the c-th cluster.

Solving the constrained optimization problem Eq. (4.8) by means of the Lagrangian multiplier method the local optimal solutions are (Krishnapuram et al., 2001):

$$u_{ic} = \frac{1}{\sum_{c'=1}^{C} \left[\frac{\|\mathbf{x}_i - \tilde{\mathbf{x}}_c\|}{\|\mathbf{x}_i - \tilde{\mathbf{x}}_{c'}\|}\right]^{\frac{2}{m-1}}}. \tag{4.9}$$

Notice that:

- Each cluster is represented by an observed representative object and not by a fictitious representative object (prototype, i.e., centroid). The possibility of obtaining non-fictitious representative prototypes in the clusters is very appealing and useful in a wide range of applications. This is very important for the interpretation of the selected clusters. In fact, as remarked by Kaufman and Rousseeuw (2009) "in many clustering problems one is particularly interested in a characterization of the clusters by means of typical or representative objects. These are objects that represent the various structural aspects of the set of objects being investigated. There can be many reasons for searching for representative objects. Not only can these objects provide a characterization of the clusters, but they can often be used for further work or research, especially when it is more economical or convenient to use a small set of c objects".

- FcMd clustering method does not depend on the order in which the objects are presented (except when equivalent solutions exist, which very rarely occurs in practice). This is not the case for many other algorithms present in the literature (Kaufman and Rousseeuw, 2009).

- Since the FcMd clustering method belongs to the class of procedures for partitioning around medoids, it attempts to alleviate the negative effects of the presence of outliers in the dataset; thus, FcMd can be considered more robust than its possible c-means version in the presence of noise and outliers because a medoid is less influenced by outliers or other extreme values than a mean. However, as remarked by García-Escudero and Gordaliza (1999, 2005), the FcMd provides only a timid robustification of the FcM. In fact, it attempts to alleviate the negative effects of presence of outliers in the dataset, but it does not solve the problem.

- When the objective function in Eq. (4.8) is minimized, the medoids $\tilde{\mathbf{X}} = \{\tilde{\mathbf{x}}_1, \ldots, \tilde{\mathbf{x}}_i, \ldots, \tilde{\mathbf{x}}_I\}$ corresponding to the solution provide a fuzzy partition via (4.9). However, the objective function in Eq. (4.8) cannot be minimized by means of the alternating optimization algorithm, because the necessary conditions cannot be derived by differentiating it with respect to the medoids. Nonetheless, following the heuristic algorithm of Fu (1982) for a crisp version of the objective function in Eq. (4.8), a fuzzy clustering algorithm that minimizes the objective function in Eq. (4.8) can be built up Krishnapuram et al. (2001).

- As for the classical case, the algorithm utilized for Eq. (4.8) - Eq. (4.9) falls in the category of the Alternating Cluster Estimation paradigm (Runkler and Bezdek, 1999). Moreover, it is not guaranteed to find the global minimum. Thus, more than one random start is suggested.

- The algorithm utilized for Eq. (4.8) - Eq. (4.9) is based on an exhaustive search for the medoids, which with large datasets could be too computationally intensive. The computational complexity of FcMd can be reduced by considering the "linearized" algorithm introduced by Krishnapuram et al. (2001) and Nasraoui et al. (2002). In this way, when we update the medoids for the generic cluster c we do not examine all the units, but only a subset that corresponds to those with the higher membership degree in cluster c.

- Since the medoid always has a membership of 1 in the cluster, raising its membership to the power m has no effect. Thus, when m is high, the mobility of the medoids may be lost. For this reason, a value between 1 and 1.5 for m is recommended; see Kamdar and Joshi (2000).

4.5 Fuzzy clustering with entropy regularization

As shown in Section 4.2, in the objective function $\sum_{i=1}^{I} \sum_{c=1}^{C} u_{ic}^m d_{ic}^2$, we have the weighting exponent m that controls the fuzziness of the partition. The fuzzification of the standard c-means clustering by introducing m has been viewed by some researchers as an artificial device, lacking a strong theoretical justification. Consequently, a new line of research has been started, based on the adoption of regularization terms to be juxtaposed to the maximum internal homogeneity criterion (see, e.g., Miyamoto and Mukaidono, 1997). In this case, the burden of representing fuzziness is shifted to the regularization term, in the form of a weighting factor multiplying the contribution of the regularization function to the clustering criterion. In this framework, the regularization function has been thought of as measuring the overall fuzziness of the obtained clustering pattern. Such measure is the entropy function (i.e. the Shannon entropy) which, if applied to the degrees of membership, may be called fuzzy entropy (Coppi and D'Urso, 2006).

In particular, Li and Mukaidono (1995) remark that this "strange" parameter is unnatural and does not have a physical meaning. Then, in the above objective function m may be removed, but in this case, the procedure cannot generate the membership update equations. For this purpose, Li and Mukaidono (1995, 1999) suggest a new approach to fuzzy clustering, the so-called Maximum Entropy Inference Method:

$$\max : -\sum_{i=1}^{I} \sum_{c=1}^{C} u_{ic} \log u_{ic}, \quad \sum_{c=1}^{C} u_{ic} = 1, u_{ic} \geq 0, \quad J_i = \sum_{c=1}^{C} u_{ic}^m d_{ic}^2 = \kappa_i(\sigma^2)$$

(4.10)

where, at each step i of the optimization algorithm, $\kappa_i(\sigma^2)$ represents the value of the loss function J_i (the within clusters sum-of-squares-error) due to object i. It is shown that this value depends on parameter σ which gets a physical interpretation in terms of "temperature" in statistical physics.

The optimal value of σ can be determined by the simulated annealing method. The term to be extremized in Eq. (4.10) defines the entropy of a fuzzy partition, and it is clearly inspired by the Shannon index concerning a finite set of random events.

We underline that the Maximum Entropy principle, as applied to fuzzy clustering, provides a new perspective to facing the problem of fuzzifying the clustering of the objects, while ensuring the maximum of compactness of the obtained clusters.

The former objective is achieved by maximizing the entropy (and, therefore, the uncertainty) of the clustering of the objects into the various clusters. The latter objective is obtained by constraining the above maximization process in such a way as to minimize the overall distance of the objects from the cluster prototypes (i.e. to maximize cluster compactness) Coppi and D'Urso (2006).

The idea underlies the entropy-based fuzzy clustering method proposed by Miyamoto and Mukaidono (1997) in which the trade off between fuzziness and compactness is dealt with by introducing a unique objective function reformulating the maximum entropy method in terms of "regularization" of the FcM function. In particular, by introducing an entropy regularization, the minimization problem becomes (Miyamoto and Mukaidono, 1997):

$$\min : \sum_{i=1}^{I}\sum_{c=1}^{C} u_{ic}\|\mathbf{x}_i - \mathbf{h}_c\|^2 + p\sum_{i=1}^{I}\sum_{c=1}^{C} u_{ic}\log u_{ic}; \quad \sum_{c=1}^{C} u_{ic} = 1, \, u_{ic} \geq 0 \quad (4.11)$$

where p is a weight factor, called degree of fuzzy entropy, similar to the weight exponent m.

By means of Eq. (4.11) the authors minimize a functional depending on the desired solution regularized by maximizing the total amount of information. By solving Eq. (4.11) using the Lagrangian multiplier method, we have $u_{ic} = \left[\sum_{c'=1}^{C}\left[\frac{\exp(1/p\|\mathbf{x}_i-\mathbf{h}_c\|^2)}{\exp(1/p\|\mathbf{x}_i-\mathbf{h}_{c'}\|^2)}\right]\right]^{-1}$.

For more references on entropy-based fuzzy clustering, see Coppi and D'Urso (2006).

4.6   Robust fuzzy clustering

In this section, we introduce some robust fuzzy clustering capable of neutralizing the negative effects of outliers in the clustering process.

4.6.1   Fuzzy clustering with noise cluster

An interesting objective function-based variants of the FcM useful for neutralizing the negative effects of noise data in the clustering process is the Fuzzy c-Means clustering method with noise cluster (FcM-NC). FcM-NC was initially proposed by Davé (1991), who uses a criterion similar to Ohashi (1984), and later extended by Davé and Sen (1997). This method consists of adding, beside the c clusters to be found in a dataset, the so-called *noise cluster*. It aims at grouping points that are badly represented by normal clusters, such as noisy data points or outliers. It is not explicitly associated with a prototype, but directly with the distance between an implicit prototype and the data points: the center of the noise cluster is considered to be at a constant distance from all data points.

Thus, the noise cluster is represented by a *fictitious prototype* (*noise prototype*) that has a constant distance (*noise distance*) from every object. An object belongs to a *real cluster* only if its distance from a prototype (centroid) is lower than the noise distance; otherwise, the object belongs to the noise cluster.

The FcM-NC clustering method can be formalized as follows:

$$\min : \sum_{i=1}^{I} \sum_{c=1}^{C-1} u_{ic}^m \|\mathbf{x}_i - \mathbf{h}_c\|^2 + \sum_{i=1}^{I} \delta^2 \left(1 - \sum_{c=1}^{C-1} u_{ic}\right)^m \qquad \sum_{c=1}^{C-1} u_{ic} \leq 1, \, u_{ic} \geq 0$$
(4.12)

where δ is a suitable scale parameter, the so-called *noise distance*, to be chosen in advance. Such a parameter plays the role of increasing (for high values of δ) or decreasing (for low values of δ) the emphasis of the "noise component" in the minimization of the objective function in Eq. (4.12), e.g. $\delta^2 = \lambda[I(C-1)]^{-1}[\sum_{I=1}^{I} \sum_{c=1}^{C-1} \|\mathbf{x}_i - \mathbf{h}_c\|^2]$, where λ is a scale multiplier that needs to be selected depending on the type of data.

It has to be observed that the model provides C clusters, but only $(C-1)$ are "real" clusters, with the extra cluster serving as the noise cluster. The difference in the second term of the objective function shown in Eq. (4.12) expresses the membership degree of each object to the noise cluster, and shows that the sum of the membership degrees over the first $(C-1)$ clusters is lower than or equal to 1. Indeed, the membership degree (u_{i*}) of the i-th object to the *noise cluster* is defined as $u_{i*} = 1 - \sum_{c=1}^{C-1} u_{ic}$ and the usual constraint of the FcM ($\sum_{c=1}^{C-1} u_{ic} = 1$) is not required. Thus, the membership constraint for the *real clusters* is relaxed to $\sum_{c=1}^{C-1} u_{ic} \leq 1$. This allows the noise object to have small membership values in *good clusters* (Davé and Sen, 2002).

By solving Eq. (4.12), we obtain

$$u_{ic} = \left[\sum_{c'=1}^{C-1} \left[\frac{\|\mathbf{x}_i - \mathbf{h}_c\|}{\|\mathbf{x}_i - \mathbf{h}_{c'}\|}\right]^{\frac{2}{m-1}} + \left[\frac{\|\mathbf{x}_i - \mathbf{h}_c\|}{\delta}\right]^{\frac{2}{m-1}}\right]^{-1} .$$

A FcMd version of Eq. (4.12), called FcMd-NC, can be obtained considering the medoid $\tilde{\mathbf{x}}_c$ instead of the centroid $\mathbf{h}_c$.

4.6.2 Fuzzy clustering with exponential distance

Another robust fuzzy clustering is the so-called Fuzzy c-Means clustering with Exponential distance (FcM-Exp):

$$\min : \sum_{i=1}^{I} \sum_{c=1}^{C} u_{ic}^m \left[1 - \exp\left\{ -\beta \|\mathbf{x}_i - \mathbf{h}_c\|^2 \right\} \right] \qquad \text{s.t.} \sum_{c=1}^{C} u_{ic} = 1, \, u_{ic} \geq 0$$

(4.13)

where $m > 1$ is a weighting exponent that controls the fuzziness of the obtained partition.

Following Wu and Yang (2002), the local optimal solutions for the objective function in Eq. (4.13) are:

$$u_{ic} = \left(\sum_{c'=1}^{C} \left[\frac{1 - \exp\left\{ -\beta \|\mathbf{x}_i - \mathbf{h}_c\|^2 \right\}}{1 - \exp\left\{ -\beta \|\mathbf{x}_i - \mathbf{h}_c'\|^2 \right\}} \right]^{\frac{1}{m-1}} \right)^{-1}$$

(4.14)

and

$$\mathbf{h}_c = \frac{\sum_{i=1}^{I} u_{ic}^m \exp\left\{ -\beta \|\mathbf{x}_i - \mathbf{h}_c\|^2 \right\} \mathbf{x}_i}{\sum_{i=1}^{I} u_{ic}^m \exp\left\{ -\beta \|\mathbf{x}_i - \mathbf{h}_c\|^2 \right\}}.$$

(4.15)

Wu and Yang (2002) showed that the c-means clustering model based on the Exponential distance is more robust than the model based on the Euclidean norm.

The value of β, determined as the inverse of the variability in the data (the more the variability in the data the less the value of β), appropriately affects the membership degree Eq. (4.14) in terms of robustness to outliers.

Wu and Yang (2002) used the fixed-point iterative method to solve $\mathbf{h}_c$ in (4.15).

Notice that the medoids version of the FcM Exp method (i.e., FcMd-Exp) can be considered by using the medoid $\tilde{\mathbf{x}}_c$ instead of centroid $\mathbf{h}_c$.

4.6.3   Trimmed fuzzy clustering

The Trimmed Fuzzy c-Means clustering model (Tr-FcM), which is a robust version of the Fuzzy c-Means clustering, achieves its robustness by adopting the "impartial trimming" procedure (García-Escudero and Gordaliza, 1999; García-Escudero et al., 2010) to identify the objects more distant from the bulk of data. The procedure is said to be "impartial" because there is not a privileged direction in the trimming of the data, but the trimming is led by the data at hand. This approach is also suitable to detect both "outlying clusters" (outliers grouped in one small cluster) and "radial outliers" (isolated outliers) (García-Escudero et al., 2003).

Given a trimming size α which ranges between 0 and 1, we solve the double minimization problem:

$$\min_{Y} \min_{u_{ic}} : \sum_{i=1}^{H(\alpha)} \sum_{c=1}^{C} u_{ic}^m \|\mathbf{x}_i - \mathbf{h}_c\|^2 \qquad \sum_{c=1}^{C} u_{ic} = 1, \quad u_{ic} \geq 0,$$

(4.16)

where u_{ic} is the membership degree of the i-th object to the c-th cluster; $m > 1$ is the fuzziness parameter — the greater the value of m the more fuzzy is the obtained partition; Y ranges on all the subsets of the objects $\{\mathbf{x}_i = (x_{i1}, \ldots, x_{ij}, \ldots, x_{iJ})' : i = 1, \ldots, I\}$, containing $H(\alpha) = \lfloor I \cdot (1 - \alpha) \rfloor$ objects ($\lfloor . \rfloor$ is the integer part of a given value). Using the above described trimming rule we allow for a proportion α of objects to be left unassigned García-Escudero et al. (2010). Notice that Eq. (4.16) includes FcM as a limit case when $\alpha = 0$. Then, each non-trimmed object is allocated into the cluster corresponding to its closest centroid.

The local optimal solutions are:

$$u_{ic} = \frac{\|\mathbf{x}_i - \mathbf{h}_c\|^{-\frac{2}{m-1}}}{\sum_{c'=1}^{C} \|\mathbf{x}_i - \mathbf{h}_{c'}\|^{-\frac{2}{m-1}}}, \qquad \mathbf{h}_c = \frac{\sum_{i=1}^{I} u_{ic}^m \mathbf{x}_i}{\sum_{i=1}^{I} u_{ic}^m}. \qquad (4.17)$$

where i ranges on the subset of the non-trimmed objects.

For more details, see, e.g., D'Urso et al. (2017b)

Notice that also in this case we can obtain the partitioning around the medoids version.

5

Observation-based clustering

CONTENTS

5.1 Introduction

In the literature different distance measures and clustering models have been proposed for classifying observed or transformed time series (observation-based-clustering). As we can see, in this chapter, this clustering approach is particularly useful when the time series are not very long. In this chapter, we show, firstly, some distance measures for observed or transformed time series; successively, we present some models for clustering time series able to capture the instantaneous and longitudinal characteristics of the observed time series. Lastly, we report some applicative examples.

5.2 Observation-based distance measures

A "direct" approach for clustering time series can be based on a comparison of the observed time series or a suitable transformation of the observed time series. This clustering approach is particularly useful when we want to cluster (univariate or multivariate) time series based on their geometric profiles. In general, the observation-based approach distances could be recommended when the aim is to identify similar geometric profiles.

To this purpose, in the literature, there are various distance measures based on the time observations or their suitable transformations. In a multivariate framework, some distances based on the time observations (position) and/or the slope and/or concavity/convexity of the time series have been proposed (D'Urso, 2000). By denoting two generic multivariate time series, respectively, with $\mathbf{x}_{it} = (x_{i1t}, \ldots, x_{ijt}, \ldots, x_{iJt})'$ and $\mathbf{x}_{lt} = (x_{l1t}, \ldots, x_{ljt}, \ldots, x_{lJt})'$ - where, e.g., x_{ijt} and x_{ljt} represent the j-th variable observed in the i-th and l-th unit at time t - an easy distance measure is:

$$_1d(x_i, x_l) = \sqrt{\sum_{t=1}^{T} \left(\|\mathbf{x}_{it} - \mathbf{x}_{lt}\|_1 w_t\right)^2} \tag{5.1}$$

where $_1w_t$ is a suitable weight at time t.

Distance measures based on suitable transformations of the observed time series, that is, on the slope and concavity/convexity, are (D'Urso, 2000):

$$_2d(x_i, x_l) = \sqrt{\sum_{t=2}^{T} \left(\|\mathbf{v}_{it} - \mathbf{v}_{lt}\|_2 w_t\right)^2} \tag{5.2}$$

$$_3d(x_i, x_l) = \sqrt{\sum_{t=3}^{T} \left(\|\mathbf{a}_{it} - \mathbf{a}_{lt}\|_3 w_t\right)^2} \tag{5.3}$$

where $_2w_t$ and $_3w_t$ are suitable weights, respectively, for the time intervals $[t - 1, t]$ and $[t - 2, t]$; $\mathbf{v}_{it} = (\mathbf{x}_{it} - \mathbf{x}_{it-1})$ and $\mathbf{v}_{lt} = (\mathbf{x}_{lt} - \mathbf{x}_{lt-1})$; $\mathbf{a}_{it} = \frac{1}{2}(\mathbf{v}_{it} - \mathbf{v}_{it-1})$ and $\mathbf{a}_{lt} = \frac{1}{2}(\mathbf{v}_{lt} - \mathbf{v}_{lt-1})$. Notice that, in $\mathbb{R}^2$, the $\mathbf{v}_{it}$ in each segment of the time series is the *slope* of the straight line passing through it: if it is negative (positive) the slope will be negative (positive) and the angle made by each segment of the time series with the positive direction of the t-axis will be obtuse (acute); the $\mathbf{a}_{it}$ in each pair of segments of time series represents its convexity or concavity: if it is positive (negative) the trajectory of the two segments is convex (concave) (D'Urso, 2000).

The distances Eq. (5.1) - Eq. (5.3) can be utilized separately in a clustering procedure, e.g., in a hierarchical clustering. In order to take into account simultaneously in the time series clustering process the features captured by the distances Eq. (5.1) - Eq. (5.3), different mixed distance measures, based on a suitable linear combination of the distances Eq. (5.1) - Eq. (5.3), have been proposed. To this purpose different criteria have been suggested for computing objectively the weights of the linear combination. See, D'Urso and Vichi (1998), D'Urso (2000), Coppi and D'Urso (2001).

For a lagged time version of the previous distances see D'Urso and De Giovanni (2008). Furthermore, we remark that Coppi and D'Urso (2000) have extended the distances Eq. (5.1) - Eq. (5.3) and the mixed version for comparing imprecise time series.

D'Urso (2000) suggested a distance for observed time series is based on the computation, e.g., for univariate time series, of the area between each pair of time series.

Furthermore, D'Urso (2000) proposed a distance measure for clustering observed time series based on the following *polygonal* representation of a (univariate) time series:

$$x_{it'} = \sum_{t=1}^{T} b_{it}|t' - t| \qquad t' = 1, T$$

where $b_{it}(i = 1, I; t = 1, T)$ are the *polygonal coefficients*, obtained by solving the previous system of equations; that is, setting $A = \frac{x_{i1} + x_{iT}}{T-1}$, we have $b_{i1} = \frac{1}{2}(x_{i2} - x_{i1} + A)$, $b_{it} = \frac{1}{2}[(x_{it+1} - x_{it}) - (x_{it} - x_{it-1})]$ $(t = 1, T - 2)$ and $b_{it} = \frac{1}{2}(A - x_{it} + x_{iT-1})$. Notice that, the polygonal coefficients b_{it} represent the semi-difference of the variation of the (univariate) time series in the different time intervals; that is, indicates the "weights" of some time circumstances that determinate the vertices of the polygonal line representing each time series. Moreover, the coefficients b_{it} supply indications of the "oscillations" of each time series. In fact, since, for definition, in a time series there is an oscillation if a set of consecutive values x_{it-1}, x_{it}, x_{it+1}, such as $x_{it-1} < x_{it}$, $x_{it} > x_{it+1}$ or $x_{it-1} > x_{it}$, $x_{it} < x_{it+1}$, exists we have that the existence of vertices in the polygonal line (which depends on the non-negative values of the polygonal coefficients b_{i1}, b_{it+1} and b_{iT}) is the necessary condition for the existence of the oscillations. Then, the oscillations of the time series depend on

Thus, a distance for (multivariate) observed time series based on the polygonal coefficients of each component of the multivariate time series is: Polygonal coefficients

$$_4d(x_i, x_l) = \sqrt{\sum_{t=1}^{T} \|\mathbf{b}_{it} - \mathbf{b}_{lt}\|^2} \qquad (5.4)$$

where $\mathbf{b}_{it}$, $\mathbf{b}_{lt}$ represent the J-dimensional polygonal coefficients vectors of the i-th and l-th multivariate time series. Notice that $\mathbf{b}_{it} = \mathbf{a}_{it+1}$.

The distance measures $_1d()$, $_2d()$, $_3d()$, $_4d()$ are useful for identifying similar geometric profiles of the time series and in general, clustering based on these distances will be mainly dominated by local comparisons. Furthermore, we remark that these distances are useful for comparing time series of equal length and with the same domain (the time series are observed in the same times).

5.2.1 Dynamic time warping

In the literature there are various distances for time series based on dynamic time warping (DTW). This is a technique used to find an optimal alignment between two given time series across time points under certain restrictions. It is preferred to the Euclidean distance measures over all the time points because Euclidean distances may fail to produce an intuitively correct measure of similarity between two sequences that is very sensitive to small distortions in time.

In DTW, the time series are warped in a nonlinear fashion to match each other. DTW was introduced to the data mining community by Berndt and Clifford (1994). Although they demonstrate the utility of the approach, they acknowledge that the algorithm's time complexity is a problem and has limitations for very large data bases of time series. Many authors have used dynamic time warping and variations of it to compare or to cluster time series and it has been extensively used in data mining.

Despite this shortcoming of DTW, it has been widely used in various fields. In bioinformatics, Aach and Church (2001) applied DTW to time series of gene (RNA) expression data. Several researchers including Vullings et al. (1998) and Caiani et al. (1998) have demonstrated the use of DTW for ECG pattern matching. In robotics, Oates et al. (2000) demonstrated that DTW may be used for clustering an agent's sensory outputs.

Keogh and Pazzani (2000) introduced a technique which speeds up DTW by a large constant. The value of the constant is data dependent but is typically one to two orders of magnitude. The algorithm that they proposed, referred to as piecewise dynamic time warping (PDTW), takes advantage of the fact that they can efficiently approximate most time series by a piecewise aggregate approximation. Keogh and Pazzani (2001) also introduced another modification of DTW called derivative dynamic time warping (DDTW) where rather than using the raw data, they consider only the (estimated) local derivatives of the data.

Chu et al. (2002) proposed another variation of DTW for time series, namely, iterative deepening dynamic time warping (IDDWT) by which for any given level of approximation, a model can be created describing the distribution of the distance approximation errors. Then, for any two time series, the approximations of DTW can be calculated at increasingly finer levels of representation and the stored distribution models are used to filter out poor matches with some user-specified tolerance. They compare IDDTW to DTW and Euclidean distance for clustering real and synthetic time series.

Jeong et al. (2011) proposed a weighted DTW (WDTW), which is a penalty-based DTW. Their approach penalizes points with higher phase difference between a reference point and a testing point in order to prevent minimum distance distortion caused by outliers. The rationale underlying the proposed distance measure is demonstrated with some illustrative examples. A new weight function, called the modified logistic weight function (MLWF), is also proposed to systematically assign weights as a function of the phase difference between a reference point and a testing point. By applying different weights to adjacent points, the proposed algorithm is able to enhance the detection of similarity between two time series. They show that DTW and Euclidean distance are special cases of our proposed WDTW measure. They extend the proposed idea to other variants of DTW such as derivative dynamic time warping (DDTW) and propose the weighted version of DDTW. They have compared the performances of their proposed procedures with other popular approaches using public data sets available through the UCR Time

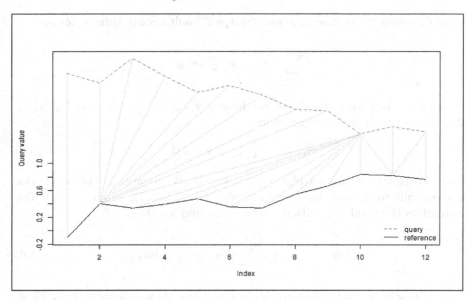

FIGURE 5.1: Dynamic time warping distance (D'Urso et al. 2018).

Series Data Mining Archive for both time series classification and clustering problems. The experimental results indicate that the proposed approaches can achieve improved accuracy for time series classification and clustering problems.

We now illustrate a distance measure based on DTW. In particular, the DTW distance for time series stretches or compresses two series locally, in order to make their shape as similar as possible.

Given a "query" (or test) time series $\mathbf{x}_i$ and a "reference" time series, $\mathbf{x}_{i'}$, with length respectively T, T' ($T \gtreqless T'$), in the following, we assume that $t = 1, \ldots, T$ and $t' = 1, \ldots, T'$ are the time indices of the elements in $\mathbf{x}_i$ and $\mathbf{x}_{i'}$.

The total distance between $\mathbf{x}_i$ and $\mathbf{x}_{i'}$ is then computed through the so called "warping curve", or "warping path", which ensures that each data point in $\mathbf{x}_i$ is compared to the "closest" data point in $\mathbf{x}_{i'}$. The warping path is defined as follows: Let

$$\Phi_l = (\varphi_l, \psi_l), \ l = 1, \ldots, L.$$

under the following constraints.

1. boundary condition: $\Phi_1 = (1,1)$, $\Phi_L = (T, T')$;
2. monotonicity condition: $\varphi_1 \leq \ldots \leq \varphi_l \leq \ldots \leq \varphi_L$ and $\psi_1 \leq \ldots \leq \psi_l \leq \ldots \leq \psi_L$.

The effect of applying the warping curve to the two multivariate time series is to realign the time indices of $\mathbf{x}_i$ and $\mathbf{x}_{i'}$ through the functions φ and ψ. The total dissimilarity between the two "warped" multivariate time series is:

$$\sum_{l=1}^{L} d(\mathbf{x}_{i,\varphi_l}, \mathbf{x}_{i',\psi_l}) m_{l,\Phi}$$

where $m_{l,\Phi}$ is a local weighting coefficient; $d(.,.)$ is, usually, the Euclidean distance for multivariate time series:

$$d(i, i') = (\|\mathbf{x}_{it} - \mathbf{x}_{i't'}\|)^{\frac{1}{2}}. \tag{5.5}$$

Since there are several warping curves, the DTW distance is the one which corresponds to the optimal warping curve, $\hat{\Phi}_l = (\hat{\varphi}_l, \hat{\psi}_l)$, $l = 1, \ldots, L$ which minimizes the total dissimilarity between $\mathbf{x}_i$ and $\mathbf{x}_{i'}$ (Figure 5.1):

$$d_{DTW}(\mathbf{x}_i, \mathbf{x}_{i'}) = \sum_{l=1}^{L} d(\mathbf{x}_{i,\hat{\varphi}_l}, \mathbf{x}_{i',\hat{\psi}_l}) m_{l,\hat{\Phi}}. \tag{5.6}$$

The finding of the optimal warping curve consists of the following steps. First, a $T \times T'$ "local cost" (or "local distance") matrix which contains the distances between each pair of points is computed. Second, the DTW algorithm finds the path that minimizes the alignment between $\mathbf{x}_i$ and $\mathbf{x}_{i'}$, starting at $d(1, 1)$ and finishing at $d(T, T')$, and aggregating the cost, that is, the total distance. At each step, the algorithm finds the direction in which the distance increases the least, under the given constraints.

5.3   Clustering methods

All the distances presented in Section 5.2 can be suitable to utilize for classifying time series by means of hierarchical and non-hierarchical clustering.

Considering a hierarchical approach (that is, average linkage method) D'Urso and Vichi (1998) clustered time series by proposing a suitable combination of the distances Eq. (5.1) - Eq. (5.3).

Following a non-hierarchical scheme, particularly interesting and promising is the fuzzy clustering approach. This clustering approach shows great sensitivity in capturing the details characterizing the time series. In fact, often the dynamics are drifting or switching (switching time series) and then the standard clustering approaches are likely to fail to find and represent underlying structure in given data related to time. Thus, the switches from one time state to another, which are usually vague and not focused on any particular instant of time, can be naturally treated by means of fuzzy clustering (D'Urso, 2005).

By considering a distance for observed time series, D'Urso (2004, 2005) proposed the following fuzzy c-means clustering model for observed time series:

$$\min \sum_{i=1}^{I} \sum_{c=1}^{C} {}_1 u_{ic}^2 \sum_{t=1}^{T} ({}_1 w_t \| \mathbf{x}_{it} - {}_1 \mathbf{h}_{ct} \|)^2 \qquad (5.7)$$

with the constraints

$$\sum_{c=1}^{C} {}_1 u_{ic} = 1, \ {}_1 u_{ic} \geq 0, \qquad (5.8)$$

$$\sum_{t=1}^{T} {}_1 w_t = 1, \ {}_1 w_t \geq 0, \qquad (5.9)$$

where ${}_1 u_{ic}$ indicates the membership degree of the i-th time series to the c-th cluster and $m > 1$ is a weighting exponent that controls the fuzziness of the obtained partition.

Notice that $\sum_{t=1}^{T} ({}_1 w_t \| \mathbf{x}_{it} - {}_1 \mathbf{h}_{ct} \|)^2$ is a sum of squared weighted Euclidean distances between unit i and centroid c at each instant of time. The weight ${}_1 w_t$ is intrinsically associated with the distance $({}_1 w_t \| \mathbf{x}_{it} - {}_1 \mathbf{h}_{ct} \|)^2$ at time t, whereas the overall squared distance is just a sum of the squares of these weighted distances. This allows us to appropriately tune the influence of the various times when computing the dissimilarity between time series. The weight ${}_1 w_t$ constitutes a specific parameter to be estimated within the clustering model. D'Urso (2004, 2005) derived iterative solutions for (5.7)-(5.9) as follows:

$$
\begin{aligned}
{}_1 u_{ic} &= \frac{1}{\sum_{c'=1}^{C} \left[\frac{\sum_{t=1}^{T} ({}_1 w_t \| \mathbf{x}_{it} - {}_1 \mathbf{h}_{ct} \|)^2}{\sum_{t=1}^{T} ({}_1 w_t \| \mathbf{x}_{it} - {}_1 \mathbf{h}_{c't} \|)^2} \right]^{\frac{1}{m-1}}}, \\[2ex]
{}_1 w_t &= \frac{1}{\sum_{t'=1}^{T} \left[\frac{\sum_{i=1}^{I} \sum_{c=1}^{C} ({}_1 u_{ic}^m \| \mathbf{x}_{it} - {}_1 \mathbf{h}_{ct} \|)^2}{\sum_{i=1}^{I} \sum_{c=1}^{C} ({}_1 u_{ic}^m \| \mathbf{x}_{it'} - {}_1 \mathbf{h}_{ct'} \|)^2} \right]}, \qquad (5.10) \\[2ex]
{}_1 \mathbf{h}_{ct} &= \frac{\sum_{i=1}^{I} {}_1 u_{ic}^m \mathbf{x}_{it}}{\sum_{i=1}^{I} {}_1 u_{ic}^m}.
\end{aligned}
$$

Looking at the iterative solutions Eq. (5.10), we observe that the time weights have a statistical meaning. In fact, they appear to mirror the heterogeneity of the total intracluster "deviances" (that is, $\sum_{i=1}^{I} \sum_{c=1}^{C} ({}_1 u_{ic}^m \| \mathbf{x}_{it} - {}_1 \mathbf{h}_{ct} \|)^2$) across the different times. In particular, weight ${}_1 w_t$ increases as long as the total intracluster "deviance" at time t decreases (compared with the remaining time occasions). Thus, the optimization procedure tends to give more emphasis to the time observations capable of increasing the within cluster similarity among the time series.

As remarked by D'Urso (2004, 2005), in the model Eq. (5.7) - Eq. (5.9), we do not take into account the evolutive features of the time series, but we consider only their instantaneous positions. In fact the clustering model Eq. (5.7) - Eq. (5.9) is based on the instantaneous differences between the time series.

Since in a time series, the successive observations are dependent, that is, the set of observed time points holds the strict monotonic ordering property, and any permutation of the time points destroys this natural dependence, it is useful to build a (squared) distance that should take into account the ordering property of the time points and should be sensitive to any permutation of the time points.

When the interest is in capturing the differences concerning the *variational* pattern of the time series, we can consider a clustering model based on the comparison of the so-called variation vectors associated with the time series (D'Urso, 2004, 2005). For this purpose, in order to take into account the variational information of each observed time series in the clustering process, D'Urso (2004, 2005) proposed to cluster time series utilising the same modeling structure as Eq. (5.7) - Eq. (5.9) but with a new comparison measure, namely, the variation-based (squared) distance which compares the dynamic features in each time interval of the time series. In particular, in the interval $[t - 1, t]$ the variations of the time series are compared by considering the following (squared) distance between the i-th observed time series and the c-th centroid time series:

$$\sum_{t=2}^{T} ({}_2w_t \|\mathbf{v}_{it} - {}_2\mathbf{h}_{ct}\|)^2$$

where ${}_2w_t$ is a weight in $[t - 1, t]$ (*"variation" weight*); $\|\mathbf{v}_{it} - {}_2\mathbf{h}_{ct}\| = \|(\mathbf{x}_{it} - \mathbf{x}_{it-1}) - ({}_1\mathbf{h}_{ct} - {}_1\mathbf{h}_{ct-1})\|$ is the Euclidean distance between the variations of the i-th observed time series the c-th centroid time series in the time interval $[t - 1, t]$, in which ${}_2\mathbf{h}_{ct} = ({}_1\mathbf{h}_{ct} - {}_1\mathbf{h}_{ct-1})$ is the variation vector of the c-th centroid time series in $[t - 1, t]$ and $\mathbf{v}_{it} = (\mathbf{x}_{it} - \mathbf{x}_{it-1})$ is the variation vector of the i-th time series.

In this case, the weight ${}_2w_t$ is intrinsically associated with the distance $({}_2w_t\|\mathbf{v}_{it} - {}_2\mathbf{h}_{ct}\|)^2$ at time interval $[t - 1, t]$. Analogous observations, indicated for instantaneous weights ${}_1w_t$, instantaneous (position) squared distance and clustering model Eq.(5.7) - Eq. (5.9), can be considered on the task of the variation weights in the variation (squared) distance and then in the variation (squared) distance-based clustering model.

Then, the squared Euclidean distance $\|\mathbf{v}_{it} - {}_2\mathbf{h}_{ct}\|$ compares the slopes in each time interval $[t - 1, t]$ of the segments of each time series concerning the i-th time series with the corresponding slopes of the c-th centroid time series.

Summing up, this distance is able to capture and so to measure similarity of shapes of the time series, which are formed by the relative change of amplitude and corresponding temporal information. In this way, the problem is approached by taking into account the time series as piecewise linear functions and measuring the difference of slopes between them.

Thus, by taking the previous variation-based (squared) distance, we can obtain a *variational fuzzy c-means clustering model* following a similar mathematical formalization to Eq. (5.7) - Eq. (5.9), that is,

$$\min \sum_{i=1}^{I} \sum_{c=1}^{C} {}_2 u_{ic}^m \sum_{t=2}^{T} ({}_2 w_t \| \mathbf{v}_{it} - {}_2 \mathbf{h}_{ct} \|)^2 \tag{5.11}$$

subject to the constraints

$$\sum_{c=1}^{C} {}_2 u_{ic} = 1, \; {}_2 u_{ic} \geq 0, \tag{5.12}$$

$$\sum_{t=2}^{T} {}_2 w_t = 1, \; {}_2 w_t \geq 0. \tag{5.13}$$

By solving Eq. (5.11) - Eq. (5.13), we have the following optimal solutions (D'Urso, 2004, 2005):

$$
\begin{aligned}
{}_2 u_{ic} &= \frac{1}{\sum_{c'=1}^{C} \left[\frac{\sum_{t=2}^{T} ({}_2 w_t \| \mathbf{v}_{it} - {}_2 \mathbf{h}_{ct} \|)^2}{\sum_{t=2}^{T} ({}_2 w_t \| \mathbf{v}_{it} - {}_2 \mathbf{h}_{c't} \|)^2} \right]^{\frac{1}{m-1}}}, \\
{}_2 w_t &= \frac{1}{\sum_{t'=2}^{T} \left[\frac{\sum_{i=1}^{I} \sum_{c=1}^{C} ({}_2 u_{ic}^m \| \mathbf{v}_{it} - {}_2 \mathbf{h}_{ct} \|)^2}{\sum_{i=1}^{I} \sum_{c=1}^{C} ({}_2 u_{ic}^m \| \mathbf{v}_{it'} - {}_2 \mathbf{h}_{ct'} \|)^2} \right]}, \\
{}_2 \mathbf{h}_{ct} &= \frac{\sum_{i=1}^{I} {}_2 u_{ic}^m \mathbf{v}_{it}}{\sum_{i=1}^{I} {}_2 u_{ic}^m}.
\end{aligned}
\tag{5.14}
$$

As noticed for the model Eq. (5.7) - Eq. (5.9), time weights ${}_2 w_t$, now referring to pairs of successive times, are connected with the heterogeneity of the total intracluster "deviations".

In the model Eq. (5.11) - Eq. (5.13) this is obviously related to the time series of "variations". Larger weights are then given to the time intervals which increase the within cluster similarity among the above time series.

Refer to D'Urso (2000, 2005) for the fuzzy clustering model based on a mixed (squared) distance, in which the instantaneous and slope features of the time series are simultaneously taken into account.

Several variants of the previous fuzzy clustering models have been proposed in the literature. Fuzzy clustering models with entropy regularization and spatial additional information have been suggested, respectively, by Coppi and D'Urso (2006) and Coppi et al. (2010).

In particular, Coppi and D'Urso (2006) proposed an entropy version of the clustering models Eq. (5.7) - Eq. (5.9) and Eq. (5.11) - Eq. (5.13). The entropy version of the clustering model Eq. (5.7) - Eq. (5.9) is:

$$\min \sum_{i=1}^{I} \sum_{c=1}^{C} u_{ic} \sum_{t=1}^{T} ({}_1 w_t \|\mathbf{x}_{it} - {}_1 \mathbf{h}_{ct}\|)^2 + p \sum_{i=1}^{I} \sum_{c=1}^{C} u_{ic} \log u_{ic} \qquad (5.15)$$

subject to the constraints

$$\sum_{c=1}^{C} u_{ic} = 1, \, u_{ic} \geq 0, \qquad (5.16)$$

$$\sum_{t=1}^{T} {}_1 w_t = 1, \, {}_1 w_t \geq 0, \qquad (5.17)$$

with the following iterative solutions:

$$
{}_1 u_{ic} = \cfrac{1}{\sum_{c'=1}^{C} \left[\cfrac{\exp\left[\frac{1}{p} \sum_{t=1}^{T} ({}_1 w_t \|\mathbf{x}_{it} - {}_1 \mathbf{h}_{ct}\|)^2\right]}{\exp\left[\frac{1}{p} \sum_{t=1}^{T} ({}_1 w_t \|\mathbf{x}_{it} - {}_1 \mathbf{h}_{c't}\|)^2\right]} \right]},
$$

$$
{}_1 w_t = \cfrac{1}{\sum_{t'=1}^{T} \left[\cfrac{\sum_{i=1}^{I} \sum_{c=1}^{C} (u_{ic} \|\mathbf{x}_{it} - {}_1 \mathbf{h}_{ct}\|)^2}{\sum_{i=1}^{I} \sum_{c=1}^{C} (u_{ic} \|\mathbf{x}_{it'} - {}_1 \mathbf{h}_{ct'}\|)^2} \right]}, \qquad (5.18)
$$

$$
{}_1 \mathbf{h}_{ct} = \cfrac{\sum_{i=1}^{I} u_{ic} \mathbf{x}_{it}}{\sum_{i=1}^{I} u_{ic}}.
$$

The entropy version of the clustering model Eq. (5.11) - Eq. (5.13) is:

$$\min \sum_{i=1}^{I} \sum_{c=1}^{C} u_{ic} \sum_{t=1}^{T} ({}_2 w_t \|\mathbf{v}_{it} - {}_2 \mathbf{h}_{ct}\|)^2 + p \sum_{i=1}^{I} \sum_{c=1}^{C} u_{ic} \log u_{ic} \qquad (5.19)$$

subject to the constraints

$$\sum_{c=1}^{C} u_{ic} = 1, \, u_{ic} \geq 0, \qquad (5.20)$$

$$\sum_{t=1}^{T} {}_2 w_t = 1, \, {}_2 w_t \geq 0, \qquad (5.21)$$

where the iterative solutions can be obtained similarly to the clustering model Eq. (5.15) - Eq. (5.17).

We may pick up the differential features between the fuzzy C-means clustering models Eq. (5.7) - Eq.(5.9) and Eq. (5.11) - Eq.(5.13) and the entropy-based fuzzy clustering models Eq. (5.15) - Eq. (5.17) and Eq. (5.19) - Eq. (5.21) with particular reference to the specific parameters associated with the time series (time weights and prototype time series). In fact, these parameters are computed as functions of weighted means of squared distances or of "variation" vectors, where the weights depend on the computed degrees of membership. However, in the fuzzy c-means clustering models, the degrees of membership must be elevated to power m (the fuzziness coefficient) while as, in the entropy-based fuzzy clustering models, they are taken linearly. This is a consequence of having the fuzzy entropy coefficient p in an additive form in the objective function of the models Eq. (5.15) - Eq. (5.17) and Eq. (5.19) - Eq. (5.21), as opposed to the exponential form of m in the objective function of the models Eq. (5.7) - Eq. (5.9) and Eq. (5.11) - Eq. (5.13). Furthermore, in the entropy-based fuzzy clustering models, the search for a balance between "within group" homogeneity of time series and degree of entropy associated with the assignment of a time series to one element of the clustering typology, appears to express in an explicit form the two-fold objective that the researcher sets out to achieve when trying to realistically classify elusive objects such as time series (Coppi and D'Urso, 2006).

In the literature, there are other observation-based clustering models for time series. Coppi et al. (2006) proposed fuzzy clustering models for time series adopting a partitioning around medoids approach. Other clustering models have been suggested by Košmelj and Batagelj (1990), Izakian et al. (2015) and Huang et al. (2016). Robust observation-based clustering of time series which neutralize the negative effects of the outlier time series in the clustering process have been proposed following different robust strategies by D'Urso (2005), D'Urso et al. (2018).

For instance, D'Urso et al. (2018) proposed a robust fuzzy clustering c-medoids model based on a robust distance measure; that is, by considering the variational case, we have:

$$^{\exp}_{2}d_{ii'}^2 = 1 - \exp\left\{-\beta \sum_{t=2}^{T} \left(_2 w_t \| \mathbf{v}_{it} - \mathbf{v}_{i't} \|\right)^2\right\} \tag{5.22}$$

where β is a suitable parameter (positive constant) determined according to the variability of the data. Based on Eq. (5.22) the model is formalized as follows (D'Urso et al., 2018):

$$\min : \quad \sum_{i=1}^{I} \sum_{c=1}^{C} u_{ic}^{m\,\exp}_{\;2}d_{ic}^2 =$$
$$\sum_{i=1}^{I} \sum_{c=1}^{C} u_{ic}^m \left[1 - \exp\left\{-\beta \sum_{t=2}^{T} \left(_2 w_t \| \mathbf{v}_{it} - \tilde{\mathbf{v}}_{ct} \|\right)^2\right\}\right]$$
$$\sum_{c=1}^{C} u_{ic} = 1, \; u_{ic} \geq 0$$
$$\sum_{t=2}^{T} {}_2 w_t = 1, \; {}_2 w_t \geq 0.$$

where $\mathbf{v}_{it}$ and $\tilde{\mathbf{v}}_{ct}$ are the t-th component of the variation of multivariate time trajectories of the i-th unit and of the c-th medoid in the interval $[t-1, \, t]$, respectively; $_2 w_t$ is the t-th time weight, which is a parameter of the clustering model.

The optimal solutions for Eq. (5.23) are:

$$u_{ic} = \frac{1}{\sum_{c'=1}^{C} \left[\frac{\left[1-\exp\left\{-\beta \sum_{t=2}^{T}(2w_t\|\mathbf{v}_{it}-\tilde{\mathbf{v}}_{ct}\|)^2\right\}\right]}{\left[1-\exp\left\{-\beta \sum_{t=2}^{T}(2w_t\|\mathbf{v}_{it}-\tilde{\mathbf{v}}_{c't}\|)^2\right\}\right]} \right]^{\frac{1}{m-1}}} \tag{5.23}$$

$$2w_t = \frac{1}{\sum_{t'=2}^{T} \left[\frac{\sum_{i=1}^{I}\sum_{c=1}^{C} u_{ic}^m\|\mathbf{v}_{it}-\tilde{\mathbf{v}}_{ct}\|^2 \exp\left\{-\beta \sum_{t''=2}^{T}(2w_{t'}''\|\mathbf{v}_{it''}-\tilde{\mathbf{v}}_{ct''}\|)^2\right\}}{\sum_{i=1}^{I}\sum_{c=1}^{C} u_{ic}^m\|\mathbf{v}_{it'}-\tilde{\mathbf{v}}_{ct'}\|^2 \exp\left\{-\beta \sum_{t''=2}^{T}(2w_{t'}''\|\mathbf{v}_{it''}-\tilde{\mathbf{v}}_{ct''}\|)^2\right\}} \right]} \tag{5.24}$$

Furthermore, by considering the DTW distance Eq. (5.6), D'Urso et al. (2018) proposed the following robust DTW-based fuzzy c-medoids cluster model:

$$\begin{aligned}
\min: \quad & \sum_{i=1}^{I}\sum_{c=1}^{C} u_{ic}^m \,_{exp}d_{DTW}^2(\mathbf{X}_i, \tilde{\mathbf{X}}_c) = \\
& \sum_{i=1}^{I}\sum_{c=1}^{C} u_{ic}^m \left[1 - \exp\left\{-\beta\, d_{DTW}(\mathbf{X}_i, \tilde{\mathbf{X}}_c)^2\right\}\right] \\
& \sum_{c=1}^{C} u_{ic} = 1, \ u_{ic} \geq 0
\end{aligned}$$

where

$$u_{ic} = \frac{1}{\sum_{c'=1}^{C} \left[\frac{\left[1-\exp\left\{-\beta\, d_{DTW}(\mathbf{X}_i, \tilde{\mathbf{X}}_c)^2\right\}\right]}{\left[1-\exp\left\{-\beta\, d_{DTW}(\mathbf{X}_i, \tilde{\mathbf{X}}_{c'})^2\right\}\right]} \right]^{\frac{1}{m-1}}}. \tag{5.25}$$

See D'Urso et al. (2018) for another DWT-based model and other details.

Finally, we remark that different fuzzy clustering models for imprecise time series have been proposed by Coppi and D'Urso (2002, 2003) and Coppi et al. (2006).

Example 5.1 In order to show the usefulness and performance of the fuzzy clustering model Eq. (5.7) - Eq. (5.9), in this section, an applicative example (drawn from D'Urso, 2005) of the model Eq. (5.7) - Eq. (5.9) to a set of synthetic time series (see Figure 5.2) - consisting of three well-separated clusters of time series (respectively with 4, 2 and 2 time series) and one switching time series (the 7-th time series)- is illustrated.

Notice that the switching time series presents, in the first times, instantaneous position and slope similar to the time series belonging to cluster 2 (time series 5 and 6), while, in the final times, it has instantaneous position and slope similar to the time series belonging to cluster 3 (time series 8 and 9). As we can see in Table 5.1, by applying the fuzzy clustering model Eq. (5.7) - Eq. (5.9) (with $C = 3$ and $m = 2.3$) the real situation is well captured.

Example 5.2 In this example, drawn from D'Urso (2005), we consider a set of 9 synthetic bivariate time series (see Figure 5.3). As we can see, we have three clusters of time series with similar instantaneous positions, but diverse slopes, respectively:

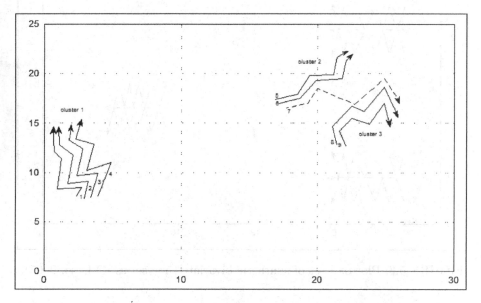

FIGURE 5.2: Plot of a set of synthetic bivariate time series (with switching time series) (D'Urso, 2015).

TABLE 5.1: Example 5.1 Cluster solution.

	cluster 1	cluster 2	cluster 3
1	0.973	0.013	0.014
2	0.991	0.005	0.004
3	0.995	0.003	0.002
4	0.961	0.024	0.015
5	0.003	0.977	0.02
6	0.001	0.997	0.002
7	0.084	0.497	0.419
8	0.004	0.027	0.969
9	0.001	0.002	0.997

time weighting system
(0.196; 0.198; 0.171; 0.136; 0.119; 0.18)

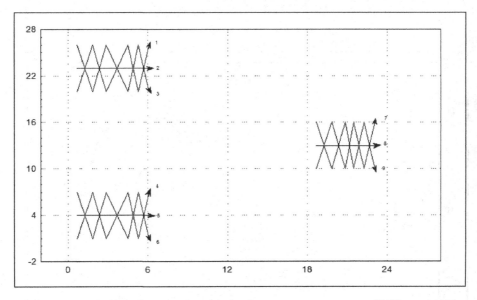

FIGURE 5.3: Plot of a set of synthetic bivariate time series (D'Urso, 2005).

time series 1, 2, 3;
time series 4, 5, 6;
time series 7, 8, 9.

Furthermore, we have also three clusters of time series with the same slopes, but different positions, respectively:
time series 1, 4, 7;
time series 2, 5, 8;
time series 3, 6, 9.

Then, we expect that by applying the clustering model Eq. (5.7) - Eq. (5.9), we have the three clusters of time series with similar positions, and by considering the slope (velocity)-based version of the model Eq. (5.7) - Eq. (5.9), we get a partition in the three expected clusters of time series with the same slopes. In fact, by applying these two models (fixing $C = 3$, $m = 2.3$), we obtain the results shown in Table 5.2.

Application 5.1 Coppi and D'Urso (2006) analyzed a set of 25 multivariate climatic time series (that is, 25 European countries (places); 5 climatic variables, that is, minimum and maximum temperature (centigrades), humidity (percentage), rain (mm per m^2), hours of sunlight; 7 times, that is, months from May to November 2001). For each of the 25 places (the capitals of 24 countries, plus North Cape) the monthly average of each variable was computed. By adopting suitable cluster validity criteria (Coppi and D'Urso, 2006), the membership degrees of the fuzzy c-means clustering model

TABLE 5.2: Example 5.2 Cluster solution.

Membership degrees matrix Clustering model (5.7)-(5.9)		
cluster 1	*cluster 2*	*cluster 3*
1 0.9009	0.0473	0.0518
2 1.0000	0.0000	0.0000
3 0.9009	0.0473	0.0518
4 0.0516	0.0490	0.8994
5 0.0000	0.0000	1.0000
6 0.0516	0.0490	0.8994
7 0.0475	0.9033	0.0492
8 0.0000	1.0000	0.0000
9 0.0475	0.9033	0.0492
time weighting system (0.16, 0.16, 0.17, 0.17, 0.17, 0.17)		

Clustering model (5.11)-(5.13)		
cluster 1	*cluster 2*	*cluster 3*
1 1.0000	0.0000	0.0000
2 0.0000	0.0000	1.0000
3 0.0000	1.0000	0.0000
4 1.0000	0.0000	0.0000
5 0.0000	0.0000	1.0000
6 0.0000	1.0000	0.0000
7 1.0000	0.0000	0.0000
8 0.0000	0.0000	1.0000
9 0.0000	1.0000	0.0000
time weighting system (0.28, 0.04, 0.02, 0.33, 0.33)		

TABLE 5.3: Membership degrees of the fuzzy c-means clustering model (5.7)-(5.9).

European countries	Membership degrees				
Austria	0.85	0.02	0.05	0.06	0.02
Belgium	0.07	0.02	0.02	0.89	0.00
Croatia	0.02	0.01	0.03	0.01	0.93
Czech Republic	0.68	0.02	0.03	0.26	0.01
Denmark	0.95	0.01	0.01	0.03	0.00
Finland	0.16	0.18	0.03	0.62	0.01
France	0.09	0.02	0.04	0.85	0.00
Germany	0.87	0.01	0.01	0.10	0.01
Great Britain	0.04	0.02	0.02	0.92	0.00
Greece	0.02	0.00	0.04	0.01	0.93
Holland	0.08	0.04	0.03	0.84	0.01
Hungary	0.58	0.04	0.20	0.11	0.07
Iceland	0.03	0.92	0.01	0.04	0.00
Ireland	0.14	0.07	0.05	0.73	0.01
Malta	0.05	0.02	0.83	0.04	0.06
North Cape	0.03	0.94	0.01	0.02	0.00
Norway	0.79	0.07	0.04	0.08	0.02
Poland	0.54	0.03	0.05	0.37	0.01
Portugal	0.01	0.00	0.98	0.01	0.00
Russia	0.13	0.07	0.02	0.77	0.01
Slovenia	0.09	0.02	0.03	0.85	0.01
Spain	0.15	0.03	0.61	0.08	0.13
Sweden	0.78	0.07	0.03	0.11	0.01
Switzerland	0.17	0.02	0.03	0.77	0.01
Turkey	0.03	0.01	0.92	0.03	0.01

Eq. (5.7) - Eq. (5.9) and the entropy-based fuzzy clustering model Eq. (5.15) - Eq. (5.17) are shown, respectively, in Table 5.3 and Table 5.4.

Looking at Table 5.3 the following 5 clusters can be set up (based on the maximum degree of membership rule):

1. Austria, Czech Republic, Denmark, Germany, Hungary, Norway, Poland, Sweden;
2. Iceland, North Cape;
3. Malta, Portugal, Spain, Turkey;
4. Belgium, Finland, France, Great Britain, Ireland, Netherlands, Russia, Slovenia, Switzerland;
5. Croatia, Greece.

Notice that, in this partition, Hungary, Finland, Norway, Poland and Sweden have the lowest degrees of membership in their clusters, although always greater than 0.50. The partition obtained by the entropy-based fuzzy cluster-

TABLE 5.4: Membership degrees of the fuzzy c-means clustering model (5.15)-(5.17).

European countries	Membership degrees				
Austria	0.21	0.05	0.72	0.00	0.02
Belgium	0.64	0.05	0.31	0.00	0.00
Croatia	0.00	0.00	0.00	1	0.00
Czech Republic	0.35	0.04	0.61	0.00	0.00
Denmark	0.25	0.16	0.58	0.00	0.01
Finland	0.25	0.49	0.26	0.00	0.00
France	0.63	0.01	0.35	0.00	0.01
Germany	0.33	0.06	0.61	0.00	0.00
Great Britain	0.70	0.03	0.27	0.00	0.00
Greece	0.00	0.00	0.00	1	0.00
Holland	0.65	0.06	0.29	0.00	0.00
Hungary	0.19	0.01	0.37	0.00	0.43
Iceland	0.02	0.96	0.02	0.00	0.00
Ireland	0.61	0.07	0.32	0.00	0.00
Malta	0.00	0.00	0.00	0.00	1
North Cape	0.00	0.99	0.01	0.00	0.00
Norway	0.21	0.51	0.28	0.00	0.00
Poland	0.37	0.02	0.60	0.00	0.01
Portugal	0.00	0.00	0.01	0.00	0.99
Russia	0.53	0.22	0.25	0.00	0.00
Slovenia	0.67	0.01	0.32	0.00	0.00
Spain	0.00	0.00	0.01	0.01	0.98
Sweden	0.18	0.34	0.48	0.00	0.00
Switzerland	0.59	0.03	0.38	0.00	0.00
Turkey	0.02	0.00	0.02	0.00	0.96

TABLE 5.5: Estimated time weights for the fuzzy c-means clustering models Eq. (5.7) - Eq. (5.9) and the entropy-based fuzzy clustering models Eq. (5.15) - Eq. (5.17).

Months	Fuzzy c-means clustering model Eq. (5.7) - Eq. (5.9)	Entropy-based fuzzy clustering model Eq. (5.15) - Eq. (5.17)
May	0.12	0.13
June	0.12	0.12
July	0.13	0.11
August	0.12	0.13
September	0.16	0.15
October	0.18	0.20
November	0.17	0.16

ing model Eq. (5.15) - Eq. (5.17) (Table 5.4) is very close to the previous one, with two main distinguishing features:

a) The countries which had sufficiently high degrees of membership in their clusters in Table 5.3, are now characterized by much stronger degrees (sometimes achieving crispness) (see, e.g., Croatia, Greece, Malta, Portugal, Spain, Iceland, Cape North).

b) The countries with lower degrees of membership in Table 5.3 (notably Hungary, Finland, Norway, Sweden) show now an increased fuzziness, clearly indicating the difficulty of fitting their climatological features in the given classification framework.

Based on the above results, Coppi and D'Urso (2006) remarked that the entropy-based fuzzy clustering model Eq. (5.15) - Eq. (5.17) appears to be more sensitive to the fuzziness of classification for "doubtful" elements and the crispness for "well characterized" elements. Thus, they observed that "since, cluster analysis is a way of describing the typological structure of a set of statistical units, the entropy model picks up more clearly the "critical" elements in the classification grid" (Coppi and D'Urso, 2006). In Table 5.5 are reported the estimated time weights for both models. We observe that the obtained clusters retain the information of each month with almost equal weights (notice that a slightly higher weight is given to the autumn months, especially in the entropy-based fuzzy clustering model Eq. (5.15) - Eq. (5.17)).

For the results obtained by means of the fuzzy c-means clustering model Eq. (5.11) - Eq. (5.13) and the entropy-based fuzzy clustering model Eq. (5.19) - Eq. (5.21) see Coppi and D'Urso (2006).

6

Feature-based clustering

CONTENTS

6.1   Introduction

A fundamental problem in clustering and classification analysis is the choice of a relevant metric. If a time series consists of a large number of observations, clustering time series based on the Euclidean distance in the space of points is not a desirable option because of the noise that is present, and the fact that the autocorrelation structure of the time series is ignored. Many feature-based methods have been developed to address the problem of clustering raw time series data.

While, in general, the observation-based metrics discussed in Chapter 5 are recommended when the aim is to identify similar geometric profiles, the feature-based metrics considered in this chapter are more suitable when the aim is to discriminate between generating processes, that is, between underlying dependence structures. The main concern in this case relies on the global performance so that the features highlighting higher level dynamic aspects could be useful to attain the clustering target. Some consideration about this point including illustrative examples is given in Section 4 of Montero and Villar (2014).

There are other advantages associated with the feature-based clustering approach. In particular, dimensional reduction will in general be attained and this is likely to lead to saving on computational time. In addition, the procedures based on feature extraction can be commonly applied to time series of different lengths.

However, in using feature-based clustering approaches, one needs to be aware the kinds of generating processes in order to determine what specific features will need to be considered. In particular, features extracted from stationary time series are not necessarily going to be the same as those extracted from non-stationary time series.

Methods based on features extracted in the time domain, the frequency domain and from wavelet decomposition of the time series are presented.

6.2   Time domain features - Autocorrelations and partial autocorrelations

6.2.1   Crisp clustering methods

Galeano and Peña (2000) introduced a metric for time series based on the estimated ACF. Given a time series $\{x_t, t = 1, 2, ...T\}$, let $\widehat{\rho}_{xr} = (\widehat{\rho}_1, \ldots, \widehat{\rho}_R)$ be the estimated autocorrelation function of the time series x_t up to lag R such that $\widehat{\rho}_i \cong 0$ for $i > R$. A distance between two time series x_t and y_t can be defined by

$$d_{ACF}(x_t, y_t) = \sqrt{(\widehat{\rho}_{xr} - \widehat{\rho}_{yr})'\Omega(\widehat{\rho}_{xr} - \widehat{\rho}_{yr})}, \tag{6.1}$$

where Ω is some matrix of weights (see Galeano and Peña, 2000). Caiado et al. (2006) implemented three possible ways of computing a distance by using the sample autocorrelation function (ACF).

The first uses a uniform weighting (ACFU), that is, $\Omega = I$, where I is an identity matrix, and is equivalent to the Euclidean distance between the autocorrelation coefficients. The second uses a geometric decay (ACFG), that is, $\Omega = D$, where D is a diagonal matrix with the geometric weights on the main diagonal. The third uses the Mahalanobis distance between the autocorrelations (ACFM), that is, $\Omega = M^{-1}$, where M is the sample covariance matrix of the autocorrelation coefficients given by the truncated Bartlett's formula (Brockwell and Davis, 1991, pp. 221-222).

It is straightforward to show that these ACF-based metrics fulfil the usual properties of a distance. In a Monte Carlo simulation study, Caiado et al. (2006) show that the metrics based on the autocorrelation coefficients can perform quite well in time series clustering. Alonso and Maharaj (2006) introduced a hypothesis testing procedure for the comparison of stationary time series based on the Euclidean distance between the autocorrelations.

Another autocorrelation distance measure, based on the Kullback-Leibler information (KLD), is defined by

$$d_{KLD}(x_t, y_t) = tr(L_x L_y^{-1}) - \log \frac{|L_x|}{|L_y|} - T, \tag{6.2}$$

where L_x and L_y are the $R \times R$ autocorrelation matrices of time series x_t and y_t, respectively, made at R successive lags. Since $d_{KLD}(x_t, y_t) \neq d_{KLD}(y_t, x_t)$, a symmetric distance or quasi-distance can be defined as

$$d_{KLJ}(x_t, y_t) = \frac{1}{2}d_{KLD}(x_t, y_t) + \frac{1}{2}d_{KLD}(y_t, x_t), \tag{6.3}$$

which also satisfies all the usual properties of a metric except the triangle inequality.

Caiado et al. (2006) also introduced distance measures based on the estimated partial autocorrelation function (PACF) $\widehat{\phi}_{xr} = (\widehat{\phi}_1, \ldots, \widehat{\phi}_R)$ and on the inverse estimated autocorrelation function (IACF). A PACF metric between the time series x_t and y_t is defined by

$$d_{PACF}(x_t, y_t) = \sqrt{(\widehat{\phi}_{xr} - \widehat{\phi}_{yr})'\Omega(\widehat{\phi}_{xr} - \widehat{\phi}_{yr})}, \tag{6.4}$$

where $\widehat{\phi}$ is a vector of the sample partial autocorrelation coefficients and Ω is also some matrix of weights. A distance between the inverse autocorrelations of the time series x_t and y_t is defined by

$$d_{IACF}(x_t, y_t) = \sqrt{(\widehat{\rho}_{xr}^{(I)} - \widehat{\rho}_{yr}^{(I)})'\Omega(\widehat{\rho}_{xr}^{(I)} - \widehat{\rho}_{yr}^{(I)})}, \tag{6.5}$$

TABLE 6.1: Stocks used to compute the Dow Jones Industrial Average (DJIA) Index.

Stock	Code	Sector	Stock	Code	Sector
Alcoa Inc.	AA	Basic materials	Johnson & Johnson	JNJ	Healthcare
American Int. Group	AIG	Financial	JP Morgan Chase	JPM	Financial
American Express	AXP	Financial	Coca-Cola	KO	Consumer goods
Boeing Co.	BA	Industrial goods	McDonalds	MCD	Services
Caterpillar Inc.	CAT	Financial	3M Co.	MMM	Conglomerates
Citigroup Inc.	CIT	Industrial goods	Altria Group	MO	Consumer goods
DuPont	DD	Basic materials	Merck & Co.	MRK	Healthcare
Walt Disney	DIS	Services	Microsoft Corp.	MSFT	Technology
General Electric	GE	Industrial goods	Pfizer Inc.	PFE	Healthcare
General Motors	GM	Consumer goods	Procter & Gamble	PG	Consumer goods
Home Depot	HD	Services	AT&T Inc.	T	Technology
Honeywell	HON	Industrial goods	United Technol.	UTX	Conglomerates
Hewlett-Packard	HPQ	Technology	Verizon Communic.	VZ	Technology
Int. Bus. Machines	IBM	Technology	Walmart	WMT	Services
Inter-tel Inc.	INTC	Technology	Exxon Mobile CP	XOM	Basic materials

where $\widehat{\rho}_{xr}^{(I)}$ and $\widehat{\rho}_{yr}^{(I)}$ are the sample inverse autocorrelation functions of time series x_t and y_t, respectively. As in the ACF-based distances, we can use uniform weights or weights that decrease with the autocorrelation lag.

Application 6.1 Caiado and Crato (2010) consider data from international stock markets. The autocorrelations of the squared returns provide useful information about the time series behaviour in terms of the presence of non-linear dependence and possible autoregressive heteroskedasticity (ARCH) effects. In contrast to the autocorrelation of returns, which are typically zero or very close to zero, the autocorrelations of squared returns or absolute returns are generally positive and significant for a substantial number of lags. Caiado and Crato (2010) used the discrepancy statistic in Eq. 6.1, based on the estimated autocorrelations of the squared returns, to identify similarities between the Dow Jones Industrial Average (DJIA) stocks (see Table 6.1). The data correspond to closing prices adjusted for dividends and splits and cover the period from 11 June 1990 to 12 September 2006 (4100 daily observations).

In order to better visualize and interpret similarities among stocks, the outlier INTC was dropped from the clustering analysis. Figure 6.1 shows the complete linkage dendrogram, which minimizes the maximum distance between stocks in the same group. Three groups of corporations were identified. One group is composed of basic materials (Alcoa, DuPont and Exxon Mobile), communications (AT&T and Verizon), industrial goods (Citigroup and General Electric), financial (AIG and JP Morgan Chase), consumer goods and services (Coca-Cola and Walmart Stores) corporations. The second group is composed of technology (IBM, Microsoft and Hewlett-Packard), healthcare (Johnson & Johnson and Pfizer), financial (American Express and Caterpillar), industrial

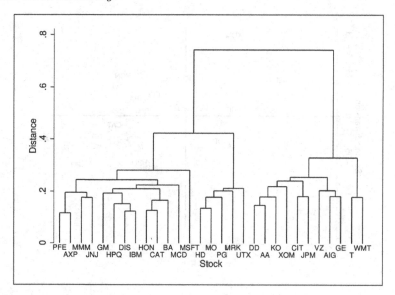

FIGURE 6.1: Complete linkage dendrogram for DJIA stocks using the ACF-based distance for squared returns observations.

goods and consumer goods (Boeing, Honeywell and General Motors), services (Walt Disney and McDonalds) and conglomerates (3M) corporations. The third group is composed of consumer goods (Altria and Procter & Gamble) and miscellaneous sector (Home Depot, Merck and United Technologies) corporations.

Figure 6.2 shows the corresponding two-dimensional map of DJIA stocks by metric multidimensional scaling (see Johnson and Wichern, 1992, p. 706-715). The first dimension accounts for 68.36% of the total variance of the data and the second dimension accounts for 5.23% of the total variance. The map tends to group the basic materials and the communications corporations in a distinct cluster and most technology, healthcare, financial, services, industrial goods and consumer goods corporations in another distinct cluster.

6.2.2 Fuzzy clustering methods

D'Urso and Maharaj (2009) proposed an Autocorrelation-based Fuzzy c-means clustering (A-FcM) model for clustering stationary time series. The model is formalized as follows:

$$min : \sum_{i=1}^{I} \sum_{c=1}^{C} u_{ic}^{m} \; d_{ic}^{2} = \sum_{i=1}^{I} \sum_{c=1}^{C} u_{ie}^{m} \sum_{r=1}^{R} (\hat{\rho}_{ir} - \hat{\rho}_{cr})^{2}, \qquad (6.6)$$

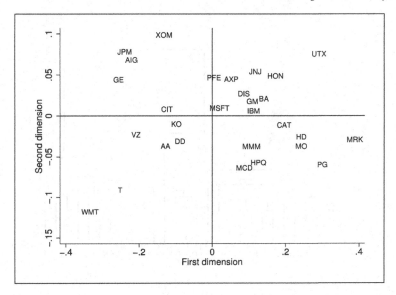

FIGURE 6.2: Two-dimensional scaling map of DJIA stocks using the ACF-based distance for squared returns observations.

with the constraints

$$\sum_{c=1}^{C} u_{ic} = 1 \qquad\qquad u_{ic} \geq 0 \qquad\qquad -1 \leq \hat{\rho_{cr}} \leq 1.$$

$d_{ic}^2 = \sum_{r=1}^{R} (\hat{\rho}_{ir} - \hat{\rho}_{cr})^2$ is the squared Euclidean distance between the i-th time series and the c-th prototype or centroid time series, based on the autocorrelation function at R lags. $m > 1$ is a parameter that controls the fuzziness of the partition (see Bezdek, 1982), u_{ic} is the membership degree of the i-th time series to the c-th cluster, I is the number of time series and C is the number of clusters. Refer to D'Urso and Maharaj (2009) for the iterative solutions to Eq. 6.6 which satisfy the autocorrelation constraints, namely, $-1 \leq \hat{\rho}_{cr} \leq 1$.

$$u_{ic} = \frac{1}{\sum_{c'=1}^{C} \left(\frac{\sum_{r=1}^{R}(\hat{\rho}_{ir} - \hat{\rho}_{cr})^2}{\sum_{r=1}^{R}(\hat{\rho}_{ir} - \hat{\rho}_{c'r})^2} \right)^{\frac{1}{m-1}}}, \qquad \hat{\rho}_{cr} = \frac{\sum_{i=1}^{I} u_{ic}^m \ \hat{\rho}_{ir}}{\sum_{i=1}^{I} u_{ic}^m}. \qquad (6.7)$$

For this purpose, by considering only the constraints on the membership degrees, D'Urso and Maharaj (2009) obtained the solutions in Eq. 6.7 for which the autocorrelation constraints, $-1 \leq \hat{\rho}_{cr} \leq 1$, are satisfied.

D'Urso and Maharaj (2009) have shown through simulation studies that when clusters are well separated, the performance of the A-FcM model is similar to that of the c-means and hierarchical methods. However, for clusters that are not well separated, the A-FcM model has the advantage of identifying time series that are members of more than one cluster simultaneously.

6.3 Time domain features - Quantile autocovariances

Let $\{X_t;\ t \in \mathbb{Z}\}$ be a strictly stationary process and denote by F the marginal distribution of X_t and by $q_\tau = F^{-1}(\tau)$, $\tau \in [0,1]$, the corresponding quantile function. With a fixed $l \in \mathbb{Z}$ and an arbitrary couple of quantile levels $(\tau, \tau') \in [0,1]^2$, consider the cross covariance of the indicator functions $I(X_t \leq q_\tau)$ and $I(X_{t+l} \leq q_{\tau'})$ given by

$$\gamma_l(\tau, \tau') = \text{cov}\{I(X_t \leq q_\tau), I(X_{t+l} \leq q_{\tau'})\} = \mathbb{P}(X_t \leq q_\tau, X_{t+l} \leq q_{\tau'}) - \tau\tau'. \tag{6.8}$$

Function $\gamma_l(\tau, \tau')$, with $(\tau, \tau') \in [0,1]^2$, is called the *quantile autocovariance function (QAF) of lag l* and can be seen as a generalization of the classical autocovariance function. While the latter measures linear dependence between different lags by evaluating covariability with respect to the average, the former studies the joint variability of the events $\{X_t \leq q_\tau\}$ and $\{X_{t+l} \leq q_{\tau'}\}$, that is, examines how a part of the range of variation of X_t helps to predict whether the series will be below quantiles in a future time. By definition, QAF captures the sequential dependence structure of a time series, thus accounting for serial features related to the joint distribution of (X_t, X_{t+l}) that the simple autocovariances cannot detect. Unlike the usual autocovariance function, QAF is well-defined even for processes with infinite moments and takes advantage of the local distributional properties inherent to the quantile methods, in particular showing a greater robustness against heavy tails, dependence in the extremes and changes in the conditional shapes (skewness, kurtosis) (Vilar et al., 2018) . See, Lee and Rao (2012), Mikosch and Stărică (2000), Davis and Mikosch (2009), Hagemann (2013), Dette et al. (2014).

An estimator of $\gamma_l(\tau, \tau')$ can be constructed replacing the theoretical quantiles by the corresponding empirical quantiles $\hat{q}_\tau$ and $\hat{q}_{\tau'}$ based on T realizations $\{X_t, 1 \leq t \leq T\}$ of the process. This way, the estimated QAF is given by

$$\hat{\gamma}_l(\tau, \tau') = \frac{1}{T - l} \sum_{t=1}^{T-l} I(X_t \leq \hat{q}_\tau) I(X_{t+l} \leq \hat{q}_{\tau'}) - \tau\tau', \tag{6.9}$$

where the empirical quantiles $\hat{q}_\alpha$, for $0 \leq \alpha \leq 1$, can be formally seen as the solution of the minimization problem (Koenker, 2005) given by

$$\hat{q}_\alpha = \arg\min_{q \in \mathbb{R}} \sum_{t=1}^{T} \rho_\alpha(X_t - q),$$

with $\rho_\alpha(x) = x(\alpha - I(x < 0))$ (Vilar et al., 2018).

Thus, Lafuente-Rego and Vilar (2015) proposed to measure dissimilarity between a pair of time series $X_t^{(1)}$ and $X_t^{(2)}$ by comparing estimates of their quantile autocovariances over a common range of selected quantiles, as proposed in Lafuente-Rego and Vilar (2015). Specifically, each time series $X_t^{(u)}$, $u = 1, 2$, is characterized by means of the vector $\mathbf{\Gamma}^{(u)}$ constructed as follows. For prefixed ranges of L lags, $l_1, \ldots, l_L$, and r quantile levels, $0 < \tau_1 < \ldots < \tau_r < 1$, the vector $\mathbf{\Gamma}^{(u)}$ is given by

$$\mathbf{\Gamma}^{(u)} = \left(\mathbf{\Gamma}_{l_1}^{(u)}, \ldots, \mathbf{\Gamma}_{l_L}^{(u)}\right), \tag{6.10}$$

where each $\mathbf{\Gamma}_{l_i}^{(u)}$, $i = 1, \ldots, L$, consists of a vector of length r^2 formed by re-arranging by rows the elements of the $r \times r$ matrix

$$\left(\hat{\gamma}_{l_i}^{(u)}(\tau_j, \tau_{j'})\right)_{j,j'=1\ldots,r}, \tag{6.11}$$

with $\hat{\gamma}$ being the sample quantile autocovariance given in Eq. (6.9). This way, the dissimilarity between $X_t^{(1)}$ and $X_t^{(2)}$ is defined as the squared Euclidean distance between the corresponding representations $\mathbf{\Gamma}^{(1)}$ and $\mathbf{\Gamma}^{(2)}$, that is,

$$d_{QAF}\left(X_t^{(1)}, X_t^{(2)}\right) = \|\mathbf{\Gamma}^{(1)} - \mathbf{\Gamma}^{(2)}\|^2 = \sum_{i=1}^{L} \sum_{j=1}^{r} \sum_{j'=1}^{r} \left(\hat{\gamma}_{l_i}^{(1)}(\tau_j, \tau_{j'}) - \hat{\gamma}_{l_i}^{(2)}(\tau_j, \tau_{j'})\right)^2 . \tag{6.12}$$

For the optimal selection of input parameters for clustering see Vilar et al. (2018).

By considering the dissimilarity measures Eq. (6.12) Lafuente-Rego and Vilar (2015) proposed clustering time series by a hierarchical approach (that is, complete linkage method). Vilar et al. (2018) adopted the dissimilarity Eq. (6.12) in a non-hierarchical framework, that is, following a non fuzzy and fuzzy partitioning around medoid approach. In the following subsection 6.3.1 we present the fuzzy C-medoids clustering model.

6.3.1   QAF-based fuzzy c-medoids clustering model (QAF–FcMdC model)

Consider a set S of I realizations of univariate time series $\left\{X_t^{(1)}, \ldots, X_t^{(I)}\right\}$ and denote the corresponding vectors of estimated quantile autocovariances computed as defined in Eq. (6.10) by $\mathbf{\Gamma} = \left\{\mathbf{\Gamma}^{(1)}, \ldots, \mathbf{\Gamma}^{(I)}\right\}$. Assume that all vectors $\mathbf{\Gamma}^{(i)}$ have the same length Lr^2, L and r being the number of lags and quantile levels considered for all the series, respectively. This way, the pairwise d_{QAF} distances between two arbitrary series can be computed according to Eq. (6.12). In this framework, we propose to perform partitional fuzzy clustering on S by means of the QAF-based Fuzzy c-Medoids Clustering model (QAF–FcMdC), which aims at finding the subset of $\mathbf{\Gamma}$ of size C,

$\widetilde{\boldsymbol{\Gamma}} = \left\{ \widetilde{\boldsymbol{\Gamma}}^{(1)}, \ldots, \widetilde{\boldsymbol{\Gamma}}^{(C)} \right\}$, and the $I \times C$ matrix of fuzzy coefficients $\boldsymbol{\Omega} = (u_{ic})$, $i = 1, \ldots, I$, $c = 1, \ldots, C$, that lead to solve the minimization problem:

$$\min_{\widetilde{\boldsymbol{\Gamma}}, \boldsymbol{\Omega}} \sum_{i=1}^{I} \sum_{c=1}^{C} u_{ic}^m \| \boldsymbol{\Gamma}^{(i)} - \widetilde{\boldsymbol{\Gamma}}^{(c)} \|^2, \text{ subject to the constraints: } \sum_{c=1}^{C} u_{ic} = 1 \text{ and } u_{ic} \geq 0,$$

(6.13)

where $u_{ic} \in [0, 1]$ represents the membership degree of the i-th series in the c-th cluster, $\widetilde{\boldsymbol{\Gamma}}^{(c)}$ is the vector of quantile autocovariances associated with the medoid series for the cluster c, and $m > 1$ is a weighting exponent that controls the fuzziness of the partition.

The iterative solutions for the membership degrees are:

$$u_{ic} = \left[\sum_{c'=1}^{C} \left(\frac{\| \boldsymbol{\Gamma}^{(i)} - \widetilde{\boldsymbol{\Gamma}}^{(c)} \|^2}{\| \boldsymbol{\Gamma}^{(i)} - \widetilde{\boldsymbol{\Gamma}}^{(c')} \|^2} \right)^{\frac{1}{m-1}} \right]^{-1}, \quad \text{for } i = 1, \ldots, I \text{ and } c = 1, \ldots, C.$$

(6.14)

For more details (also on the simulation study) see Vilar et al. (2018). Lafuente-Rego et al. (2017) proposed a different robust version of (6.13).

Application 6.2 Vilar et al. (2018) analyzed daily returns of stocks included in the IBEX-35, which groups the thirty-five companies with the highest liquidity and trading volume in the Spanish stock market. Specifically, we manage a database formed by the daily returns of twenty-four stocks located in the TOP-30 ranking according to the finance section of the Yahoo website[1]. The period of observation of the series spans from 1st January 2008 to 19th December 2016, thus resulting in realizations of length $T = 2337$. The daily adjusted closing prices for all the stocks were sourced from the mentioned website and used to obtain the daily returns by considering the first differences of their natural logarithms. The time series are displayed in Figure 6.3.

Heteroskedasticity is again observed although less pronounced for several stocks. Vilar et al. (2018) analyzed the data by means of the QAF–FcMdC clustering. By applying the fuzzy silhouette and the Xie-Beni criteria the authors obtained $C=3$.

The resulting membership degrees are shown in Table 6.2. The shaded cells enhance the highest membership degrees with each procedure and the stocks allocated in a fuzzy way between two or three clusters are indicated with memberships in bold font.

In the partition generated by the QAF–FcMdC model there is a large cluster, C_1, gathering together most of the stocks, including the ones of the sectors of energy and materials, industry and construction (except for Arcelormittal-MTE), and also the three banks with the highest capitalization level in the financial services sector, namely BBVA, Santander-SAN and Caixabank-CABK. The cluster C_3 classifies the company Arcelormittal-MTE

---

[1] https://finance.yahoo.com/

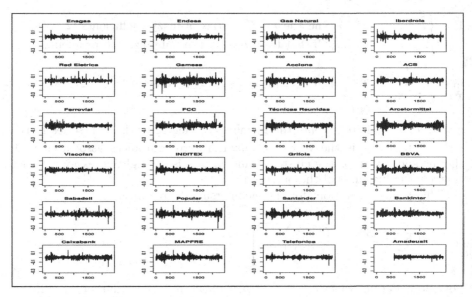

FIGURE 6.3: Daily returns of 24 stocks included in the IBEX-35. Sample period: 1st January 2008 to 19th December 2016.

together with the smaller banks Banco Popular-POP, Banco Sabadell-SAB and Bankinter-BKT, although SAB and BKT could be allocated in C_1 by exhibiting similar memberships for both clusters. The cluster C_2 classifies together two important companies of the consumer goods industry (Viscofan-VIS and Inditex-ITX), the only insurance company (Mapfre-MAP), and a technological company related to the travel sector (Amadeus-AMS). The fuzzy partition provided by the QAF–FcMdC model seems to be congruent with features like company size and business area. Notice that the motivation of the authors is to illustrate the capability of their model to identify similar dependence structures. In this sense, a relevant point of treating with daily returns is to analyze their dispersion, that is, the underlying volatility patterns. To bring insight into this issue, nonparametric approximations of the variance between returns were obtained. The estimated volatility curves grouped according to the three clusters identified with the QAF–FcMdC model are depicted in Figure 6.4.

Notice that all the curves in Figure 6.4 (a) present a very similar fluctuation pattern, with some bumps of different sizes in similar periods of time. The curves in Figure 6.4 (b) corresponding to the cluster C_2 are characterized by a flat profile throughout the second half of the sample period. In fact, only Mapfre-MAP shows a few periods with moderate rise in the level of volatility. The cluster C_3 brings together stocks exhibiting a marked pickup in volatility in the last year, particularly Arcelormittal-MTE and Banco Popular-POP. This effect is less evident for Banco Sabadell-SAB, which could account for its

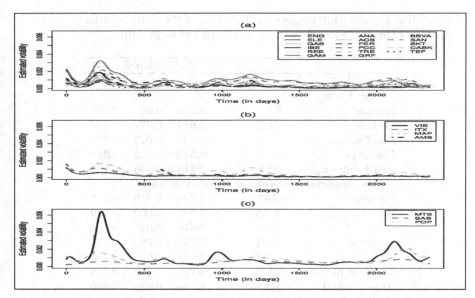

FIGURE 6.4: Nonparametric estimators of the volatility for the daily returns of the 24 analyzed stocks.

vague allocation in this cluster (with a membership of 0.516). It is worthy noting that Arcelormittal-MTE presented a sharp rising of volatility during the first year and a half of the sample period, fairly above the rest of the analyzed stocks. This significant behaviour might determine the atypical character of this time series. Overall, Figure 6.4 allows us to describe representative volatility patterns for each of the clusters determined by the QAF–FcMdC model.

6.4 Time domain features – Variance ratios

6.4.1 Variance ratio tests

The question of whether a time series follows a random walk has been studied extensively in the financial and economic literature. Lo and Mackinlay (1988) introduced a variance ratio test for both homoskedastic and heteroskedastic random walks, using asymptotic normal distribution. Wright (2000) proposed non-parametric variance ratio tests based on ranks and signs, with bootstrap evaluation of significance.

Let p_t, $t = 0, 1, ..., T$ denote a time series of asset prices and y_t denote the continuously compounded return at time t, $y_t = \log(p_t/p_{t-1})$, $t = 1, ..., T$. Given the time series of asset returns $y_t = \mu + \epsilon_t$, where μ is a drift parameter,

TABLE 6.2: Membership degrees in clustering of the daily returns of 24 stocks included in the IBEX-35 ($C = 3$, $m = 1.5$ for QAF–FCMdC).

		QAF-FCMdC		
		$\mathcal{C}_1$	$\mathcal{C}_2$	$\mathcal{C}_3$
Sector: Energy				
Enagás	ENG	0.558	0.275	0.167
Endesa	ELE	0.684	0.072	0.244
Gas Natural	GAS	0.946	0.013	0.041
Iberdrola	IBE	**0.579**	0.052	**0.369**
Red Eléctrica	REE	0.814	0.054	0.132
Sector: Materials, Industry and Construction				
Gamesa	GAM	0.703	0.079	0.218
Acciona	ANA	1.000	0.000	0.000
ACS	ACS	0.816	0.020	0.164
Ferrovial	FER	0.754	0.095	0.151
FCC	FCC	0.821	0.025	0.154
Técnicas Reunidas	TRE	0.710	0.147	0.143
Arcelormittal	MTS	0.084	0.020	0.896
Sector: Consumer Goods				
Viscofan	VIS	0.087	0.849	0.064
Inditex	ITX	1.000	0.000	
Grifols	GRF	**0.539**	0.070	**0.391**
Sector: Financial Services				
BBVA	BBVA	0.860	0.017	0.123
Santander	SAN	0.801	0.076	0.123
Caixabank	CABK	0.860	0.037	0.103
Banco Sabadell	SAB	**0.316**	0.168	**0.516**
Banco Popular	POP	0.000	0.000	1.000
Bankinter	BKT	**0.501**	0.040	**0.459**
Sector: Insurance				
Mapfre	MAP	0.821	0.061	
Sector: Technology and Telecommunications				
Telefónica	TEF	0.955	0.006	0.039
Amadeus	AMS	0.708	0.107	

we want to test the null hypothesis that: i) ϵ_t are identical and independently distributed (iid), or ii) ϵ_t are independent and conditional heteroskedastic.

If we assume the time series follows a random walk, the variance of k-period return should be k times the variance of the one-period return. Therefore, if a return series is a random walk the ratio of $1/k$ times the variance of $\log(p_t/p_{t-k})$ to the variance of $\log(p_t/p_{t-1})$ should be close to 1.

This variance ratio is given by

$$\text{VR}(k) = \frac{\frac{1}{Tk}\sum_{t=k}^{T}\left(y_t + y_{t-1} + \ldots + y_{t-k+1} - k\hat{\mu}\right)^2}{\frac{1}{T}\sum_{t=1}^{T}\left(y_t - \hat{\mu}\right)^2}, \tag{6.15}$$

where $\hat{\mu} = T^{-1} \sum_{t=1}^{T} y_t$. Lo and MacKinlay (1988) showed that, if the returns are i.i.d. then the test statistic

$$M_1(k) = (\text{VR}(k) - 1)\, \phi(k)^{-1/2}, \qquad (6.16)$$

where

$$\phi(k) = \frac{2(2k-1)(k-1)}{3kT}, \qquad (6.17)$$

has asymptotic normal distribution under the null hypothesis that $\text{VR}(k) = 1$. Lo and MacKinlay (1988) proposed an alternative test statistic which is robust against the presence of conditional heteroskedasticity, given by

$$M_2(k) = (\text{VR}(k) - 1) \left[\sum_{j=1}^{k-1} \left[\frac{2(k-j)}{k} \right]^2 \delta_j \right]^{-1/2}, \qquad (6.18)$$

where

$$\delta_j = \frac{\sum_{t=j+1}^{T} (y_t - \hat{\mu})^2 (y_{t-j} - \hat{\mu})^2}{\left[\sum_{t=1}^{T} (y_t - \hat{\mu})^2 \right]^2}. \qquad (6.19)$$

conventional critical values for the standard normal distribution hold for both tests.

Wright (2000) suggests modifying the usual variance ratio tests using two non-parametric tests based on standardized ranks of the increments y_t,

$$r_{1t} = \frac{r(y_t) - \frac{T+1}{2}}{\sqrt{\frac{T^2 - 1}{12}}} \qquad (6.20)$$

and

$$r_{2t} = \Phi^{-1}\left(\frac{r(y_t)}{T+1} \right), \qquad (6.21)$$

where Φ is the standard normal cumulative distribution function. The proposed test statistics are given by

$$R_1(k) = \left[\frac{\frac{1}{Tk} \sum_{t=k}^{T} (r_{1t} + r_{1t-1} + \cdots + r_{1t-k+1})^2}{\frac{1}{T} \sum_{t=1}^{T} r_{1t}^2} - 1 \right] \cdot \phi(k)^{-1/2}, \qquad (6.22)$$

and

$$R_2(k) = \left[\frac{\frac{1}{Tk} \sum_{t=k}^{T} (r_{2t} + r_{2t-1} + \cdots + r_{2t-k+1})^2}{\frac{1}{T} \sum_{t=1}^{T} r_{2t}^2} - 1 \right] \cdot \phi(k)^{-1/2}. \qquad (6.23)$$

Under the null hypothesis that ϵ_t is i.i.d., the exact sampling distribution of $R_1(k)$ and $R_2(k)$ may be derived from a permutation bootstrap.

Wright (2000) also suggests a modification of the homoskedasticity statistic of Lo and MacKinlay (1988) in which y_t is replaced by its sign. The sign-based test is given by

$$S_1(k) = \left[\frac{\frac{1}{Tk} \sum_{t=k}^{T} \left(s_t + s_{t-1} + \dots + s_{t-k+1} \right)^2}{\frac{1}{T} \sum_{t=1}^{T} s_t^2} - 1 \right] \cdot \phi(k)^{-1/2}. \tag{6.24}$$

where s_t is equal to 1 if $y_t > 0$ and equal to -1 otherwise.

To control the size distortion of the individual tests of Lo and MacKinlay (1988) and Wright (2000), Chow and Denning (1993) proposed a conservative joint test that examines the maximum absolute value of a set of multiple variance ratio statistics.

6.4.2　Variance ratio-based metric

Bastos and Caiado (2014) introduced a distance measure between the vectors of the variance ratio statistics M_1, M_2, R_1, R_2 and S_1. Denoting by $v_x' = [\text{VR}_{1x}, \text{VR}_{2x}, ..., \text{VR}_{px}]$ and $v_y' = [\text{VR}_{1y}, \text{VR}_{2y}, ..., \text{VR}_{py}]$ the p-dimensional vectors of standardized variance ratios for time series x_t and y_t, respectively, the distance measure between these vectors is

$$d_{\text{VR}}(x_t, y_t) = \sqrt{\sum_{j=1}^{p} (\text{VR}_{jx} - \text{VR}_{jy})^2} \tag{6.25}$$

where the vectors include variance ratios evaluated at several lags k in order to capture the serial dependence of the returns. Bastos and Caiado (2014) used the proposed metric for classification and clustering of financial time series with applications to international stock market returns. They found that this metric discriminates stock markets reasonably well according to their size and level of development.

6.5　Other time domain clustering methods

Several other authors have used other time domain features to cluster time series. Clustering of financial and economic time series with correlation or cross-correlation coefficients include those by Dose and Cincotti (2005), Basalto et al. (2007), Takayuki et al. (2006), Miskiewicz and Ausloos (2008), and Ausloos and Lambiotte (2007), while Goutte et al. (1999) clustered functional magnetic resonance image (fMRI) time series using cross-correlations.

Wang et al. (2006) proposed a characteristic-based method for clustering time series, where global features are extracted from each time series. These features include trend, seasonality, autocorrelations, non-linearity, skewness, kurtosis, self-similarity, chaos and periodicity. They fed these features into several clustering algorithms, including unsupervised neural networks and self organising maps for visualization and interpretation. Wang et al. (2007) extended this characteristic-based method for clustering time series to multivariate time series.

6.6 Frequency domain features - Spectral ordinates

Spectral analysis provides useful information about the time series behaviour in terms of cyclic patterns and periodicity. In this sense, nonparametric methods based on spectral analysis can be useful for classification and clustering of time series data. For these purposes, some distance-based methods in the frequency domain that have been proposed in the literature are presented.

6.6.1 Crisp clustering methods

Caiado et al. (2006) proposed a spectral domain method for clustering time series of equal length. Let $P_x(\omega_j) = T^{-1}|\sum_{t=1}^{T} x_t e^{-it\omega_j}|^2$ be the periodogram of time series x_t at frequencies $\omega_j = 2\pi j/T$, $j = 1, ..., [T/2]$, with $[T/2]$ the largest integer less or equal to $T/2$ (similar expression applies to series y_t). The Euclidean distance between the periodograms of x_t and y_t is given by

$$d_P(x_t, y_t) = \sqrt{\sum_{j=1}^{[T/2]} [P_x(\omega_j) - P_y(\omega_j)]^2}. \tag{6.26}$$

Since the variance of the periodogram ordinates is proportional to the spectrum at the corresponding Fourier frequencies, Caiado et al. (2006) suggest the use of sample variances to normalize the periodograms and then take logarithms to attain homoskedasticity. Thus the distance becomes

$$d_{LNP}(x_t, y_t) = \sqrt{\sum_{j=1}^{[T/2]} \left[\log \frac{P_x(\omega_j)}{\widehat{\sigma}_x^2} - \log \frac{P_y(\omega_j)}{\widehat{\sigma}_y^2}\right]^2}, \tag{6.27}$$

where $\widehat{\sigma}_x^2$ and $\widehat{\sigma}_y^2$ are the sample variances of x and y, respectively. These metrics satisfy the usual properties of a metric: positivity, symmetry, identity and triangle inequality.

The Kullback-Leibler information distance in the frequency domain (Kakizawa et al., 1998) which is asymptotically equivalent to Eq. (6.2) but much easier to compute, is given by

$$d_{KLF}(x_t, y_t) = \sum_{j=1}^{[T/2]} \left(\frac{P_x(\omega_j)}{P_y(\omega_j)} - \log \frac{P_x(\omega_j)}{P_y(\omega_j)} - 1\right). \tag{6.28}$$

This distance measure is greater or equal to zero, with equality if and only if $P_x(\omega_j) = P_y(\omega_j)$ almost everywhere. In a simulation study Caiado et al. (2006) show that (6.27) and the normalized periodogram version of (6.28) for high frequency components can perform quite well in distinguishing between nonstationary and near-nonstationary time series.

Diggle and Fisher (1991) proposed a graphical method for comparison of two periodograms and developed a nonparametric approach to test the hypothesis that two underlying spectra are the same. Let $P_x(\omega_j)$ and $P_y(\omega_j)$ denote the periodogram ordinates of time series x and y, as defined in (6.26). The corresponding normalized cumulative periodogram is

$$F_x(\omega_j) = \frac{\sum_{i=1}^{j} P_x(\omega_i)}{\sum_{i=1}^{[T/2]} P_x(\omega_i)} ,   \tag{6.29}$$

and a similar definition for $F_y(\omega_j)$. Since $P_x(\omega_i)$ and $P_x(\omega_j)$, for $i \neq j$, are asymptotically independent, as are $P_y(\omega_j)$ and $P_y(\omega_i)$, to test the null hypothesis that $F_x(\omega_j)$ and $F_y(\omega_j)$ are independent and identically distributed, for each $j = 1, \ldots, [T/2]$, Diggle and Fisher (1991) proposed two measures of the distance between $F_x(\omega)$ and $F_y(\omega)$, based on the Kolmogorov-Smirnov and Cramér-von Mises statistics,

$$D_{KS} = \sup |F_x(\omega) - F_y(\omega)| ,   \tag{6.30}$$

and

$$D_{CVM} = \int_0^\pi [F_x(\omega) - F_y(\omega)]^2 \, d\bar{F}(\omega) ,   \tag{6.31}$$

where $\bar{F}(\omega) = \frac{1}{2}[F_x(\omega) + F_y(\omega)]$. Monte Carlo simulations suggested that the statistic D_{KS} is often competitive with existing semiparametric tests, as the ones of Coates and Diggle (1986). For comparison of more than two periodograms, Diggle and Fisher (1991) proposed the use of the extended Kolmogorov-Smirnov statistic given by Kiefer (1959).

Maharaj (2002) introduced a nonparametric test to compare the evolutionary spectra of two time series. Let $\{X_t, t = 1, 2, \ldots\}$ be a process that may or may not be stationary in the mean but is nonstationary in variance, with spectral density function $f(\omega)$.

A smoothed estimate of the spectrum is given by

$$\hat{f}(\omega) = \sum_{k=-m}^{m} W(k)\hat{\gamma}_k e^{-i\omega k} ,   \tag{6.32}$$

where $W(k)$ is a suitable lag window and $\hat{\gamma}_k$ is the sample autocovariance function. The estimate of the evolutionary spectrum is given by

$$\hat{h}(\omega) = \sum_v g_t \left| \hat{f}_t(\omega) \right|^2 ,   \tag{6.33}$$

where g_t is a weight function of suitable length and $\hat{f}_t(\omega)$ is the smoothed estimate of the spectrum in the neighbourhood of t. Two measures of distance between the estimated evolutionary spectra $\hat{h}_x(\omega_j)$ and $\hat{h}_y(\omega_j)$, $j = 1, \ldots, [T/2]$, of two time series x_t and y_t, were considered by Maharaj (2002). For related time series, she used

$$D_{ESR} = \sum_{j=1}^{[T/2]} \left[\hat{h}_x(\omega_j) - \hat{h}_y(\omega_j) \right] \tag{6.34}$$

and, for independent time series,

$$D_{ESI} = \sum_{j=1}^{[T/2]} \hat{h}_x(\omega_j) - \sum_{j=1}^{[T/2]} \hat{h}_y(\omega_j) . \tag{6.35}$$

6.6.2 Fuzzy clustering methods

Maharaj and D'Urso (2011) proposed a class of frequency domain-based fuzzy clustering models which can be formalized as follows:

$$min : \sum_{i=1}^{I} \sum_{c=1}^{C} u_{ic}^m \, d_{ic}^2 = \sum_{i=1}^{I} \sum_{c=1}^{C} u_{ic}^m \sum_{r=1}^{R} (\tilde{p}_{ir} - \tilde{p}_{cr})^2, \tag{6.36}$$

with the constraints

$$\sum_{c=1}^{C} u_{ic} = 1 \qquad u_{ic} \geq 0 \qquad \tilde{p}_L < \tilde{p}_{ic} < \tilde{p}_U.$$

$d_{ic}^2 = \sum_{r=1}^{R} (\tilde{p}_{ir} - \tilde{p}_{cr})^2$ is now based on the relevant frequency domain features, with m, μ_{ic}, i and c defined as in Eq. (6.36). $\tilde{p}_L$ and $\tilde{p}_U$ are the upper and lower limits of the frequency domain feature if they exist. Maharaj and D'Urso (2011) derived iterative solutions to Eq. (6.36) which satisfy the constraints pertinent to the specific frequency domain features, namely, normalized periodogram ordinates, log normalized periodogram ordinates and cepstral coefficients of the cepstrum. The cepstrum of a time series is the spectrum of the logarithm of the spectrum. Refer to Boets et al. (2005) for more details of the cepstrum.

For the normalized periodogram-based fuzzy clustering model, $\tilde{p}_{ir} \equiv np_{ir}$, the normalized periodogram ordinate of the i-th time series at the r-th frequency and $\tilde{p}_{cr} \equiv np_{cr}$, the normalized periodogram ordinate of the centroid time series at the r-th frequency. $d_{ic}^2 \equiv \sum_{r=1}^{R} (np_{ir} - np_{cr})^2$ the squared Euclidean distance measure between the i-th time series and the centroid time series of the c-th cluster based on the normalized periodogram at r-th frequency, $R = [(T-1)/2]$ and T is the length of the time series. $0 < np_{ir} < 1$ is the constraint on the normalized periodogram ordinates.

For the log normalized periodogram-based fuzzy clustering model, $\tilde{p}_{ir} \equiv lnp_{ir}$, the log normalized periodogram ordinate of the i-th time series at the r-th frequency and $\tilde{p}_{cr} \equiv lnp_{cr}$, the lognormalized periodogram ordinate of the centroid time series at the r-th frequency. $d_{ic}^2 \equiv \sum_{r=1}^{R}(lnp_{ir} - lnp_{cr})^2$ the squared Euclidean distance measure between the i-th time series and the centroid time series of the c-th cluster based on the log normalized periodogram at r-th frequency, $R = [(T - 1)/2]$. and T is the length of the time series. $-\infty < lnp_{ir} < 0$ is the constraint on the log normalized periodogram ordinates.

For the cepstral-based fuzzy clustering model, $\tilde{p}_{ir} \equiv cp_{ir}$, the cepstral ordinate of the i-th time series at the r-th frequency and $\tilde{p}_{cr} \equiv cp_{cr}$, the cepstral ordinate of the centroid time series at the r-th frequency. $d_{ic}^2 \equiv \sum_{r=1}^{R}(cp_{ir} - cp_{cr})^2$ the squared Euclidean distance measure between the i-th time series and the centroid time series of the c-th cluster based on the cepstrum at r-th frequency, and in this case I is just a small fraction of $R = [(T - 1)/2]$. and T is the length of the time series. There are no constraints on cp_{ir} since $-\infty < cp_{ir} < \infty$.

Maharaj and D'Urso (2011) conducted a a number of simulation studies using time series generated from both linear and non linear models and they found that the cepstral-based fuzzy clustering model generally performs better than the normalized and log normalized periodogram-based fuzzy clustering models, the autocorrelation-based fuzzy c-means Clustering from D'Urso and Maharaj (2009), and a fuzzy clustering model based on discrete wavelet transform (DWT) coefficients. The DWT decomposes the time series into different frequency bands (scales) and hence the total energy of the time series is decomposed into frequency bands (from high frequency to low). Some of the results of the application to electroencephalogram (EEG) time series to differentiate between patterns associated with a sample of healthy volunteers and a sample of epileptic patients during seizure activity, are presented below.

Application 6.3 Maharaj and D'Urso (2011) considered a subset of 200 electroencephalogram (EEG) time series from a suite studied by Andrzejak et al. (2001). These 200 series are divided into two sets denoted by A and E, each containing 100 EEG segments of 23.6 seconds duration (4096 observations). Set A EEG recordings are of healthy volunteers while Set E consists of EEG recordings of epileptic patients during seizure activity. Figure 6.5 shows a typical EEG record from each of Sets A and E from where it can be observed that there does appear to be an overall difference in patterns. However, since there is much noise present in both types of records, misclassifications are likely to occur.

Using adaptive neuro fuzzy inference system networks to discriminate among the patterns A and E, Kannathal et al. (2005) achieved a classification error rate of 7.8% while Nigam and Graupe (2004) used Large-Memory Storage and Retrieval neural networks to discriminate among the patterns A and E and achieved a classification error rate of 2.8%. On the other hand

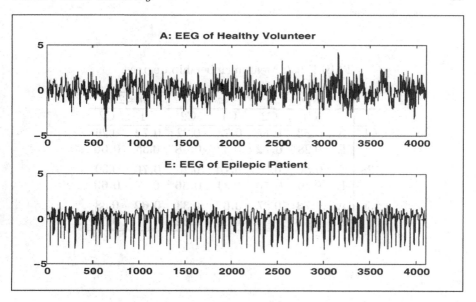

FIGURE 6.5: Standardized EEG recordings from each of sets A and E.

Maharaj and Alonso (2007) achieved a 0% classification error rate using time dependent wavelet variances in a quadratic discriminant analysis procedure.

While the aim of cluster analysis is to find groups in data when usually the groupings are not known a priori, Maharaj and D'Urso (2011) demonstrate that clustering with cepstral coefficients using the c-means algorithm can discriminate between the EEG patterns of sets A and E with error rates comparable to Kannathal et al. (2005), while fuzzy c-means clustering can explain some of the misclassifications.

Since each EEG record is of length $T = 2^{12} = 4096$, using the guidelines they put forward for the minimum number of cepstral coefficients p to achieve successful classification, they performed the analysis for $p= 64, 128$ and 256 and for fuzzy parameter values of $m = 1.8, 2$ and 2.2. For all (m, p) combinations, the same 5 EEG recordings from Set A were misclassified as having patterns of the Set E records, and the same 10 EEG recordings from Set E were misclassified as having patterns of the Set A records. For the 200 EEG records, c-means clustering achieved a classification error rate of 7.5%.

Table 6.3 shows the mean membership degrees across the 100 cases of Set A EEG records in Cluster 1 (C1) and in Cluster 2 (C2), and the 100 cases of Set E EEG records in Cluster 1 and in Cluster 2. Table 6.4 shows the membership degrees from fuzzy c-means clustering of the Set A and E EEG records that were misclassified into Clusters 2 and 1 respectively, by c-means clustering for $p = 64$.

TABLE 6.3: Mean membership degrees.

		m=1.8		m=2.0		m=2.2	
p		C1	C2	C1	C2	C1	C2
64	A	**0.83**	0.17	**0.78**	0.22	**0.74**	0.26
	E	0.28	**0.72**	0.32	**0.68**	0.35	**0.65**
128	A	**0.80**	0.20	**0.74**	0.26	**0.70**	0.30
	E	0.30	**0.70**	0.34	**0.66**	0.37	**0.63**
256	A	**0.73**	0.27	**0.67**	0.33	**0.62**	0.38
	E	0.33	**0.67**	0.38	**0.62**	0.41	**0.59**

TABLE 6.4: Membership degrees of the Set A and E EEG records that were misclassified by c-means clustering for p=64.

p=64	c-means		fuzzy c-means					
EEG Record	Set	Cluster	m=1.8		m=2.0		m=2.2	
			C1	C2	C1	C2	C1	C2
1	A	C2	0.49	0.51	0.49	0.51	0.49	0.51
27	A	C2	0.45	0.55	0.46	0.54	0.46	0.54
52	A	C2	0.47	0.53	0.47	0.53	0.47	0.53
78	A	C2	0.45	0.55	0.46	0.54	0.46	0.54
99	A	C2	0.33	0.67	0.36	0.64	0.38	0.62
107	E	C1	0.58	0.42	0.56	0.44	0.55	0.45
117	E	C1	**0.75**	0.25	**0.70**	0.30	**0.66**	0.34
131	E	C1	0.62	0.38	0.60	0.40	0.58	0.42
132	E	C1	0.58	0.42	0.56	0.44	0.54	0.46
134	E	C1	0.56	0.44	0.55	0.45	0.54	0.46
135	E	C1	0.69	0.31	0.65	0.35	0.62	0.38
143	E	C1	0.69	0.31	0.65	0.35	0.62	0.38
172	E	C1	0.61	0.39	0.58	0.42	0.56	0.44
181	E	C1	0.63	0.37	0.60	0.40	0.58	0.42
190	E	C1	**0.79**	0.21	**0.74**	0.26	**0.69**	0.31

On comparing the mean membership degrees (Table 6.3) of the

1. Set A EEG records in Cluster 1 with that of the five misclassified Set A records (Table 6.4), it can be observed that in all cases the membership degrees are smaller than the mean and are fairly fuzzy; hence these five records have fuzzy membership in both clusters.

2. Set E EEG record in Cluster 2 with that of the ten misclassified Set E records (Table 6.4), it can be observed that of the ten records, only 117 and 190 have greater membership degrees than the mean membership degrees in Table 6.3 while the remaining eight records have fuzzy membership in both clusters.

Similar observations were made for $p = 128$ and 256. It can be concluded from the 200 EEG records that only two EEG records are clearly misclassified while the other thirteen have fuzzy membership in both clusters. Refer to Maharaj and D'Urso (2011) for the validation of these results. From the results of this application, they concluded, that while classification error rates for discriminating between the patterns of the EEG records in Sets A and E, achieved by c-means clustering, are not always comparable to those achieved by other methods, fuzzy c-means clustering adds a new dimension to the analysis of EEG records that are misclassified. Namely, the advantage of fuzzy clustering in a situation such as this is that those time records that are potentially misclassified are identified and hence could be rechecked using another method such as a human reader.

6.7 Frequency domain clustering methods for time series of unequal lengths

In many real applications, it is often the case that the data sets have different lengths and the sets of frequencies at which the periodogram ordinates are usually computed are different. A solution to the problem is to extend the length of the shorter series to the length of the longer series by adding zeros to the shorter series and computing the periodogram. This matches the frequencies of the longer series and produces a smoothed periodogram. This approach, known as the "zero-padding" procedure, is widely used in the pattern recognition and signal processing literature, e.g., Wang and Bolstein (2004) due to its simplicity and applicability.

Let x_t and y_t be two time series with different sample sizes, $n_x > n_y$. Let $P_x(\omega_j)$ with $\omega_j = 2\pi j/n_x$, $j = 1, ..., m_x = [n_x/2]$ and $P_y(\omega_p)$ with $\omega_p = 2\pi p/n_y$, $j = 1, ..., m_y = [n_y/2]$ be the periodograms of series x_t and y_t, respectively. Caiado et al. (2009) define a zero-padding periodogram discrepancy statistic between x_t and y_t by

$$d_{ZP}(x_t, y_t) = \sqrt{\frac{1}{m_x} \sum_{j=1}^{m_x} [P_x(\omega_j) - P_{y'}(\omega_j)]^2}, \qquad (6.37)$$

where $P_{y'}(\omega_j)$ is the periodogram of $y'_t = \begin{cases} y_t, & t = 1, ..., n_y \\ 0, & t = n_y + 1, ..., n_x, \end{cases}$. This metric performs reasonably well for the comparison of stationary time series with similar autocorrelation structure. However, it is not able to distinguish between longer stationary and shorter nonstationary time series due to distortion of the zero-padding approach for very unbalanced sample sizes.

As put forward by Caiado et al. (2009), a second solution to the problem of clustering of time series of unequal lengths is to compute both periodograms at a common frequency. For instance, the periodogram ordinates of the longer series x_t at the frequencies of the shorter series y_t may be calculated and then the following reduced periodogram discrepancy statistic can be used.

$$d_{RP}(x_t, y_t) = \sqrt{\frac{1}{m_y} \sum_{p=1}^{m_y} [P_x^{RP}(\omega_p) - P_y(\omega_p)]^2}, \qquad (6.38)$$

where $P_x^{RP}(\omega_p) = \frac{1}{n_x} \left| \sum_{t=1}^{n_x} x_t e^{-it\omega_p} \right|^2$ with $\omega_p = 2\pi p/n_y$, $p = 1, ..., m_y < m_x$ is the reduced periodogram. From the results of a simulation study, Caiado et al. (2009) concluded that the distance (6.38) performs poorly for classifying stationary and nonstationary time series of short length.

A third solution proposed by Caiado et al. (2009) for handling series of unequal lengths in the frequency domain is to construct interpolated periodogram ordinates for the longer series at the frequencies defined by the shorter series. Without loss of generality, let $r = [p\frac{m_x}{m_y}]$ be the largest integer less or equal to $p\frac{m_x}{m_y}$ for $p = 1, ..., m_y$, and $m_y < m_x$. The periodogram ordinates of x_t can be estimated as

$$
\begin{aligned}
P_x^{IP}(\omega_p) &= P_x(\omega_r) + (P_x(\omega_{r+1}) - P_x(\omega_r)) \times \frac{\omega_{p,y} - \omega_{r,x}}{\omega_{r+1,x} - \omega_{r,x}} \\
&= P_x(\omega_r)\left(1 - \frac{\omega_{p,y} - \omega_{r,x}}{\omega_{r+1,x} - \omega_{r,x}}\right) + P_x(\omega_{r+1})\left(\frac{\omega_{p,y} - \omega_{r,x}}{\omega_{r+1,x} - \omega_{r,x}}\right).
\end{aligned}
$$
$$(6.39)$$

This procedure will yield an interpolated periodogram with the same Fourier frequencies of the shorter periodogram $P_y(\omega_p)$. If one is interested only in the dependence structure and not in the process scale, then the periodograms can be standardized by dividing them by the sample variances, and then taking the logarithms: $\log NP_x^{IP}(\omega_p) = \log\left(P_x^{IP}(\omega_p)/\hat{\sigma}_x^2\right)$ and $\log NP_y(\omega_p) = \log\left(P_y(\omega_p)/\hat{\sigma}_y^2\right)$.

They define the interpolated periodogram discrepancy statistic by

$$d_{IP}(x_t, y_t) = \sqrt{\frac{1}{m_y} \sum_{p=1}^{m_y} [P_x^{IP}(\omega_p) - P_y(\omega_p)]^2}, \qquad (6.40)$$

or, by using the log normalized periodogram,

$$d_{ILNP}(x_t, y_t) = \sqrt{\frac{1}{m_y} \sum_{p=1}^{m_y} \left[\log \frac{P^{IP}(\omega_p)}{\widehat{\sigma}_x^2} - \log \frac{P_y(\omega_p)}{\widehat{\sigma}_y^2} \right]^2}. \qquad (6.41)$$

6.7.1 Hypothesis testing

Caiado et al. (2012) introduced a periodogram-distance based test of the hypothesis that two time series of unequal lengths are realizations of the same stochastic process. Given two independent stationary series x_t and y_t, with $n_x = n_y = m$, the null hypothesis to be tested is $H_0 : f_x(\omega_j) = f_y(\omega_j)$; that is, there is no difference between the underlying spectra of the series $\{x_t\}$ and $\{y_t\}$ at all Fourier frequencies ω_j.

They proposed a test of significance for comparing the log normalized periodograms of time series x_t and y_t based on the following statistic:

$$D_{NP} = \frac{\overline{x}_{LNP} - \overline{y}_{LNP}}{\sqrt{\left(s_{LNP,x}^2 + s_{LNP,y}^2\right)/m}}. \qquad (6.42)$$

where $\overline{x}_{LNP}$ and $s_{LNP,x}^2$ are the sample mean and sample variance of the log normalized periodogram of x_t ($\overline{y}_{LNP}$ and $s_{LNP,y}^2$ apply to the log normalized periodogram of y_t). This statistic is approximately normally distributed with zero mean and unit variance. For different lengths, $m_x \neq m_y$, regular periodograms cannot be used as the Fourier frequencies are different. One approach could be the use of the interpolated periodogram for the longer series x_t at the frequencies $\omega_p = 2\pi p/n_y$, for $p = 1, ..., m_y$, as defined in Eq. (6.39), and use the test statistic

$$D_{NP}^I = \frac{\overline{x}_{LNP^I} - \overline{y}_{LNP}}{\sqrt{\left(s_{LNP^I,x}^2 + s_{LNP,y}^2\right)/m_y}}, \qquad (6.43)$$

where $\overline{x}_{LNP^I} = \frac{1}{m_y} \sum_{p=1}^{m_y} \log NP_x^I(\omega_p)$, $s_{LNP^I,x}^2 = \frac{1}{m_y} \sum_{p=1}^{m_y} \left[\log NP_x^I(\omega_p) - \overline{x}_{LNP^I} \right]^2$ and $m_y < m_x$.

6.7.2 Comparison of processes with similar sample characteristics with simulated time series

Application 6.4: To illustrate the performance of the interpolated periodogram based metric, two series of different sample sizes, $(n_1, n_2) = \{(50, 100), (100, 100), (200, 100), (500, 250), (1000, 500), (2000, 1000)\}$, were simulated from each of the following processes (Caiado et al., 2009). So, four different series were simulated for each replication on each of the following (a) through (i) comparisons:

(a) AR(1), $\phi = 0.9$ versus AR(1), $\phi = 0.5$ (Table 6.5);
(b) MA(1), $\theta = -0.9$ versus MA(1), $\theta = -0.5$ (Table 6.6);
(c) ARMA(1,1), $\phi = 0.5$, $\theta = -0.2$ versus ARMA(1,1), $\phi = 0.2$, $\theta = -0.8$ (Table 6.7);
(d) AR(1), $\phi = 0.9$ versus ARIMA(0,1,0) (Table 6.8);
(e) IMA(1,1), $\theta = 0.8$ versus ARMA(1,1), $\phi = 0.95$, $\theta = 0.74$ (Table 6.9);
(f) ARFIMA(0,0.45,0) versus white noise (Table 6.10);
(g) ARFIMA(0,0.45,0) versus ARMA(1,0), $\phi = 0.95$ (Table 6.11);
(h) ARFIMA(1,0.45,0), $\phi = 0.3$ versus ARIMA(1,1,0), $\phi = 0.3$ (Table 6.12);
(i) Determinist trend, $x_t = 1 + 0.02t + \varepsilon_t$ versus stochastic trend, $x_t = 0.02 + x_{t-1} + (1 - 0.9B)\varepsilon_t$ (Table 6.13).

In cases (a), (b) and (c), we compare models of similar type, but with low order parameters and similar autocorrelation functions. In case (d), we compare a nonstationary process and a stationary process with AR parameter value very close to the random walk model. In case (e), we compare nonstationary and near nonstationary processes of Wichern (1973). In cases (f), we compare stationary processes with different characteristics of persistence. In case (g), we compare long-memory and short-memory near nonstationary processes. In case (h), we compare a near nonstationary process with long memory and a nonstationary process. In case (i), we compare the trend-stationary and difference-stationary processes of Enders, 1995, p. 252), but with a near unit root in the MA component of the stochastic formulation in order to have the two processes with similar properties.

The fractional noise was simulated using the finite Fourier method of Davies and Harte (1987). The four generated series with zero mean and unit variance white noise were grouped into two clusters by the hierarchical method of complete linkage using the Euclidean mean distance between the log normalized periodogram ordinates defined in (6.41). This was repeated 1000 times. The mean percentages of success of the comparison in cases (a) to (i) are provided in Tables 6.5 to 6.13, respectively. For instance, in Table 6.5, the value 61.2 in the upper-left cell means that 61.2% of the times the two AR(1), $\phi = 0.9$, $n_1 = 50$ and $n_2 = 100$ processes were grouped into one cluster and the two AR(1), $\phi = 0.5$, $n_1 = 50$ and $n_2 = 100$ processes were grouped into another cluster.

In the comparisons among stationary processes with ARMA and ARFIMA formulations, the interpolated periodogram based metric shows a remarkable good performance. The simulations results of the comparison between ARMA versus ARIMA processes show a performance that increases significantly with the sample size. The exception to this is case (i), in which the metric is unable to distinguish successfully between trend-stationary and difference-stationary processes of similar lengths, in particular for large data samples. This can be easily explained by noting that periodograms of both processes are dominated by a divergence at low frequencies that conceals differences when the sample size is large. For unequal lengths, the discrimination between the two models works well.

TABLE 6.5: Percentages of successes of the comparison between AR(1): $\phi = 0.5$ and AR(1):$\phi = 0.9$.

AR(1): $\phi = 0.9$	AR(1): $\phi = 0.5$					
	(50,100)	(100,100)	(200,100)	(500,250)	(1000,500)	(2000,1000)
(50,100)	61.2	58.6	73.4	98.4	100.0	100.0
(100,100)	73.2	72.1	71.9	95.6	100.0	100.0
(200,100)	84.8	81.1	87.9	95.4	99.9	100.0
(500,250)	99.1	98.0	98.6	99.2	99.9	100.0
(1000,500)	100.0	100.0	100.0	99.9	100.0	100.0
(2000,1000)	100.0	100.0	100.0	100.0	100.0	100.0

TABLE 6.6: Percentages of successes of the comparison between MA(1): $\theta =$ -0.5 and MA(1): $\theta =$ -0.9.

MA(1): $\theta = -0.9$	MA(1): $\theta = -0.5$					
	(50,100)	(100,100)	(200,100)	(500,250)	(1000,500)	(2000,1000)
(50,100)	43.3	39.2	58.6	95.5	100.0	100.0
(100,100)	36.0	43.9	42.0	88.1	100.0	100.0
(200,100)	58.0	43.1	64.2	85.8	99.6	100.0
(500,250)	93.3	86.6	82.5	92.0	95.3	99.2
(1000,500)	100.0	99.8	99.4	96.3	99.4	99.6
(2000,1000)	100.0	100.0	100.0	99.7	100.0	100.0

TABLE 6.7: Percentages of successes of the comparison between ARMA(1,1): $\phi = 0.2$, $\theta = -0.8$ and ARMA(1,1): $\phi = 0.5$, $\theta = -0.2$.

ARMA(1,1): $\phi = 0.5$, $\theta = -0.2$	ARMA(1,1): $\phi = 0.2$, $\theta = -0.8$					
	(50,100)	(100,100)	(200,100)	(500,250)	(1000,500)	(2000,1000)
(50,100)	36.6	26.3	48.7	92.8	100.0	100.0
(100,100)	30.1	31.4	33.8	84.4	100.0	100.0
(200,100)	50.7	32.4	54.7	77.5	98.2	100.0
(500,250)	93.7	82.7	74.5	84.9	92.1	98.7
(1000,500)	100.0	99.8	98.1	91.5	97.1	98.3
(2000,1000)	100.0	100.0	100.0	99.0	98.5	99.8

TABLE 6.8: Percentages of successes of the comparison between AR(1) and ARIMA(0,1,0).

AR(1): $\phi = 0.9$	ARIMA(0,1,0)					
	(50,100)	(100,100)	(200,100)	(500,250)	(1000,500)	(2000,1000)
(50,100)	16.4	26.2	42.4	88.0	99.7	100.0
(100,100)	11.6	22.7	30.8	78.9	98.3	100.0
(200,100)	22.8	19.4	36.0	76.6	96.4	100.0
(500,250)	82.4	59.8	58.2	74.8	92.0	97.7
(1000,500)	99.8	100.0	96.4	79.4	89.0	96.8
(2000,1000)	100.0	100.0	100.0	99.5	95.3	95.0

TABLE 6.9: Percentages of successes of the comparison between IMA(1,1) and ARMA(1,1).

IMA(1,1): $\theta = 0.8$	ARMA(1,1): $\phi = 0.95$, $\theta = 0.74$					
	(50,100)	(100,100)	(200,100)	(500,250)	(1000,500)	(2000,1000)
(50,100)	14.6	11.2	26.6	84.8	100.0	100.0
(100,100)	11.6	11.1	8.2	60.7	100.0	100.0
(200,100)	26.9	10.2	20.6	46.2	92.7	100.0
(500,250)	81.8	60.1	48.7	41.1	54.4	90.3
(1000,500)	99.6	97.3	90.4	62.6	60.4	77.6
(2000,1000)	100.0	100.0	100.0	88.5	76.1	74.1

TABLE 6.10: Percentages of successes of the comparison between ARFIMA(0,0.45,0) and white noise.

ARFIMA(0,0.45,0)	White noise					
	(50,100)	(100,100)	(200,100)	(500,250)	(1000,500)	(2000,1000)
(50,100)	45.5	35.1	54.6	95.3	100.0	100.0
(100,100)	34.8	41.0	40.1	88.1	100.0	100.0
(200,100)	63.8	44.5	66.7	82.8	99.4	100.0
(500,250)	95.5	87.4	87.0	93.7	95.9	99.4
(1000,500)	100.0	100.0	99.1	98.2	99.5	99.5
(2000,1000)	100.0	100.0	100.0	99.9	100.0	100.0

6.7.3   Clustering ARMA and ARIMA processes with simulated time series of unequal lengths

Application 6.5: To investigate the affinity between the ARMA and ARIMA processes, Caiado et al. (2006) carried out a cluster analysis from the following simulated processes:

Small samples: Model (A) AR(1), $\phi = 0.9$, $n = 100$;

TABLE 6.11: Percentages of successes of the comparison between ARFIMA(0,0.45,0) and ARMA(1,0).

ARFIMA(0,0.45,0)	ARMA(1,0): $\phi = 0.95$					
	(50,100)	(100,100)	(200,100)	(500,250)	(1000,500)	(2000,1000)
(50,100)	63.5	82.9	86.3	98.2	100.0	100.0
(100,100)	57.7	83.1	86.0	96.0	99.8	100.0
(200,100)	74.9	82.5	85.2	95.2	99.7	100.0
(500,250)	98.7	95.1	93.4	93.9	97.6	99.9
(1000,500)	100.0	100.0	99.9	96.5	97.8	99.6
(2000,1000)	100.0	100.0	100.0	100.0	99.4	99.5

TABLE 6.12: Percentages of successes of the comparison between ARFIMA(1,0.45,0) and ARIMA(1,1,0).

ARFIMA(1,0.45,0): $\phi = 0.3$	ARIMA(1,1,0): $\phi = 0.3$					
	(50,100)	(100,100)	(200,100)	(500,250)	(1000,500)	(2000,1000)
(50,100)	49.9	70.4	79.0	95.4	99.8	99.9
(100,100)	43.1	67.6	75.1	94.2	98.7	100.0
(200,100)	56.1	64.0	73.0	92.3	97.6	99.9
(500,250)	95.3	85.4	84.0	91.1	95.1	99.4
(1000,500)	100.0	99.8	98.8	93.0	96.0	98.9
(2000,1000)	100.0	100.0	100.0	99.8	97.9	98.8

TABLE 6.13: Percentages of successes of the comparison between deterministic trend and stochastic trend.

$x_t = 1 + 0.02t + \varepsilon_t$	$x_t = 0.02 + x_{t-1} + (1 - 0.9B)\varepsilon_t$					
	(50,100)	(100,100)	(200,100)	(500,250)	(1000,500)	(2000,1000)
(50,100)	16.6	10.0	26.7	84.7	99.9	100.0
(100,100)	9.3	9.8	14.4	58.4	97.8	100.0
(200,100)	24.8	7.0	14.4	36.9	93.7	100.0
(500,250)	80.1	46.2	18.3	2.3	18.3	78.5
(1000,500)	99.9	99.9	88.5	7.8	0.2	6.2
(2000,1000)	100.0	100.0	100.0	57.6	3.8	0.0

Model (B) AR(1), $\phi = 0.9$, $n = 200$;
Model (C) AR(2), $\phi_1 = 0.7$, $\phi_2 = 0.2$, $n = 100$;
Model (D) AR(2), $\phi_1 = 0.7$, $\phi_2 = 0.2$, $n = 200$;
Model (E) MA(1), $\theta = -0.9$, $n = 100$;
Model (F) MA(1), $\theta = -0.9$, $n = 200$;
Model (G) MA(2), $\theta_1 = -0.7$, $\theta_2 = -0.2$, $n = 100$;
Model (H) MA(2), $\theta_1 = -0.7$, $\theta_2 = -0.2$, $n = 200$;
Model (I) ARMA(1,1), $\phi = 0.8$, $\theta = -0.2$, $n = 100$;

Model (J) ARMA(1,1), $\phi = 0.8$, $\theta = -0.2$, $n = 200$;
Model (K) ARMA(1,1), $\phi = 0.2$, $\theta = -0.8$, $n = 100$;
Model (L) ARMA(1,1), $\phi = 0.2$, $\theta = -0.8$, $n = 200$;
Model (M) White noise, $n = 100$;
Model (N) White noise, $n = 200$;
Model (O) ARIMA(0,1,0), $n = 100$;
Model (P) ARIMA(0,1,0), $n = 200$;
Model (Q) ARIMA(1,1,1), $\phi = 0.1$, $\theta = -0.1$, $n = 100$;
Model (R) ARIMA(1,1,1), $\phi = 0.1$, $\theta = -0.1$, $n = 200$.
Large samples: **Model (A1)** AR(1), $\phi = 0.9$, $n = 500$;
Model (B1) AR(1), $\phi = 0.9$, $n = 1000$;
Model (C1) AR(2), $\phi_1 = 0.7$, $\phi_2 = 0.2$, $n = 500$;
Model (D1) AR(2), $\phi_1 = 0.7$, $\phi_2 = 0.2$, $n = 1000$;
Model (E1) MA(1), $\theta = -0.9$, $n = 500$;
Model (F1) MA(1), $\theta = -0.9$, $n = 1000$;
Model (G1) MA(2), $\theta_1 = -0.7$, $\theta_2 = -0.2$, $n = 500$;
Model (H1) MA(2), $\theta_1 = -0.7$, $\theta_2 = -0.2$, $n = 1000$;
Model (I1) ARMA(1,1), $\phi = 0.8$, $\theta = -0.2$, $n = 500$;
Model (J1) ARMA(1,1), $\phi = 0.8$, $\theta = -0.2$, $n = 1000$;
Model (K1) ARMA(1,1), $\phi = 0.2$, $\theta = -0.8$, $n = 500$;
Model (L1) ARMA(1,1), $\phi = 0.2$, $\theta = -0.8$, $n = 1000$;
Model (M1) White noise, $n = 500$;
Model (N1) White noise, $n = 1000$;
Model (O1) ARIMA(0,1,0), $n = 500$;
Model (P1) ARIMA(0,1,0), $n = 1000$;
Model (Q1) ARIMA(1,1,1), $\phi = 0.1$, $\theta = -0.1$, $n = 500$;
Model (R1) ARIMA(1,1,1), $\phi = 0.1$, $\theta = -0.1$, $n = 1000$.

In Figure 6.6 we show the dendrogram of those processes for small samples using the complete linkage method for the interpolated periodogram based metric. This dendrogram was obtained 14 times in 50 simulations. The method can split the series into two distinct clusters: Cluster 1 = (B, P, R, O, C, D, F, Q, A, J) and Cluster 2 = (E, F, K, L, G, H, M, N). Cluster 1 includes all the AR(1), AR(2), ARMA(1,1) with large autoregressive coefficients and ARIMA(1,1,1) processes. Cluster 2 grouped the MA(1), MA(2), ARMA(1,1) processes with larger magnitude in the moving average component and white noises processes together. We also got two clusters with all the near nonstationary processes and all the nonstationary processes respectively 8 times in 50 simulations.

Figure 6.7 gives the clustering results for large samples. The method split the near nonstationary ARMA and nonstationary ARIMA processes into two distinct clusters 45 times in 50 simulations. This confirms the high performance of the metric for this type of comparison, for large data samples.

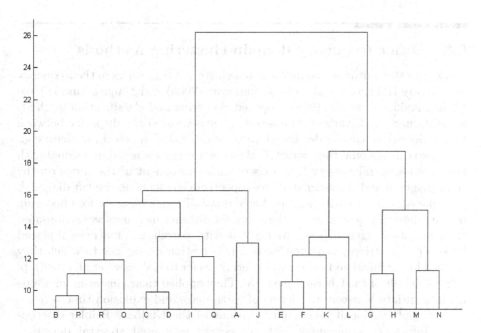

FIGURE 6.6: Dendrogram of near nonstationary and nonstationary processes for small samples using the interpolated periodogram based metric.

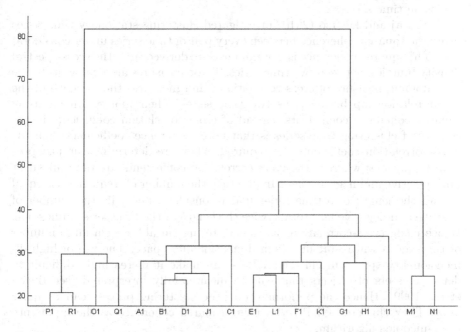

FIGURE 6.7: Dendrogram of near nonstationary and nonstationary processes for large samples using the interpolated periodogram based metric.

6.8   Other frequency domain clustering methods

Amongst other authors who investigated clustering time series in the frequency domain are Kakizawa et al. (1998), Shumway (2003) and Maharaj and D'Urso (2010). Kakizawa et al. (1998) proposed clustering and classification methods for stationary multivariate time series. They measured the disparity between two multivariate time series based on their estimated spectral matrices; e.g., for a two dimensional time series X, the spectral matrix is 4-dimensional with estimated spectral density functions of each component of the series on the right diagonal and the estimated cross spectrum elements on the left diagonal. This measure of disparity was used as a quasi-distance measure for clustering multivariate time series. Approximations for distance measures were computed from the J-divergence (refer to Eq. 6.3 with correlation matrices replaced by spectral matrices) and the Chernoff information divergence to which they applied hierarchical and c-means clustering. Refer to Kakizawa et al. (1998), p. 332 for details of the Chernoff measure. They applied their clustering methods to differentiate between waveforms of earthquake and explosion time series.

By applying locally stationary versions of the Kullback-Leibler discriminant information measures with respect to estimated spectral densities, Shumway (2003) proposed the clustering of non-stationary time series and also applied his method to differentiate between waveforms of earthquake and explosion time series.

Maharaj and D'Urso (2010) investigated clustering stationary time series using the squared coherence between every pair of time series under consideration. The squared coherence is a useful measure derived from the cross-spectral density function between two time series. These measures are analogous to the time domain measure of cross-correlations, and measures the strength of the linear relationship between the two time series. Their motivation for using squared coherence coefficients instead of cross correlation coefficients in the context of clustering time series is that fewer coherence coefficients than the cross-correlation coefficients are required. They are determined at just positive frequencies whereas the cross-correlation coefficients are determined at both positive and negative lags. In practice, the number of frequencies is equal to half the length of a time series under consideration while the number of positive and negative lags totals twice the length of the time series minus one. Hence using cross-correlations as the clustering variables for a large number of time series will result in a high dimensionality space. The use of high dimensionality spaces in cluster analysis can make it increasingly difficult to detect clusters of objects that can be meaningfully interpreted (see Beyen et al., 1999). Hence the performance of the clustering process can be quite poor. They clustered GDP series using squared coherence as the input into the c-medoids algorithm.

6.9 Wavelet-based features

Amongst the authors who have used features from the wavelet decomposition of time series in clustering are Zhang et al. (2005), Maharaj et al. (2010) and D'Urso and Maharaj (2012). Zhang et al. (2005) used discrete wavelet transform (DWT) coefficients to cluster univariate time series. They considered the DWT in a k-means clustering process, keeping as features, the wavelet coefficients of only those frequency bands that have low energy. To reduce the noise effect, they remove the coefficients of the high frequency bands.

Maharaj et al. (2010) considered the modified discrete wavelet transform (MODWT) variances at all the frequency bands as the extracted features in the clustering process, using hierarchical, non-hierarchical and fuzzy cluster analysis. Refer to Section 2.6 and to Percival and Walden (2000) for more details about the DWT and MODWT. Since the wavelet coefficients are not used as they are by Zhang et al. (2005), but the wavelet variances associated with each frequency band are used, the dimensionality of the data set is reduced to just the number of frequency bands. Maharaj et al. (2010) proposed a fuzzy c-means clustering approach with the wavelet variances to enable the identification of time series that may simultaneously belong to more than one cluster based on their patterns of variability. As in Eq. (6.36) they formalized the fuzzy model with the wavelet variances and derived the iterative solutions subject to constraints on the wavelet variances. . D'Urso and Maharaj (2012) proposed traditional and fuzzy clustering methods based on a combination of univariate and multivariate wavelet features for clustering multivariate time series.

Application 6.6 Maharaj et al. (2010) examined the variability of a sample of developed and emerging equity market returns at different timescales through wavelet decomposition. They adopted the crisp and fuzzy clustering procedures to classify equity markets into two groups. The importance of understanding the variability in financial time series is well documented. See for example, Taylor (2007). They considered daily returns of sixteen emerging market indices and eighteen developed market indices available in the Morgan Stanley Capital Indices (MSCI) database. The data for several emerging markets in the MSCI database start from December 1992. The data for each market spans from 18 January 1993 to 23 February 2007 (3680 observations). The daily returns are computed as the change in the logarithm of the closing prices of successive days. All return series are stationary in the mean.

A list of the markets and some summary statistics of daily returns is given in Table 6.14. Two distinguishing features of the two types of markets are in the standard deviation and kurtosis in daily returns. The variance and kurtosis of the returns in emerging markets are generally high compared to those in the developed markets. The average variance of developed and emerging markets are 1.547 and 4.003 respectively, while the average kurtosis are 3.924 and 15.478 respectively. The return distributions of eleven emerging markets and fourteen developed markets are negatively skewed.

Venezuela records the highest kurtosis (120.5) and the greatest skewness (-5.02) in the return distribution and Turkey records the greatest spread (3.28 per cent) in the returns. The two highest mean daily returns are observed for Poland and Peru (0.070 and 0.058 per cent) and the mean daily return of all the other markets is below 0.053 per cent. All observed extreme values of return distribution characteristics are associated with emerging markets-Venezuela, Turkey, Poland and Peru.

Wavelet variance for each return series for the optimal numbers of scales for a given wavelet filter width were generated. The Haar, DB(4), DB(6), DB(8), LA(8), LA(12) and the CF(6) filters were considered. Given that the sample size is 3680, series of 3680 wavelet coefficients were obtained at each of the eight time scales. The maximum number of time scales for a series of this length is J = 11, since $2^{11} < 3680 < 2^{12}$. Each time scale reflects a different frequency. Scale 1 reflects changes at the highest frequency and Scale 11 reflects changes at the lowest frequency. Scale 1 reflects 2-4 day dynamics inherent in the series; Scale 2 reflects 4-8 day dynamics and so on. Scales 7 and 8 reflect dynamics over a long period of time: 128-256 day (approximately one year) and 256-512 day (approximately two years) dynamics respectively. Given that the interest is in the dynamics only over the medium-term, only the first 8 scales were considered.

Figure 6.8 shows the wavelet variances of developed and emerging market returns up to eight scales using the LA(8) filter. It is clear that at all scales, there are differences in the wavelet variances of developed and emerging market returns. It can be observed that (i) wavelet variance of equity markets associated with time scales is such that the higher the time scale the lower the variance and (ii) developed markets are generally less volatile than emerging markets and the difference in the volatility is more pronounced at the lower time scales. Therefore, given the high variation in the wavelet variances of equity market returns, compared to that of the developed markets, especially at the lower scales, the crisp and fuzzy clustering procedures on wavelet variances are adopted to identify two clusters. Since wavelet variances at the higher scales are very small, only the wavelet variances of the first five scales are used as clustering variables. The aim is to investigate the extent to which the equity markets in the two clusters match their known type of market: developed and emerging.

Table 6.15 shows the membership degrees for both fuzzy and crisp clustering when the LA(8) filter is used to generate the wavelet variances. The fuzzy approach reveals that all the developed markets and four emerging markets (Ireland, Israel, Jordan and South Africa) form one cluster. The emerging markets–Colombia, India, Peru and Taiwan–display fuzzy membership (0.4 $< u <$ 0.6) in both clusters. This would imply that emerging markets with fuzzy membership belong to the cluster of developed markets over some pe-

TABLE 6.14: Some summary statistics of emerging and developed market daily returns.

	Mean	Variance	Kurtosis	Skewness
D Developed markets (n=18)				
Australia	0.038	1.169	2.560	-0.169
Austria	0.039	1.140	2.440	-0.398
Belgium	0.038	1.250	4.723	0.108
Canada	0.043	1.198	5.884	-0.637
Denmark	0.054	1.235	2.416	-0.281
France	0.037	1.484	2.288	-0.152
Germany	0.037	1.848	2.745	-0.200
Hong Kong	0.027	2.531	9.526	0.054
Italy	0.040	1.798	2.129	-0.064
Japan	0.012	1.939	3.509	0.198
Netherlands	0.037	1.471	4.090	-0.201
Norway	0.050	1.668	4.016	-0.462
Singapore	0.025	1.783	8.172	0.123
Spain	0.052	1.646	2.498	-0.097
Sweden	0.057	2.501	3.585	-0.100
Switzerland	0.047	1.153	3.370	-0.116
UK	0.029	1.022	2.377	-0.182
USA	0.033	1.007	4.297	-0.123
Average	0.039	1.547	3.924	-0.150
E Emerging markets (n=16)				
Chile	0.031	1.332	3.676	0.019
Colombia	0.045	2.265	11.931	0.089
India	0.037	2.459	3.787	-0.295
Indonesia	0.008	8.008	31.163	-1.230
Ireland	0.044	1.336	4.085	-0.411
Israel	0.021	2.280	4.383	-0.262
Jordan	0.028	1.023	10.355	0.064
Korea	0.030	5.777	12.937	0.308
Mexico	0.040	3.697	14.125	-0.104
Pakistan	0.014	3.693	6.798	-0.450
Peru	0.058	2.534	5.083	-0.076
Poland	0.070	4.972	4.143	-0.160
South Africa	0.042	2.371	5.944	-0.440
Taiwan	0.016	3.003	2.749	0.029
Turkey	0.052	10.768	6.004	-0.236
Average	0.034	4.003	15.478	-0.511

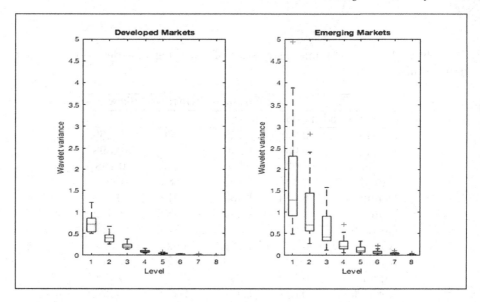

FIGURE 6.8: Wavelet variance of developed and emerging markets.

riods of time, while at other periods of time they belong to the cluster with the most emerging markets. All the other emerging markets form the second cluster.

In the crisp clustering procedure the four markets classified as fuzzy members are distributed to the two clusters. In this case Colombia, India and Peru join the cluster which includes all developed markets and Taiwan joins the other cluster.

When other wavelet filters are used, the same clusters and the same emerging markets with fuzzy membership are identified. Hence the performance of fuzzy procedure is not influenced by the wavelet filters of different width. However, the crisp clustering procedure is not as robust with the groupings and a slight variation in membership is observed.

When fuzzy clustering is used to form clusters based on variances of equity market returns rather than on wavelet variances, eleven of the sixteen emerging markets are grouped with the eighteen developed markets, one emerging market is classified as fuzzy and four emerging markets form one cluster. One emerging market, namely, Poland, is identified as being fuzzy. In the crisp clustering procedure this emerging market moves into the cluster of four emerging markets observed in the fuzzy clustering procedure. The results are reported in Table 6.16.

It is clear from comparing the variances (see Table 6.14 of the emerging markets which are now classified with the developed markets by both the crisp c-means and and fuzzy-c-means procedures using time series variances), namely, those of Mexico, Pakistan and Peru are more compatible with those

TABLE 6.15: Membership degrees for the fuzzy and crisp clustering approaches using wavelet variances.

	Fuzzy clustering		Crisp clustering	
	Cluster 1	Cluster 2	Cluster 1	Cluster 2
Australia	0.029	0.971	0	1
Austria	0.027	0.973	0	1
Belgium	0.011	0.989	0	1
Canada	0.021	0.980	0	1
Denmark	0.024	0.976	0	1
France	0.006	0.994	0	1
Germany	0.027	0.973	0	1
Hong Kong	0.341	0.659	0	1
Italy	0.027	0.973	0	1
Japan	0.040	0.960	0	1
Netherlands	0.006	0.994	0	1
Norway	0.015	0.985	0	1
Singapore	0.064	0.936	0	1
Spain	0.006	0.994	0	1
Sweden	0.311	0.690	0	1
Switzerland	0.030	0.970	0	1
UK	0.071	0.929	0	1
USA	0.070	0.930	0	1
Colombia	0.418	0.582	0	1
India	0.438	0.562	0	1
Indonesia	0.936	0.064	1	0
Ireland	0.007	0.993	0	1
Israel	0.197	0.803	0	1
Jordan	0.060	0.940	0	1
Korea	0.982	0.018	1	0
Mexico	0.878	0.122	1	0
Pakistan	0.887	0.113	1	0
Peru	0.401	0.599	0	1
Poland	0.993	0.007	1	0
South Africa	0.292	0.708	0	1
Taiwan	0.604	0.396	1	0
Turkey	0.885	0.115	1	0
Venezuela	0.932	0.068	1	0

TABLE 6.16: Membership degrees for the fuzzy and crisp clustering approaches using equity market variances.

	Fuzzy clustering		Crisp clustering	
	Cluster 1	Cluster 2	Cluster 1	Cluster 2
Australia	0.010	0.990	0	1
Austria	0.010	0.990	0	1
Belgium	0.008	0.992	0	1
Canada	0.009	0.991	0	1
Denmark	0.008	0.992	0	1
France	0.003	0.997	0	1
Germany	0.000	1.000	0	1
Hong Kong	0.013	0.987	0	1
Italy	0.000	1.000	0	1
Japan	0.000	1.000	0	1
Netherlands	0.003	0.997	0	1
Norway	0.001	0.999	0	1
Singapore	0.000	1.000	0	1
Spain	0.001	0.999	0	1
Sweden	0.012	0.988	0	1
Switzerland	0.010	0.990	0	1
UK	0.014	0.987	0	1
USA	0.014	0.986	0	1
Chile	0.006	0.994	0	1
Colombia	0.005	0.996	0	1
India	0.010	0.990	0	1
Indonesia	0.999	0.002	1	0
Ireland	0.006	0.994	0	1
Israel	0.005	0.995	0	1
Jordan	0.013	0.987	0	1
Korea	0.715	0.285	1	0
Mexico	0.140	0.861	0	1
Pakistan	0.139	0.861	0	1
Peru	0.014	0.987	0	1
Poland	0.474	0.526	1	0
South Africa	0.007	0.993	0	1
Taiwan	0.045	0.955	1	1
Turkey	0.926	0.074	1	0
Venezuela	0.998	0.002	1	0

of emerging markets than developed markets. The variance of the emerging market, Poland (4.97) which has fuzzy membership is far more compatible with that of emerging markets than that of developed markets and hence its fuzziness would appear to be doubtful.

Overall, we observe that there are some differences in the membership of the two clusters when formed with (i) variances and wavelet variances and (ii) fuzzy clustering and crisp clustering. The procedure that sorts equity markets to two clusters in line with the known types in the existing literature of equity markets is fuzzy clustering with wavelet variances.

Given the robustness of the fuzzy clustering procedure with wavelet variances when applied to this data, regardless of the type and length of the wavelet filter used, and the fact that it can assign some time series to more than one cluster simultaneously, the fuzzy clustering method appears more appealing than the crisp clustering procedure. Furthermore the results generated by fuzzy clustering with wavelet variances appear to be more credible than fuzzy clustering with variances.

D'Urso and Maharaj (2012) extended the approach used by Maharaj et al. (2010) but this time using MODWT wavelet variances and wavelet correlations to cluster multivariate time series. As in Eq. 6.36 they formalized the fuzzy model but this time with the wavelet variances and wavelet correlations and derived the iterative solutions subject to constraints on the wavelet variances and correlations. These features were input into the c-means, c-medoids, fuzzy c-means and fuzzy relational algorithms. Comparison of their approach to some other methods for clustering multivariate time series, in particular by Maharaj (1999), Singhal and Seborg (2005) and Wang et al. (2007), reveal a favourable performance of their approach.

6.10 Other feature-based applications

6.10.1 Comparison between trend-stationary and difference-stationary processes

Application 6.7: Caiado (2006) discussed the problem of discrimination between stochastic trend and deterministic trend processes. Many economic time series, such as GNP, money supply, and investment exhibit a time-dependent trend which may contain either deterministic or stochastic components. However, it can be quite difficult to distinguish between the two components.

There are different types of nonstationary processes. One can consider a deterministic linear trend process $y_t = a + bt + \varepsilon_t$ (with ε_t a white noise term), that can be transformed into a stationary process by subtracting the trend $a + bt$, and a stochastic linear trend process such as the so-called random

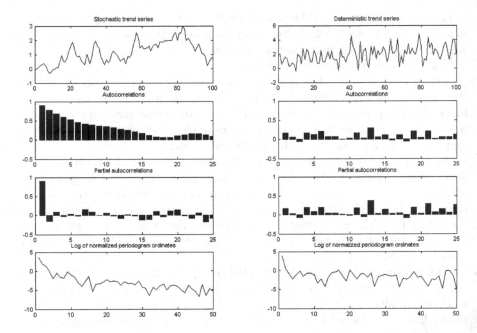

FIGURE 6.9: Typical shapes of stochastic and deterministic trend processes of length $n = 100$.

walk model $(1 - B)y_t = \varepsilon_t$ or $y_t = y_{t-1} + \varepsilon_t$. An interesting, but sometimes difficult problem is to determine whether a linear process contains a trend, and whether a linear process exhibits a deterministic or a stochastic trend. In particular, it is useful to distinguish between a random walk plus drift $y_t = \mu + y_{t-1} + \varepsilon_t$ and a deterministic trend in the form $y_t = a + \mu t + \varepsilon_t$.

For the Monte Carlo simulations we chose the determinist trend and random walk plus drift models studied by Enders (1995, p. 252)

$$y_t = 1 + 0.02t + \varepsilon_t$$

and

$$y_t = 0.02 + y_{t-1} + \varepsilon_t/3 \,,$$

with ε_t a zero mean and unit variance white noise. We performed 250 replicated simulations of five deterministic trend models and five random walk models with those specifications, with sample sizes of 50, 100, 200, 500 and 1000 observations. They used the previously discussed metrics ACFU (Eq. 6.1 with uniform weights), ACFG (Eq. 6.1 with geometric weights), PACFU,(Eq. 6.4 with uniform weights) PACFG(Eq. 6.4 with geometric weights) and LNP (Eq. 6.27) to compute the distance matrices among the 10 time series and to aggregate them into two clusters (determinist trend and stochastic trend) using an hierarchical clustering algorithm (complete linkage method).

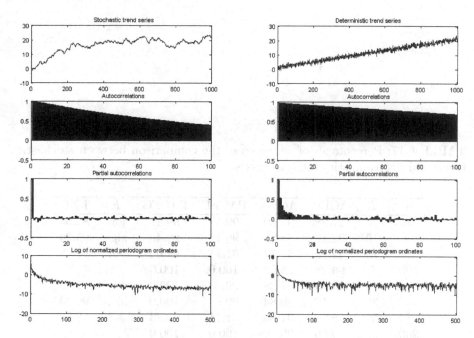

FIGURE 6.10: Typical shapes of stochastic and deterministic trend processes of length $n = 1000$.

Figures 6.9 and 6.10 show the typical shape of each series with sample sizes $n = 100, 1000$ (plots, sample autocorrelations, sample partial autocorrelations, and normalized periodogram ordinates in logarithm scale). Table 6.17 presents the percentage of successes obtained in the comparison between the two processes, where n is the sample size; L is the autocorrelation length; the sample autocorrelation and sample partial autocorrelation metrics (ACFG and PACFG metrics) use a geometric decay of $p = 0.05$; F for low frequencies corresponds to periodogram ordinates from 1 to $\sqrt{n}$ and F for high frequencies corresponds to periodogram ordinates from $\sqrt{n+1}$ to $n/2$ (LNP metric).

The ACF based metrics can discriminate quite well between the deterministic trend models and random walk models. This is particularly evident for the first few autocorrelations, since the ACF of the random walk process is close to unity and the ACF of the deterministic trend tends to approach zero. The partial autocorrelation based metrics perform quite well across sample sizes and PACF orders considered. The LNP metric performs quite well for periodogram ordinates dominated by high frequencies, which concerns the short-term information of the processes.

TABLE 6.17: Percentages of successes of the comparison between stochastic trend and deterministic trend processes.

n	L	ACFU	ACFG	PACFU	PACFG	F	LNP
50	5	97.28	97.60	99.57	99.27	low	85.04
	10	92.12	94.88	99.11	99.46	high	95.24
	25	92.12	91.52	61.78	64.00	all	94.48
100	5	99.28	98.92	100.0	100.0		
	10	95.68	97.28	99.78	100.0	low	92.48
	25	88.16	89.84	99.94	100.0	high	99.04
	50	85.08	91.80	61.11	70.73	all	98.72
200	5	99.56	99.36	100.0	100.0		
	10	95.40	97.36	100.0	100.0	low	96.08
	20	87.80	91.20	100.0	100.0	high	99.28
	50	72.76	81.80	100.0	100.0	all	99.20
	100	70.56	82.56	60.22	94.37		
500	5	97.68	97.64	100.0	100.0		
	10	89.52	92.12	100.0	100.0	low	94.32
	20	78.00	81.28	100.0	100.0	high	98.56
	50	68.24	70.32	100.0	100.0	all	98.16
	100	68.72	70.04	100.0	100.0		
	250	67.92	70.12	na	na		
1000	5	94.48	94.60	100.0	100.0		
	10	83.04	83.56	100.0	100.0	low	90.40
	20	72.52	73.92	100.0	100.0	high	96.72
	50	67.36	68.65	100.0	100.0	all	93.92
	100	67.52	67.86	100.0	100.0		
	500	65.12	67.36	na	na		

6.10.2 Comparison of processes with different characteristics of persistence

Application 6.8: Caiado (2006) compared stationary processes with different characteristics of persistence. It is well known that in a fractional ARIMA(0,d,0) process (Granger and Joyeux, 1980, Hosking, 1981) the parameter d corresponds to the long-term dependency, whereas in a ARMA(p,q) process the parameters p and q represent the short-term behaviour. In many economic time series, it can be very difficult to distinguish between stationary, near nonstationary and nonstationary processes, as shown by Diebold and Rudebusch (1991) and Hassler and Wolters (1994).

Table 6.18 presents the Monte Carlo simulations on the comparison between the ARFIMA(0,0.45,0) process and the ARMA(1,0), $\phi = 0.95$ process. We can see that the ACF and the PACF based metrics perform fairly well for short lags and the LNP metric works well using high frequency ordinates. Figures 6.11 and 6.12 show the typical shapes of each series with sample sizes $n = 100, 1000$. Stationary processes with fractional integration present several characteristics like those of near nonstationary processes. Long-memory processes exhibit autocorrelations that decay very slowly, in a way like the autocorrelations of near non-stationary processes with short memory.

TABLE 6.18: Percentages of successes of the comparison between long-memory and short-memory processes.

n	L	ACFU	ACFG	PACFU	PACFG	F	LNP
50	5	84.24	83.32	84.24	83.64	low	74.64
	10	78.04	78.20	78.36	84.12	high	85.00
	25	73.96	77.68	61.24	61.76	all	81.72
100	5	90.92	91.24	97.00	97.08		
	10	84.04	83.24	93.24	95.72	low	82.92
	25	74.96	81.04	84.92	92.88	high	94.96
	50	74.04	80.28	61.12	64.04	all	92.36
200	5	95.96	95.52	99.68	99.48		
	10	89.96	91.60	99.44	99.24	low	91.52
	20	81.80	86.20	99.20	99.60	high	98.88
	50	76.04	84.72	93.00	99.60	all	98.80
	100	71.00	82.20	60.88	92.16		
500	5	98.20	98.44	100.0	100.0		
	10	95.68	96.40	100.0	100.0	low	96.60
	20	89.20	91.20	99.96	100.0	high	99.92
	50	73.96	87.88	99.92	99.52	all	100.0
	100	69.52	89.52	98.83	99.36		
	250	67.88	88.24	na	na		
1000	5	99.00	99.24	100.0	100.0		
	10	97.56	98.20	100.0	100.0	low	98.76
	20	91.08	94.28	100.0	100.0	high	100.0
	50	80.24	92.32	99.76	100.0	all	100.0
	100	73.32	92.48	99.64	99.72		
	500	67.28	92.48	na	na		

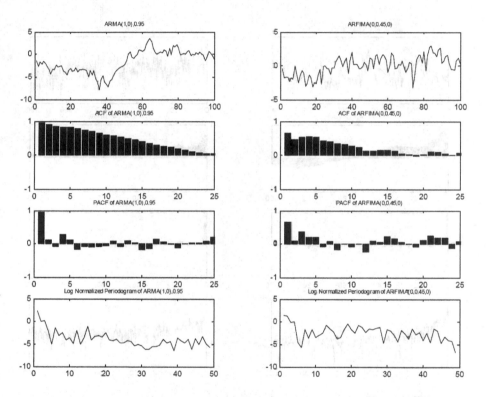

FIGURE 6.11: Typical shapes of short-memory and long-memory near non-stationary processes of length $n = 100$.

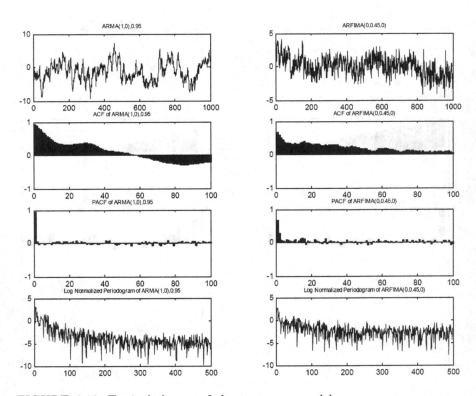

FIGURE 6.12: Typical shapes of short-memory and long-memory near non-stationary processes of length $n = 1000$.

7

Model-based clustering

CONTENTS

7.1   Introduction

For most model-based methods, the time series under consideration are assumed to have been generated from specific underlying models or by a combination of probability distributions, and the similarity between fitted models is evaluated. One the earliest works on model-based time series clustering was that by Piccolo (1990) where ARIMA models were fitted to every pair of time series under consideration, and the Euclidean distance between their corresponding autoregressive expansions were used as the metric. Hierarchical methods were then applied to cluster the time series. Another early piece of research on model-based time series clustering was that by Tong and Dabas (1990) who fitted linear and non-linear models to the time series and applied hierarchical methods to the residuals of the fitted models for clustering the time series. Their paper is a seminal piece of work on time series clustering and it has motivated much of the subsequent research on this topic.

While in many cases, time series can be easily clustered using the parameter estimates of the fitted models, the challenge is how to handle situations where all the time series under consideration are not associated with the same number of parameter estimates. Maharaj (1996, 2000) addressed this for stationary time series, by fitting trucated $AR(\infty)$ models to all series under consideration and using the maximum order for all series.

Another challenge is how to cluster time series that are non-stationary in the variance, namely, heteroscedastic time series. Several authors including Otranto (2008, 2010), Caiado and Crato (2010), and D'Urso et al. (2013b, 2016) rose to this challenge by proposing methods based on the estimated parameters of the fitted generalized autoregressive conditional heteroskedasticity (GARCH) model.

While Piccolo's method can be extended to clustering seasonal time series by fitting seasonal ARIMA models, authors such as Scotto et al. (2010), Maharaj et al. (2016) and D'Urso et al. (2017a) proposed different aspects of clustering of seasonal time series based on the estimates of fitted generalized extreme value models.

Time series clustering methods based on forecast densities (Alonso et al., 2006; Vilar et al., 2010, Liu et al., 2014) can also be considered to be model-based approaches to time series clustering. However, these forecast density methods aim to identify similar forecasts so that series with similar forecasts at a specific horizon may be grouped together in the same cluster, even though they may have been generated by different models. In contrast, the similarity principle of all other model-based time series clustering methods relies on the proximity between the generating processes.

Some of these above-mentioned methods together with other methods are discussed in the following sections.

7.2 Autoregressive expansions

7.2.1 AR(∞) and MA(∞) coefficients-based distances

Let $x_t, t = 1, 2, \ldots, n$ be an observable time series represented by an autoregressive and moving average or ARMA(p,q) process,

$$\phi_p(B)X_t = \theta_q(B)\varepsilon_t, \tag{7.1}$$

where $\phi_p(B) = 1 - \phi_1 B - \ldots - \phi_p B^p$ and $\theta_q(B) = 1 - \theta_1 B - \ldots - \theta_q B^q$ are polynomials of orders p and q, B is the back-shift operator, such that $B^k x_t = x_{t-k}$, and ε_t is a white noise process with zero mean and constant variance σ_ε^2. For the process (7.1) to be causal and invertible, $\phi_p(B)$ and $\theta_q(B)$ must have all roots outside the unit circle and no common roots. If the series x_t is generated from an ARMA(p,q) process, then the series $y_t = (1-B)^d x_t$ is considered to be generated from an autoregressive integrated moving average or ARIMA(p,d,q) process.

Piccolo (1990) defined a metric for the class of invertible ARIMA models as the Euclidean distance between their autoregressive expansions. Let X_t be a zero mean stochastic process following an invertible ARIMA(p,0,q) model: $\phi_p(B)X_t = \theta_q(B)\varepsilon_t$. Then it can be represented by the AR(∞) operator $\pi(B) = \theta_q^{-1}(B)\phi_p(B) = 1 - \pi_1 B - \pi_2 B^2 - \cdots$, and the π coefficients contain all the information about the stochastic dependence structure of a time series. Similar definitions and distributional results apply to the time series y_t. Piccolo introduced a metric by comparing the respective π sequences, defined by the distance

$$d_{AR}(x_t, y_t) = \sqrt{\sum_{j=1}^{\infty}(\pi_{j,x} - \pi_{j,y})^2}, \tag{7.2}$$

which satisfies the usual properties of a distance, namely, non-negativity, symmetry and triangularity. This metric can be used for the comparison of any ARIMA models. However, it cannot distinguish between series generated from ARMA processes with large autoregressive parameters and ARIMA processes with parameter values close to the random walk. Its statistical properties are discussed in Corduas and Piccolo (2008). A limitation of the Piccolo's metric is the requirement to first fit an ARMA model to each of the time series under consideration, before computing the distances.

If the processes X_t and Y_t are stationary, we can also use the Euclidean distance between the coefficients of the MA(∞) operator $\psi(B) = \phi_p^{-1}(B)\theta_q(B) = 1 - \psi_1 B - \psi_2 B^2 - \cdots = \pi^{-1}(B)$, defined as

$$d_{MA}(x_t, y_t) = \sqrt{\sum_{j=1}^{\infty}(\psi_{j,x} - \psi_{j,y})^2}. \tag{7.3}$$

7.2.2   AR coefficients-based distance

Maharaj (1996) extended the model-based clustering idea of Piccolo (1990) by developing a testing procedure for differences between underlying models of each pair of independent time series by using equivalent autoregressive (AR) expansions and using the p-values of each test in an algorithm to cluster the time series. Maharaj (2000) extended the testing procedure for significant differences between underlying models of each pair of independent time series to that of related series. In what follows, the more generalized procedure of Maharaj (2000) of which the procedure of Maharaj (1996) is a special case will be discussed here.

Following on from the ARMA(p,q) model

$$\phi(B)Z_t = \theta(B)\varepsilon_t. \tag{7.4}$$

the AR expansion can be expressed as

$$Z_t = \Sigma_{j=1}^{\infty}\pi_j Z_{t-j} + \varepsilon_t$$

where

$$\Pi(B) = \phi(B)\theta^{-1}(B) = 1 - \pi_1 B - \pi_2 B^2 - \ldots.$$

If x_t and y_t are two stationary time series that are assumed to be generated from AR(∞) models, selection criteria such as Akaike's information criterion (AIC) or Schwartz's Bayesian information criterion (BIC) are used to select fitted truncated AR(∞) models of order k_1 and k_2, respectively.

Expressing the vector of AR(k_1) and AR(k_2) parameters of generating processes X_t and Y_t, respectively as

$\pi_x = [\pi_{1x}\pi_{2x}\ldots\pi_{k_1 x}]'$ and $\pi_y = [\pi_{1y}\pi_{2y}\ldots\pi_{k_2 y}]'$

and the parameter estimates as

$\hat{\pi}_x = [\hat{\pi}_{1x}\hat{\pi}_{2x}\ldots\hat{\pi}_{k_1 x}]'$ and $\hat{\pi}_y = [\hat{\pi}_{1y}\hat{\pi}_{2y}\ldots\hat{\pi}_{k_2 y}]'$, respectively,

in constructing the test statistic, the order $k = max(k_1, k_2)$ is fitted to both the series.

The test of hypothesis is H_0: $\pi_x = \pi_y$; H_1: $\pi_x \neq \pi_y$

The test statistic is constructed based on a form of the "seemingly unrelated regressions model" proposed by Zellner (1962). The models fitted to the time series can be expressed as

$$\mathbf{X} = \mathbf{W}_x\pi_x + \varepsilon_x \tag{7.5}$$

$$\mathbf{Y} = \mathbf{W}_y\pi_y + \varepsilon_y \tag{7.6}$$

where $\mathbf{x} = [x_{k+1}\ldots x_{T-1}x_T]'$

$$\mathbf{W}_x = \begin{bmatrix} x_k & x_{k-1} & \cdots x_1 \\ \vdots & \vdots & \ddots \vdots \\ x_{T-2} & x_{T-3} & \cdots x_{T-k-1} \\ x_{T-1} & x_{T-2} & \cdots x_{T-k} \end{bmatrix}$$

and $\varepsilon_x = [\varepsilon_{k+1} \ldots \varepsilon_{T-1} \varepsilon_T]'$.

$\mathbf{y}$, $\mathbf{W_y}$ and ε are similarly defined.

$E[\varepsilon_x] = 0$, $E[\varepsilon_x \varepsilon_x'] = \sigma_x^2 \mathbf{I}_{T-k}$, $E[\varepsilon_y] = 0$, $E[\varepsilon_y \varepsilon_y'] = \sigma_y^2 \mathbf{I}_{T-k}$

where $\mathbf{I}_{T-k}$ is a $(T-k)$ x $(T-k)$ identity matrix. It is assumed that the disturbances of the two models are correlated at the same points in time but uncorrelated across observations, namely,

$$E[\varepsilon_x \varepsilon_y'] = \sigma_{xy} \mathbf{I}_{T-k}.$$

The dimensions of $\mathbf{x}$, $\mathbf{y}$, ε_x, ε_y are $(T-k)$ x 1, of π_x and π_y are k x 1, and of $\mathbf{W}_x$ and $\mathbf{W}_y$ are $(T-k)$ x k.

When a total of $2(T-k)$ observations are used in estimating the parameters of the models in Eq. (7.5) and Eq. (7.6) the combined model can be expressed as

$$\mathbf{Z} = \mathbf{W}\pi + \varepsilon, \tag{7.7}$$

where

$$\mathbf{Z} = \begin{bmatrix} \mathbf{X} \\ \mathbf{Y} \end{bmatrix},$$

$$\mathbf{W} = \begin{bmatrix} \mathbf{W}_x & \mathbf{0} \\ \mathbf{0} & \mathbf{W}_y \end{bmatrix},$$

$$\pi = \begin{bmatrix} \pi_x \\ \pi_y \end{bmatrix},$$

$$\varepsilon = \begin{bmatrix} \varepsilon_x \\ \varepsilon_y \end{bmatrix},$$

and

$E[\varepsilon] = 0$, $E[\varepsilon \varepsilon'] = \mathbf{V} = \mathbf{\Sigma} \otimes \mathbf{I}_{T-k}$, where

$$\mathbf{\Sigma} = \begin{bmatrix} \sigma_x^2 & \sigma_{xy} \\ \sigma_{xy} & \sigma_y^2 \end{bmatrix}.$$

Thus, the generalized least squares estimator is

$$\hat{\pi} = [\mathbf{W}' \mathbf{V}^{-1} \mathbf{W}]^{-1} \mathbf{W}' \mathbf{V}^{-1} \mathbf{Z}.$$

By the results in Anderson (1971) and Amemiya (1985) assuming that $\hat{\pi}$ is normally distributed can be shown to be asymptotically normally distributed.

It can also be shown that under the null hypothesis which can also be expressed as $H_0 : \mathbf{R}\pi = \mathbf{0}$, where $\mathbf{R} = [\mathbf{I}_k - \mathbf{I}_k]$, $\mathbf{R}\hat{\pi}$ is asymptotically normally distributed. Maharaj (1997) has shown that a possible test statistic is

$$\mathbf{D} = (\mathbf{R}\hat{\pi})^{'}[\mathbf{R}(\mathbf{W}^{'}\hat{\mathbf{V}}^{-1}\mathbf{W})^{-1}\mathbf{R}^{'}]^{-1}(\mathbf{R}\hat{\pi}), \qquad (7.8)$$

which is asymptotically distributed as chi-square with k degrees of freedom. $\mathbf{V}$ is estimated by $\hat{\mathbf{\Sigma}}\otimes\mathbf{I}_{T-k}$. Zellner (1962) has shown that least squares residuals can be used to estimate the elements of $\mathbf{\Sigma}$ consistently.

Maharaj (2000) in evaluating the finite sample behaviour of the test statistic $\mathbf{D}$ showed reasonably good size and power of the test under many different simulation scenarios. The clustering algorithm based on the p-values of the test for all pairs of time series under consideration is given in Maharaj (2000, p.307). This p-value clustering algorithm incorporates the principles of the agglomerative approach to hierarchical clustering but will only group together those pairs of series whose associated values are greater than some pre-specified significance level (e.g., 5%, 1%). If one of the series, x_t, is already in a cluster, then another series y_t will merge into this cluster if the p-value of the test associated with y_t and every other series in this cluster is greater than the pre-specified significance level. If each series from a pair under consideration is in a different cluster, the two clusters will merge if the p-values of the test of all pairs of series across the two clusters are greater than the pre-specified significance level.

In a fuzzy framework, D'Urso et al. (2013a) proposed an AR metric-based clustering model based on a *partitioning around medoids* procedure. Successively, robust versions of the fuzzy c-medoids clustering based on an AR metric have been suggested by D'Urso et al. (2013a, 2015, 2017b).

Application 7.1 To illustrate this p-value clustering approach by Maharaj (2000), consider monthly average temperature series recorded in 15 Australian cities from January 1971 to December 2015 (Australian Bureau of Meteorology). Seasonal and first differencing were first applied to the series to make them stationary after which AR models were fitted with the maximum order determined by the BIC information criterion. The p-value algorithm was then applied and the cities together with their locations and cluster allocation are given in Table 7.1. The results reveal that series within each cluster would most likely exhibit similar seasonal and monthly change dynamics. Profiling of the clusters based on the AR estimates of the series up to a maximum of order 8 is shown in Figures 7.1 and 7.2, while that based on the mean, standard deviation, skewness and kurtosis of the stationary series is given in Figure 7.3.

It is clear from Figures 7.1 and 7.2 that there are differences between the three clusters in the distributions of the AR coefficients at lags 1 to 8. The greatest differences are at lags 1, 3-7. From Figure 7.3, it can be observed that there

TABLE 7.1: Cities and clusters.

City	Location	Cluster
Adelaide	South	1
Broken Hill	Central	1
Newcastle	South East	1
Perth	South West	1
Sydney	South East	1
Alice Springs	Central	2
Broome	North West	2
Dubbo	Central	2
Hobart	South	2
Melbourne	South	2
Wyndham	North	2
Brisbane	Central East	3
Cairns	North East	3
Darwin	North	3
Townsville	North East	3

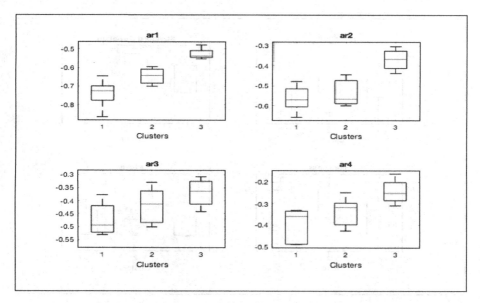

FIGURE 7.1: Box plots of AR estimates phi1 to phi4.

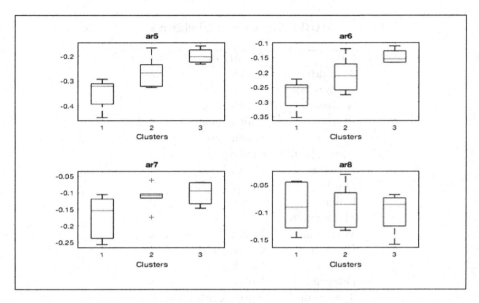

FIGURE 7.2: Box plots of AR estimates: phi5 to phi8.

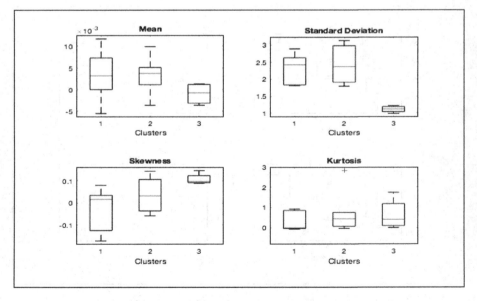

FIGURE 7.3: Box plots of summary statistics.

are distinct difference in the distribution of the skewness of the three clusters. Differences in the distributions of the means of three clusters is also apparent. While the distribution of the standard deviation for Clusters 1 and 2 do not differ all that much, that of Cluster 3 is distinctly different. The distribution of the kurtosis of the three clusters is similar.

Hence profiling the clusters obtained from the method of clustering put forward by Maharaj (2000) reveals that the method does appear to separate homogenous groupings quite well.

Maharaj (1999) extended this model-based approach to clustering time series to multivariate time series by using the parameter estimates of vector autoregressive models.

Liu and Maharaj (2013) used bias-adjusted AR estimators in the construction of a test statistic similar to that in Eq. (7.8) but which follows a non-central chi-square distribution under the null hypothesis. They showed through simulation studies that as the length of the series increases, the performance of the test improves as assessed by size and power estimates. In an application to GDP series of a number of developed European countries, they input the p-values of the test into the p-value algorithm developed by Maharaj (2000) and obtained well-explained clusters.

7.2.3 ARMA(p,q) coefficents-based distance

Caiado et al. (2012) proposed a test to compare two independent stationary time series similar to that of Maharaj(1996), but based on the parameter estimates on fitted ARMA(p,q) models

Given two independent time series x_t and y_t generated by the same ARMA(p,q) process as defined in Eq. (2.1) but with different parameter values, let the $k = p + q$ estimated parameters be grouped in the vectors $\widehat{\beta}_x$ and $\widehat{\beta}_y$ with estimated covariance matrices V_x and V_y, respectively. We want to check whether they are different realizations of the same stochastic process, so that $E[\widehat{\beta}_x] = E[\widehat{\beta}_y] = \beta$. Then $\delta = \widehat{\beta}_x - \widehat{\beta}_y$ for large samples will be an approximately normally distributed vector with zero mean and covariance matrix

$$V_\delta = V_x + V_y, \tag{7.9}$$

and therefore, we can use the statistic

$$D_P = \delta' V_\delta^{-1} \delta, \tag{7.10}$$

which is asymptotically a chi-square distribution with k degrees of freedom under the null $\beta_x = \beta_y$.

In order to test if two generating ARMA processes are equal, the model for each time series can be selected by Akaike's information criterion (AIC) or the Bayesian information criterion (BIC) selection criteria. If the obtained model is the same for the two time series, then the statistic D_P is computed by using the estimated parameters in each time series.

If the selected models are different, Caiado et al. (2012) suggested fitting both selected models, say $M1$ and $M2$, to both time series and computing the statistic D_P in these two situations, namely, $D_P(M1)$ and $D_P(M2)$. If $D_P(M1) \leq \chi^2_{k_1, \alpha/2}$ and $D_P(M2) \leq \chi^2_{k_2, \alpha/2}$, where k_1 and k_2 are the degrees of freedom associated with the models $M1$ and $M2$, the null hypothesis is not rejected and we conclude that the processes are generated by the same model. If the null hypothesis is rejected in one of the models, or in both, then we conclude that the generating processes are different. Since two comparison statements have to be made, the Bonferroni inequality suggests that each test has a significance level $\alpha/2$ to ensure the overall significance level of α.

7.3   Fitted residuals

Tong and Dabas (1990) proposed fitting linear or nonlinear models to time series and investigated the possible existence of clusters amongst the time series based on the residuals of the fitted models. They used the following measures of similarity and dissimilarity

$$1 - \left| corr\left(e_t^{(i)}, e_t^{(j)}\right) \right|$$

$$\left\{ \sum_{t=1}^{T} \left[e_t^{(i)} - e_t^{(j)} \right]^2 \right\}^{\frac{1}{2}}$$

$$\sum_{t=1}^{T} \left| e_t^{(i)} - e_t^{(j)} \right|,$$

where $e_t^{(i)}$ is the residual of the model fitted to series i and T is the length of the series, to cluster the residuals of the fitted models using both multidimensional scaling and hierarchical clustering methods.

The main idea of the clustering method of Tong and Dabas (1990) is that if the residuals of two time series have a high degree of affinity, then models generating these time series should also have a high degree of affinity.

They applied their method to the iconic Canadian lynx data and demonstrated the formation of interesting clusters.

7.4 Forecast densities

7.4.1 Clustering based on forecast densities

All the methods discussed so far in this chapter are concerned with clustering time series based on historical values. In some cases, it may be appropriate to employ clustering methods that rely directly on the properties of the time series forecasts. For example, given CO_2 emissions for several countries up to a certain year, say 2017, we may be interested in groupings of countries based on forecast CO_2 emissions for the next five years. So, the interest is this case is on how the forecasts at a specific future time period can be grouped. To this end, several authors have proposed methods based on forecast densities.

Alonso et al. (2006) proposed a clustering method based on the full probability density of forecasts. Initially a resampling method combined with a non-parametric kernel estimator provides estimates of the forecast densities. A measure of discrepancy that is defined between the estimates and the dissimilarity matrix of these measures is used to determine the clustering solution.

The intention is to cluster time series based on their full forecast densities at a specific future time $T + h$ and hence the distances between forecasts densities seems appropriate. Alonso et al. (2006) chose the squared L^2 distance for its "computational advantages and it analytic tractability".

If $\mathbf{x}^i = (x_1^{(i)}, x_2^{(i)}, \ldots, x_T^{(i)})$ is the time series in the sample corresponding to the i-th individual, $i = 1, 2, \ldots, m$, and $f_{x_{t+h}^{(i)}}$ denotes the density function of the forecast of $x_{t+h}^{(i)}$, then the chosen distance is

$$D_{ij} = \int \left(f_{x_{t+h}}(i) - f_{x_{t+h}}(j) \right)^2 dx$$

for $i, j, = 1, 2, \ldots, m$

In practice, density forecasts are unknown; the distances D_{ij} are approximated for the data. To obtain the forecasts, Alonso et al. (2006) use a sieve bootstrap procedure which is based on the residuals resampling from an autoregressive approximation of the given process. The bootstrap sample is denoted by, $(x_{T+h}^{(*1)}, x_{T+h}^{(*2)}, \ldots, x_{T+h}^{(*B)})$, where B is the number of bootstrap samples. They apply the kernel estimation technique as described by Silverman (1986) to obtain $\hat{f}_{x_{t+h}^{(i)*}}$, the h-step-ahead kernel density estimator at point x for the i-th time series. They then estimate the squared L^2 distance to be

$$\hat{D}_{ij} = \int \left(\hat{f}_{x_{t+h}}(i) - \hat{f}_{x_{t+h}}(j) \right)^2 dx,$$

and proved the consistency of $\hat{D}_{ij}$. This dissimilarity matrix is used to carry out hierarchical clustering. This clustering procedure is applied to time series that are generated from parametric models. Vilar et al. (2010) extended this approach to cover the case of non-parametric models of arbitrary autoregressions. Their approach does not assume any parametric model for the true autoregressive structure of the series, which is estimated by using kernel smoothing techniques. As a consequence, only non-parametric approximations of the true autoregressive functions are available in this new setup, and hence, the sieve bootstrap is not a valid resampling procedure. In their procedure, the mechanism used to obtain bootstrap predictions is based on mimicking the generating process using a non-parametric estimator of the autoregressive function and a bootstrap resample of the nonparametric residuals. They provide a useful device for classifying non-linear autoregressive time series, including extensively studied parametric models such as the threshold autoregressive (TAR), the exponential autoregressive (EXPAR), the smooth-transition autoregressive (STAR) and the bilinear, among others.

Vilar and Vilar (2013) extended some the above-mentioned techniques to the case where the forecast horizon of interest to perform clustering involves several future times.

7.4.2 Clustering based on the polarization of forecast densities

Liu et al. (2014) adopted an approach to time series classification and clustering based on a polarization measure of forecast densities of time series. By fitting autoregressive models, forecast replicates of each time series are obtained via the bias-corrected bootstrap, and a stationarity correction is considered when necessary. Kernel estimators are then employed to approximate forecast densities, and discrepancies of forecast densities of pairs of time series are estimated by a polarization measure, which evaluates the extent to which two densities overlap. Anderson (2004) proposed an overlap measure of two probability densities as an index of convergence and a function of its negative as a measure of alienation. It is defined as

$$\theta = \int_{-\infty}^{\infty} min[f(y), g(y)]dy.$$

θ evaluates how much the two densities have in common where $0 \leq \theta \leq 1$, and is unit free. $1 - \theta$ evaluates the extent to which the distributions are alienated. Anderson et al. (2012) derived a nonparametric estimator of θ. The asymptotic properties of $\hat{\theta}$ depend on the contact set of two distributions, namely, $C_{f,g} = (x \epsilon R^d : f(x) = g(x) > 0)$ and its complements. The bias of $\hat{\theta}$ is related to these sets.

Following the distributional properties of the polarization measure, Liu et al. (2014) developed a discriminant rule and a clustering method to conduct the supervised and unsupervised classification, respectively. They then introduced a forecast density-based clustering method using hypothesis tests.

$$H_0 : \quad \theta_{ij,h} = 1$$
$$H_1 : \quad \theta_{ij,h} < 1$$

where $\theta_{ij,h}$ denotes the extent to which the two forecast densities of the i-th and j-th time series overlap at the forecast horizon h. Under H_0, the test statistic and its asymptotic distribution are given by

$$\frac{\sqrt{n}\big(\hat{\theta}_{ij,h}^{bc} - 1\big)}{\sigma_0\sqrt{\hat{\rho}_0}} \to N(0,1),$$

where $\hat{\theta}_{ij,h}^{bc}$ is the bias-corrected estimator of $\theta_{ij,h}$, and $\sigma_0^2\hat{\rho}_0$ is the limiting variance under the null hypothesis. σ_0^2 has been calculated and reported by Anderson et al. (2012) and $\hat{\rho}_0$ is the estimator of ρ, where $\rho = P(X \epsilon C_{f,g}) = P(Y \epsilon C_{f,g})$. If H_0 is rejected, it can be concluded that the two underlying forecast densities are significantly different, and that the two corresponding time series have significantly different future behaviours at the specified forecast horizon. The test results for pairs of time series can be used for clustering using the p-value approach of Maharaj (2000).

The outline of the steps to carry out the procedures follows:

- Phase 1: for each time series, obtain bootstrap forecast replicates at each of the forecast horizons that are of interest, by fitting autoregressive (AR) models;
- Phase 2: for each time series, use the bootstrap forecast replicates to estimate forecast densities. Then for each pair of time series compute the polarization measure for the estimated forecast densities.
- Phase 3: using the estimated polarization values, the time series are classified in either a supervised or an unsupervised manner, by following a proposed discrimination rule or conducting hypothesis tests, respectively.

7.5 ARMA mixture models

Xiong and Yeung (2002) proposed an approach for clustering of time series using mixtures of autoregressive moving average (ARMA) models. Using

$$\phi(B)\mathbf{Z}_t = \theta(B)\varepsilon_t \tag{7.11}$$

where ε_t are assumed to be a sequence of independent and identically distributed (i.i.d), Gaussian white noise terms with variance σ^2, the sequence of the natural logarithm of conditional likelihood function can be expressed as

$$lnP(\mathbf{z}_t|\Phi) = -\frac{n}{2}ln(2\pi\sigma^2) - \frac{1}{2\sigma^2}\sum_1^n \varepsilon_t^2$$

where $\Phi = \{\phi_0, \phi_1, \ldots, \phi_p, \beta_0, \beta_1, \ldots, \beta_p\}$ is the set of all the model parameters and ε_t is estimated recursively. They extended the ARMA models to ARMA mixtures. They assumed that time series under consideration are generated by M different ARMA models, which correspond to M different clusters, $\omega_1, \omega_2, \ldots, \omega_M$. They then express the conditional likelihood of the mixture model in the form of a mixture density

$$P(\mathbf{z}_t|\Theta) = \sum_{k=1}^{M} P(\mathbf{z}_t|\omega_k), \Phi_k P(\omega_k)$$

where $P(\mathbf{z}_t|, \omega_k, \Phi_k)$ denotes the conditional likelihood or density function of component model k with $\Theta_k = \{\Phi_1, \Phi_2, \ldots, \Phi_M, P(\omega_1), P(\omega_2), \ldots, P(\omega_M)\}$ representing the set of all parameters for the mixture model. A time series is assigned to cluster ω_k with posterior probability, $P(\omega_k|\mathbf{z}_t)$, where $\sum_{k=1}^{M} P(\omega_k|\mathbf{z}_t)$ = 1.

Given a set $\mathbf{D} = \{\mathbf{z}_{t1}, \mathbf{z}_{t2}, \ldots, \mathbf{z}_{tN}\}$ of N time series, then under the usual assumptions that time series are conditionally independent of each other, given the underlying model parameters, the likelihood of $\mathbf{D}$ can be expressed as

$$P(\mathbf{D}|\Theta) = \prod_{i=1}^{N} P(\mathbf{z}_{ti}|\Theta)$$

Given the data set $\mathbf{D}$, model parameter learning is finding the maximum *a posterior* (MAP) parameter estimate, namely,

$$\hat{\Theta} = argmax_\Theta P[\mathbf{D}|\Theta)P(\Theta)]$$

If the noninformative prior is taken on Θ, this becomes the maximum likelihood (MLE) estimator

$$\hat{\Theta} = argmax_\Theta P(\mathbf{D}|\Theta).$$

Xiong and Yeung (2002) derived an expectation-maximization (EM) algorithm to solve the MLE problem. Model selection was addressed using the Bayesian information criterion (BIC) to determine the number of clusters in the data.

7.6 Generalized autoregressive conditional heteroskedasticity (GARCH) models

Cluster analysis of financial time series plays an important role in several areas of application, such as international equity market analysis, portfolio diversification and risk management.

Dealing with financial heteroskedastic time series, the comparison of the dynamics of the variances is pivotal. If the conditional variance follows a stochastic process, heteroskedastic time series can be represented by GARCH models. In this regards, in the literature different time series clustering models based on GARCH models have been proposed; see, for instance, Otranto (2008, 2010), Caiado and Crato (2010), D'Urso et al. (2013b, 2016).

Caiado and Crato (2010) introduced a suitable dissimilarity measure between two volatility time series based on the estimated parameters of the GARCH representation of the time series weighted with their estimated covariances. Then a hierarchical agglomerative clustering method augmented with the dissimilarity measure proposed is used.

Otranto (2008) suggested a three-level clustering of time series. The first level groups time series on the basis of the unconditional volatility. The second level subgroups time series with similar time-varying volatility within the groups characterized by similar unconditional volatility. Finally, a more accurate classification is obtained distinguishing, within the groups with equal unconditional and time-varying volatilities, the time series with equal parameters of the GARCH representation. The similarity of the time series in each of the three levels is determined using the result (p-value) of a Wald statistical test on the unconditional volatility, on the time-varying volatility, on the estimated GARCH parameters, respectively. The threshold on the p-values allows the automatic detection of the number of clusters.

D'Urso et al. (2013b) proposed two fuzzy clustering models of volatility time series in the framework of a partitioning around medoids approach. One is based on the Caiado and Crato (2010) dissimilarity and the other on the distance between the estimated parameters of the autoregressive representation of the GARCH processes generating the volatility time series.

D'Urso et al. (2016) first proposed a suitable distance measure for heteroskedastic time series; successively they proposed different GARCH-based time series clustering models for classifying heteroskedastic time series. A GARCH-based Fuzzy c-Medoids Clustering model (GARCH-FcMdC model) provides only a timid robustification with respect to the presence of possible outlier time series. The model alleviates the negative effects of the presence of outliers in the dataset but does not solve the problem. For this reason, D'Urso et al. (2016) proposed successively the following robust models which represent different types of robustification of the GARCH-FcMdC model: GARCH-based Exponential Fuzzy c-Medoids Clustering model (GARCH-E-FcMdC model), GARCH-based Fuzzy c-Medoids clustering with Noise Cluster model (GARCH-NC-FcMdC model), GARCH-based Trimmed Fuzzy c-Medoids Clustering model (GARCH-Tr-FcMdC model).

In general, the D'Urso et al. (2016) models have the following features:
1. they are based on a *partitioning around medoids* (PAM) approach;
2. they follow the fuzzy clustering approach to generate a fuzzy partition of the heteroskedastic time series;

3. they are robust to the presence of outliers, that is, time series with anomalous patterns;

4. they are based on a GARCH parametric modeling of heteroskedastic time series, more specifically on the different components of the volatility of the GARCH representation of time series, namely, the unconditional volatility (*uv*) and the time varying volatility (*tvv*) (notice that this approach also allows the comparison of time series of different lengths);

5. they are based on a suitable distance measure for heteroskedastic time series which weights differently the different components of the volatility of the GARCH representation of time series.

With respect to Caiado and Crato (2010) and to Otranto (2010), the novelty of D'Urso et al. (2016) models are: i) the use of a distance based on the components of the volatility (unconditional and time-varying) objectively weighted; ii) the robustness to the presence of outliers of the clustering algorithms in which the distance works; iii) the fuzziness of the partition.

With respect to D'Urso et al. (2013b) the novelty of D'Urso et al. (2016) models are: i) the use of a distance based on the components of the volatility (unconditional and time-varying) objectively weighted; ii) the robustness to the presence of outliers of the clustering algorithms in which the distance works.

Caiado and Crato (2010) introduced a volatility-based metric for clustering asset returns and employed their method to investigate the similarities among the "blue-chip" stocks used to compute the Dow Jones Industrial Average (DJIA) index.

7.6.1   Unconditional, Minimum and Time-varying Volatilities

Let y_t $(t = 1, \ldots, T)$ be a time series, where t is the time index, modelled as the sum of a constant term μ and a zero mean heteroskedastic univariate process ε_t (heteroskedastic disturbance):

$$
\begin{aligned}
y_t &= \mu + \varepsilon_t \\
\varepsilon_t &= u_t \sqrt{h_t}
\end{aligned}
\tag{7.12}
$$

where u_t is a univariate white noise process with mean 0 and variance 1. The conditional variance h_t follows a GARCH(p, q) process as Bollerslev (1992):

$$
h_t = \gamma + \alpha_1 \varepsilon_{t-1}^2 + \ldots + \alpha_1 \varepsilon_{t-p}^2 + \beta_1 h_{t-1} + \ldots + \beta_q h_{t-q}
\tag{7.13}
$$

with

$$
\gamma > 0, \ 0 \le \alpha_i \le 1, \ 0 \le \beta_j \le 1 \ (i = 1, \ldots, p; \ j = 1, \ldots, q), \ \sum_{i=1}^{p} \alpha_i + \sum_{j=1}^{q} \beta_j < 1.
$$

Consider the difference between ε_t^2 and h_t:

$$\eta_t = \varepsilon_t^2 - h_t \tag{7.14}$$

where η_t are zero mean errors, uncorrelated with past information. After simple algebra, from Eq. (7.13) the squared disturbances ε_t^2 can be represented as an ARMA(p^*, q) process:

$$\varepsilon_t^2 = \gamma + \sum_{i=1}^{p^*}(\alpha_i + \beta_i)\varepsilon_{t-1}^2 - \sum_{j=1}^{q}\beta_j + \eta_t \tag{7.15}$$

where $p^* = \max(p, q)$, $\alpha_i = 0$ for $i > p$, if $p^* = q$, $\beta_j = 0$ for $j > q$ if $p^* = p$.

The parameters of the GARCH(p, q) model are $(\gamma, \alpha_1, \ldots, \alpha_p, \beta_1, \ldots, \beta_q)$. Hence, the GARCH process will be denoted also as GARCH($\gamma, \alpha_1, \ldots, \alpha_p, \beta_1, \ldots, \beta_q$).

Given the usual stationarity and invertibility restrictions on the roots of $(1 - (\alpha_1 + \beta_1)z - \ldots - (\alpha_i + \beta_i)z^i - \ldots - (\alpha_{p^*} + \beta_{p^*})z^{p^*})$ and $(1 - \beta_1 z - \ldots \beta_j z^j - \ldots - \beta_q z^q)$, from Eq. (7.15) ε_t^2 can be expressed as an infinite autoregressive AR(∞) model, after recursive substitution:

$$\varepsilon_t^2 = \frac{\gamma}{1 - \sum_{j=1}^{q}\beta_j} + \sum_{k=1}^{\infty}\pi_k \varepsilon_{t-k}^2 + \eta_t. \tag{7.16}$$

As is well known, indicating with ϕ_i the generic AR parameter and with θ_j the generic MA parameter of an ARMA(p, q) model, the recursive formula:

$$\pi_k - \sum_{j=1}^{q}\theta_j \pi_{k-j} = \phi_k \qquad k = 0, 1, \ldots \tag{7.17}$$

provides the sequence of parameters π_k. In Eq. (7.17) $\phi_0 = 1$, $\phi_i = 0$ for $i > p$ and $\pi_k = 0$ for $k < 0$. From Eq. (7.15) and Eq. (7.17) the π_k parameters are:

$$\pi_k = (\alpha_k + \beta_k) - \sum_{j=1}^{q}\beta_j \pi_{k-j}. \tag{7.18}$$

From Eq. (7.16) the expected volatility at time $t+1$, given the information available at time t, can be split in a constant part and a time-varying part (which depends on the time history of the volatility) (Otranto, 2008):

$$E_t(\varepsilon_{t+1}^2) = \frac{\gamma}{1 - \sum_{j=1}^{q}\beta_j} + \sum_{k=1}^{\infty}\pi_k \varepsilon_{t-k}^2. \tag{7.19}$$

The *unconditional volatility* (*uv*) is then given by the unconditional expected value of ε_{t+1}^2:

$$uv = E(\varepsilon_{t+1}^2) = \frac{\gamma}{(1 - \sum_{j=1}^{q}\beta_j)(1 - \sum_{k=1}^{\infty}\pi_k)}. \tag{7.20}$$

The time-varying part of the volatility is an infinite weighted sum of unobservable random variables (see Eq. (7.19)). The null time-varying volatility is obtained when each of the π_k coefficients is equal to zero. Considering the metric introduced by Piccolo (1990) between two ARIMA models as the Euclidean distance between the coefficients of the AR(∞) representation of the two models, the distance of a time series from the case of null time-varying volatility (hence the case of constant volatility) is given by Otranto (2008), yielding the expression of *time varying volatility*:

$$tvv = \left(\sum_{k=1}^{\infty} \pi_k^2 \right)^{\frac{1}{2}}. \qquad (7.21)$$

7.6.2   A GARCH-based metric for time series clustering

Many time-varying volatility models have been proposed to capture the so-called "asymmetric volatility" effect. A univariate volatility model commonly used to allow for asymmetric shocks to volatility is the threshold GARCH (or TGARCH) model (see Glosten, Jagannathan and Runkle, 1993 and Zakoian, 1994). The conditional variance of a simple TGARCH(1,1) model is

$$h_t^2 = \gamma + \alpha \varepsilon_{t-1}^2 + \lambda \varepsilon_{t-1}^2 d_{t-1} + \beta h_{t-1}^2$$

where $d_t = 1$ if ε_t is negative, and $d_t = 0$ otherwise. The volatility may either diminish ($\lambda < 0$), rise ($\lambda > 0$), or not be affected ($\lambda \neq 0$) by negative shocks or "bad news" ($\varepsilon_{t-1} < 0$). Good news has an impact of α while bad news has an impact of $\alpha + \lambda$.

Caiado and Crato (2010) proposed a distance measure for clustering time series with similar volatility dynamics effects. Let $r_{x,t} = \log P_{x,t} - \log P_{x,t-1}$ denote the continuously compounded return of an asset x from time $t-1$ to t ($r_{y,t}$ is similarly defined for asset y). Suppose we fit a common TGARCH(1,1) model to both time series by the method of maximum likelihood assuming GED innovations. Let $T_x = (\widehat{\alpha}_x, \widehat{\beta}_x, \widehat{\lambda}_x, \widehat{v}_x)'$ and $T_y = (\widehat{\alpha}_y, \widehat{\beta}_y, \widehat{\lambda}_y, \widehat{v}_y)'$ be the vectors of the estimated ARCH, GARCH, leverage effect and tail-thickness parameters, with the estimated covariance matrices given by V_x and V_y, respectively.

A Mahalanobis-like distance between the dynamic features of the return series $r_{x,t}$ and $r_{y,t}$, called the TGARCH-based distance, can be defined by

$$d_{TGARCH}(x_t, y_t) = \sqrt{(T_x - T_y)' \Omega^{-1} (T_x - T_y)}, \qquad (7.22)$$

where $\Omega = V_x + V_y$ is a weighting matrix. This distance considers the information about the stochastic dynamic structure of the time series volatilities and allows for unequal length time series.

Caiado and Crato (2010) also proposed combining this model based method with features derived for the time series such as periodogram ordinates or autocorrelations lags (Caiado et al., 2006). The spectrum or the autocorrelation function of the squared return series provides useful information about the time series behaviour in terms of the ARCH effects.

Let $P_x(\omega_j) = n^{-1}|\sum_{t=1}^{n} r_{t,x} e^{-it\omega_j}|^2$ be the periodogram of the squared return series, $r_{x,t}^2$, at frequencies $\omega_j = 2\pi j/n$, $j = 1, ..., [n/2]$ (with $[n/2]$ the largest integer less or equal to $n/2$). Let s_x^2 be the sample variance of $r_{x,t}$ (a similar expression applies to asset y).

The Euclidean distance between the log normalized periodograms (Caiado et al., 2006) of the squared returns of x_t and y_t is given by

$$d_{LNP}(x_t, y_t) = \sqrt{\sum_{j=1}^{[n/2]} \left[\log \frac{P_x(\omega_j)}{s_x^2} - \log \frac{P_y(\omega_j)}{s_y^2} \right]^2}, \qquad (7.23)$$

or, using matrix notation,

$$d_{LNP}(x_t, y_t) = \sqrt{(L_x - L_y)'(L_x - L_y)}. \qquad (7.24)$$

where L_x and L_y are the vectors of the log normalized periodogram ordinates of $r_{x,t}^2$ and $r_{y,t}^2$, respectively.

Since the parametric features of the TGARCH model are not necessarily associated with all the periodogram ordinates, the parametric and nonparametric approaches can be combined to consider both the volatility dynamics and the cyclical behavior of the return series (Caiado and Crato, 2010), that is

$$d_{TGARCH-LNPSR}(x_t, y_t) = \lambda_1 \sqrt{(T_x - T_y)'\Omega^{-1}(T_x - T_y)}$$
$$+ \lambda_2 \sqrt{(L_x - L_y)'(L_x - L_y)}. \qquad (7.25)$$

where $\lambda_i, i = 1, 2$ are normalizing/weighting parameters.

It is straightforward to show that the statistic Eq. (7.25) satisfies the following distance properties: (i) $d(x, y)$ is asymptotically zero for independent time series generated by the same data generating process (DGP); (ii) $d(x, y) \geq 0$ as all the quantities are nonnegative; and (iii) $d(x, y) = d(y, x)$, as all transformations are independent of the ordering.

7.6.3 A combined distance measure for heteroskedastic time series

Following D'Urso et al. (2016), the distance between each pair of time series is measured by comparing the *unconditional volatility* and the *time-varying volatility* of the time series, that is, by separately considering the distances for the *unconditional volatility* and the *time-varying volatility* estimated parameters of the GARCH representation of the time series and using a suitable weighting system for such distance components. Thus, by considering the i-th and i'-th units, we have:

$$_{uv,tvv}d_{ii'} = [w_1^2 {}_{uv}d_{ii'}^2 + w_2^2 {}_{tvv}d_{ii'}^2]^{\frac{1}{2}} = [w_1^2(uv_i - uv_{i'})^2 + w_2^2(tvv_i - tvv_{i'})^2]^{\frac{1}{2}}$$
$$(7.26)$$

where $_{uv}d_{ii'}^2 = (uv_i - uv_{i'})^2$ is the squared Euclidean distance between the unconditional volatility of units i and i' (uv_i and $uv_{i'}$ respectively); $_{tvv}d_{ii'}^2 = (tvv_i - tvv_{i'})^2$ is the squared Euclidean distance between the time-varying volatility of units i and i' (tvv_i and $tvv_{i'}$ respectively); w_1, $w_2 \geq 0$ are suitable weights for the unconditional and time-varying components. These weights can be fixed subjectively a priori by considering external or subjective conditions (internal weighting system) or can be computed objectively within a suitable clustering procedure (external weighting system). The following conditions are assumed: $w_1 + w_2 = 1$ (normalization condition) and $w_1, w_2 \geq 0$; that is, it can set $w_1 = w$, $w_2 = (1 - w)$.

The weights w_1, w_2 are intrinsically associated with the characteristics of the time series captured by the unconditional and time-varying volatility; thus the weights allow properly tuning the influence of the two components of the volatility of the time series when calculating the distance.

Time series with similar unconditional volatility can have different dynamics, characterized by different time-varying volatilities; conversely, time series with similar time-varying volatility can have different unconditional volatilities.

Through the normalization condition $w_1 + w_2 = 1$, it is possible to assess comparatively the contribution of the components in the computation of $_{uv,tvv}d_{ii'}$.

The measure $_{uv,tvv}d_{ii'}$ is utilized for comparisons within a set of data rather than for examining a single pair of data. Thus, for a given dataset, the weighting system is optimal only for the dataset involved.

If two time series have the same unconditional volatility and the same time-varying volatility, it is not possible to conclude that they are generated by the same GARCH process. In fact the equality of the two unconditional volatilities and the two time-varying volatilities is relative to two nonlinear combinations of the parameters of the GARCH representation. The case of equality of the two data generating processes is obtained if and only if the constant γ and the parameters α_i and β_j ($i = 1, \ldots, p; j = 1, \ldots, q$) are the same for the two GARCH models. This is a stronger requirement with respect to the equality of the unconditional volatilities and the time-varying volatilities. It is obvious that the equality of the parameters of two time series implies equal unconditional and time-varying volatilities (but not vice versa).

7.6.4 GARCH-based Fuzzy c-Medoids Clustering model (GARCH-FcMdC)

D'Urso et al. (2016) proposed the GARCH Fuzzy c-Medoids Clustering model (GARCH-FcMdC), characterized as follows:

$$
\begin{aligned}
\min : & \sum_{i=1}^{I} \sum_{c=1}^{C} u_{ic}^{m} {}_{uv,tvv} d_{ic}^{2} = \\
& \sum_{i=1}^{I} \sum_{c=1}^{C} u_{ic}^{m} [w_1^2 {}_{uv} d_{ic}^2 + w_2^2 {}_{tvv} d_{ic}^2] = \\
& \sum_{i=1}^{I} \sum_{c=1}^{C} u_{ic}^{m} [w_1^2 (uv_i - uv_c)^2 + w_2^2 (tvv_i - tvv_c)^2] \\
& \sum_{c=1}^{C} u_{ic} = 1; \ w_1 + w_2 = 1; \ w_1, w_2 \geq 0
\end{aligned}
\tag{7.27}
$$

where $m > 1$ is a weighting exponent that controls the fuzziness of the obtained partition; u_{ic} indicates the membership degree of the i-th unit in the c-th cluster represented by the c-th medoid.

The iterative solutions are (D'Urso et al., 2016):

$$
\begin{aligned}
u_{ic} &= \frac{1}{\sum_{c'=1}^{C} \left[\frac{w_1^2 {}_{uv} d_{ic}^2 + w_2^2 {}_{tvv} d_{ic}^2}{w_1^2 {}_{uv} d_{ic'}^2 + w_2^2 {}_{tvv} d_{ic'}^2} \right]^{\frac{1}{m-1}}} = \\
&= \frac{1}{\sum_{c'=1}^{C} \left[\frac{w_1^2 (uv_i - uv_c)^2 + w_2^2 (tvv_i - tvv_c)^2}{w_1^2 (uv_i - uv_{c'})^2 + w_2^2 (tvv_i - tvv_{c'})^2} \right]^{\frac{1}{m-1}}}
\end{aligned}
\tag{7.28}
$$

$$
\begin{aligned}
w_1 &= \frac{\sum_{i=1}^{I} \sum_{c=1}^{C} u_{ic}^{m} {}_{tvv} d_{ic}^2}{\sum_{i=1}^{I} \sum_{c=1}^{C} u_{ic}^{m} ({}_{uv} d_{ic}^2 + {}_{tvv} d_{ic}^2)} = \\
&= \frac{\sum_{i=1}^{I} \sum_{c=1}^{C} u_{ic}^{m} (tvv_i - tvv_c)^2}{\sum_{i=1}^{I} \sum_{c=1}^{C} u_{ic}^{m} [(uv_i - uv_c)^2 + (tvv_i - tvv_c)^2]}
\end{aligned}
\tag{7.29}
$$

$$
\begin{aligned}
w_2 &= \frac{\sum_{i=1}^{I} \sum_{c=1}^{C} u_{ic}^{m} {}_{uv} d_{ic}^2}{\sum_{i=1}^{I} \sum_{c=1}^{C} u_{ic}^{m} ({}_{uv} d_{ic}^2 + {}_{tvv} d_{ie}^2)} = \\
&= \frac{\sum_{i=1}^{I} \sum_{c=1}^{C} u_{ic}^{m} (uv_i - uv_c)^2}{\sum_{i=1}^{I} \sum_{c=1}^{C} u_{ic}^{m} [(uv_i - uv_c)^2 + (tvv_i - tvv_c)^2]}.
\end{aligned}
\tag{7.30}
$$

7.6.5 GARCH-based Exponential Fuzzy c-Medoids Clustering model (GARCH-E-FcMdC)

D'Urso et al. (2016) introduced the following "robust" distance measure (Wu and Yang, 2002; Zhang and Chen, 2004):

$$
\begin{aligned}
{}_{uv,tvv}^{exp} d_{ii'} &\equiv [1 - \exp\{-\beta_{uv,tvv} d_{ii'}^2\}]^{\frac{1}{2}} \equiv \\
&\equiv [1 - \exp\{-\beta(w_1^2 {}_{uv} d_{ii'}^2 + w_2^2 {}_{tvv} d_{ii'}^2)\}]^{\frac{1}{2}} = \\
&= [1 - \exp\{-\beta[w_1^2 (uv_i - uv_{i'})^2 + w_2^2 (tvv_i - tvv_{i'})^2]\}]^{\frac{1}{2}}
\end{aligned}
\tag{7.31}
$$

where β is a suitable (positive) parameter computed according to the variability of the data (see D'Urso et al., 2016), for more details on β).

By considering the "exponential distance", D'Urso et al. (2016) proposed the following GARCH-E-FcMdC model:

$$\min : \sum_{i=1}^{I}\sum_{c=1}^{C} u_{ic}^m \left({}_{uv,tvv}^{exp}d_{ic}^2 \right) =$$

$$\sum_{i=1}^{I}\sum_{c=1}^{C} u_{ic}^m [1 - \exp\{-\beta[w_1^2(uv_i - uv_c)^2 + w_2^2(tvv_i - tvv_c)^2]\}]. \tag{7.32}$$

The iterative solutions are:

$$u_{ic} = \frac{1}{\sum_{c'=1}^{C}\left[\frac{{}_{uv,tvv}^{exp}d_{ic}^2}{{}_{uv,tvv}^{exp}d_{ic'}^2}\right]^{\frac{1}{m-1}}} =$$

$$= \frac{1}{\sum_{c'=1}^{C}\left[\frac{1-\exp\{-\beta[w_1^2(uv_i-uv_c)^2+w_2^2(tvv_i-tvv_c)^2]\}}{1-\exp\{-\beta[w_1^2(uv_i-uv_{c'})^2+w_2^2(tvv_i-tvv_{c'})^2]\}}\right]^{\frac{1}{m-1}}} \tag{7.33}$$

$$w_1 = \frac{\sum_{i=1}^{I}\sum_{c=1}^{C} u_{ic}^m {}_{tvv}d_{ic}^2 (1 - {}_{uv,tvv}^{exp}d_{ic}^2)}{\sum_{i=1}^{I}\sum_{c=1}^{C} u_{ic}^m ({}_{uv}d_{ic}^2 + {}_{tvv}d_{ic}^2)(1 - {}_{uv,tvv}^{exp}d_{ic}^2)} =$$

$$= \frac{\sum_{i=1}^{I}\sum_{c=1}^{C} u_{ic}^m (tvv_i - tvv_c)^2 \exp\{-\beta[w_1^2(uv_i - uv_c)^2 + w_2^2(tvv_i - tvv_c)^2]\}}{\sum_{i=1}^{I}\sum_{c=1}^{C} u_{ic}^m [(uv_i - uv_c)^2 + (tvv_i - tvv_c)^2] \exp\{-\beta[w_1^2(uv_i - uv_c)^2 + w_2^2(tvv_i - tvv_c)^2]\}} \tag{7.34}$$

$$w_2 = \frac{\sum_{i=1}^{I}\sum_{c=1}^{C} u_{ic}^m {}_{uv}d_{ic}^2 (1 - {}_{uv,tvv}^{exp}d_{ic}^2)}{\sum_{i=1}^{I}\sum_{c=1}^{C} u_{ic}^m ({}_{uv}d_{ic}^2 + {}_{tvv}d_{ic}^2)(1 - {}_{uv,tvv}^{exp}d_{ic}^2)} =$$

$$= \frac{\sum_{i=1}^{I}\sum_{c=1}^{C} u_{ic}^m (uv_i - uv_c)^2 \exp\{-\beta[w_1^2(uv_i - uv_c)^2 + w_2^2(tvv_i - tvv_c)^2]\}}{\sum_{i=1}^{I}\sum_{c=1}^{C} u_{ic}^m [(uv_i - uv_c)^2 + (tvv_i - tvv_c)^2] \exp\{-\beta[w_1^2(uv_i - uv_c)^2 + w_2^2(tvv_i - tvv_c)^2]\}}. \tag{7.35}$$

7.6.6 GARCH-based Fuzzy c-Medoids Clustering with Noise Cluster model (GARCH-NC-FcMdC)

D'Urso et al. (2016) proposed the Fuzzy C-Medoids clustering model with Noise Cluster (GARCH-NC-FcMdC). This model achieves its robustness with respect to outliers by introducing a noise cluster represented by a noise prototype, namely, a noise medoid, which is always at the same distance from all units. Let there be $C - 1$ good clusters and let the C-th cluster be the noise cluster. Let the noise prototype (namely, noise medoid) be the C-th prototype (medoid). It is assumed that the distance measure $_{uv,tvv}d_{iC}$ of unit i from the C-th medoid is equal to δ, $i = 1\ldots,I$.

Then the GARCH-NC-FcMdC model can be formalized as follows:

$$
\begin{aligned}
\min : & \sum_{i=1}^{I}\sum_{c=1}^{C-1} u_{ic}^m {}_{uv,tvv}d_{ic}^2 + \sum_{i=1}^{I} u_{iC}^m \delta^2 = \\
& \sum_{i=1}^{I}\sum_{c=1}^{C-1} u_{ic}^m [w_{1\,uv}^2 d_{ic}^2 + w_{2\,tvv}^2 d_{ic}^2] + \sum_{i=1}^{I} u_{iC}^m \delta^2 = \\
& \sum_{i=1}^{I}\sum_{c=1}^{C-1} u_{ic}^m [w_1^2 (uv_i - uv_c)^2 + w_2^2 (tvv_i - tvv_c)^2] + \sum_{i=1}^{I} u_{iC}^m \delta^2
\end{aligned}
\tag{7.36}
$$

where $u_{iC} = 1 - \sum_{c=1}^{C-1} u_{ic}$.

The distance from the noise cluster depends on the average distance among units $\delta^2 = \rho(I(C-1))^{-1}\sum_{i=1}^{I}\sum_{c=1}^{C-1} {}_{uv,tvv}d_{ic}^2$. In any case, the results do not seem very sensitive to the value of the multiplier ρ, (Davé, 1991). Due to the presence of δ, units that are close to good clusters are correctly classified in a good cluster while the noise units that are away from good clusters are classified in the noise cluster.

The iterative solutions are:

$$
\begin{aligned}
u_{ic} = & \frac{1}{\sum_{c'=1}^{C-1}\left[\frac{w_{1\,uv}^2 d_{ic}^2 + w_{2\,tvv}^2 d_{ic}^2}{w_{1\,uv}^2 d_{ic'}^2 + w_{2\,tvv}^2 d_{ic'}^2}\right]^{\frac{1}{m-1}} + \left[\frac{w_{1\,uv}^2 d_{ic}^2 + w_{2\,tvv}^2 d_{ic}^2}{\delta^2}\right]^{\frac{1}{m-1}}} = \\
= & \frac{1}{\sum_{c'=1}^{C-1}\left[\frac{w_1^2(uv_i - uv_c)^2 + w_2^2(tvv_i - tvv_c)^2}{w_1^2(uv_i - uv_{c'})^2 + w_2^2(tvv_i - tvv_{c'})^2}\right]^{\frac{1}{m-1}} + \left[\frac{w_1^2(uv_i - uv_c)^2 + w_2^2(tvv_i - tvv_c)^2}{\delta^2}\right]^{\frac{1}{m-1}}}
\end{aligned}
$$

for $c = 1,\ldots,C - 1$, while the membership degrees for the noise cluster are:

$$
\begin{aligned}
u_{iC} = & \frac{\left[\frac{1}{\delta^2}\right]^{\frac{1}{m-1}}}{\sum_{c'=1}^{C-1}\left[\frac{1}{w_{1\,uv}^2 d_{ic'}^2 + w_{2\,tvv}^2 d_{ic'}^2}\right]^{\frac{1}{m-1}} + \left[\frac{1}{\delta^2}\right]^{\frac{1}{m-1}}} \\
= & \frac{\left[\frac{1}{\delta^2}\right]^{\frac{1}{m-1}}}{\sum_{c'=1}^{C-1}\left[\frac{1}{w_1^2(uv_i - uv_{c'})^2 + w_2^2(tvv_i - tvv_{c'})^2}\right]^{\frac{1}{m-1}} + \left[\frac{1}{\delta^2}\right]^{\frac{1}{m-1}}}
\end{aligned}
$$

The values of w_1 and w_2 are obtained as in Eq. (7.29) - Eq. (7.30), where the inner summation ranges over the $C - 1$ good clusters.

7.6.7   GARCH-based Trimmed Fuzzy c-Medoids Clustering model (GARCH-Tr-FcMdC)

D'Urso et al. (2016) proposed the Trimmed Fuzzy c-Medoids Clustering model (GARCH-Tr-FcMdC), by considering the Least Trimmed Squares approach and using Eq. (7.28) - Eq. (7.30).

This model achieves its robustness with respect to outliers by trimming away a certain fraction of the data units and requires the specification of the "trimming ratio", τ, which is the fraction of the data units that has to be trimmed Krishnapuram et al. (2001).

The objective function is obtained by substituting in the objective function Eq. (7.27) the expression of the optimal u_{ic} Eq. (7.28):

$$\text{min}: \quad \sum_{i=1}^{I} \left(\sum_{c=1}^{C} [w_{1}^2{}_{uv} d_{ic}^2 + w_{2}^2{}_{tvv} d_{ic}^2]^{\frac{1}{1-m}} \right)^{1-m} = \sum_{i=1}^{I} harm_i$$

where

$$harm_i = \left(\sum_{c=1}^{C} [w_{1}^2{}_{uv} d_{ic}^2 + w_{2}^2{}_{tvv} d_{ic}^2]^{\frac{1}{1-m}} \right)^{1-m} =$$

$$\left(\sum_{c=1}^{C} [w_1^2 (uv_i - uv_c)^2 + w_2^2 (tvv_i - tvv_c)^2]^{\frac{1}{1-m}} \right)^{1-m} \qquad (7.37)$$

is C^{-1} times the harmonic mean of $[w_{1}^2{}_{uv} d_{ic}^2 + w_{2}^2{}_{tvv} d_{ic}^2]^{\frac{1}{1-m}}$ when $m = 2$.

The objective function of the GARCH-Tr-FcMdC model, when τI ($0 \leq \tau \leq 1$) data units are trimmed, corresponding to those with the highest values of $harm_i$ (the farthest from the medoids), is obtained by modifying the objective function in Eq. (7.27) setting to $I' = I - \tau I$ the limit of the range of the outer summation:

$$\text{min}: \sum_{i=1}^{I'} \sum_{c=1}^{C} u_{ic}^m [uv, tvv \, d_{ic}]^2 =$$

$$\sum_{i=1}^{I'} \sum_{c=1}^{C} u_{ic}^m [w_{1}^2{}_{uv} d_{ic}^2 + w_{2}^2{}_{tvv} d_{ic}^2] = \qquad (7.38)$$

$$\sum_{i=1}^{I'} \sum_{c=1}^{C} u_{ic}^m [w_1^2 (uv_i - uv_c)^2 + w_2^2 (tvv_i - tvv_c)^2]$$

and is minimized with respect to the related parameters. The values of w_1 and w_2 are obtained as in Eq. (7.29) - Eq. 7.30).

Application 7.2 D'Urso et al. (2016) applied the different models to the volatility daily index returns of the major international stock exchanges. The data includes 30 time series with unequal length, since the period of observation of time series starts from January 2000 until December 2010, but some of the time series data were available only for a shorter period (source: http://finance.yahoo.com). The aim of the application is to show the usefulness of the fuzzy clustering approach in identifying groups of countries whose daily index returns share a similar volatility pattern. The time series of daily index returns are shown in Figure 7.4.

For choosing the best GARCH(p, q) models for the time series of daily index returns, D'Urso et al. (2016) considered the Box and Jenkins modelling procedure. The final results of this procedure are shown in Table 7.2. The best model selected for all time series is the GARCH$(1, 1)$. All estimated coefficients are significant. In Table 7.2 are shown the models' coefficients, their standard error (in brackets) and some diagnostic tests with the related p-value. Q and Q^2 are the values of the Ljung-Box test up to twenty lags for serial correlation in the residuals and the LM is the Lagrange multiplier test for ARCH (AutoRegressive Conditional Heteroskedasticity) effects in the residuals. The clustering algorithms use the truncated AR(∞) representation. First the GARCH(1,1) process in the ARMA(1,1) process is represented; then the time series transformed in the ARMA process are fitted with truncated AR(∞) models and those time series fitted with AR models retain their coefficients.

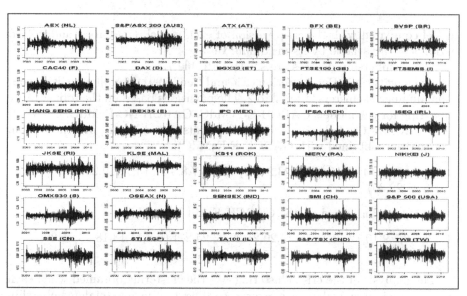

FIGURE 7.4: Daily index returns of 30 international stock exchanges.

D'Urso et al. (2016) applied the GARCH-FcMdC model, the GARCH-E-FcMdC model, the GARCH-NC-FcMdC model, the GARCH-Tr-FcMdC

TABLE 7.2: Estimated coefficients of GARCH(1,1) processes for the daily index returns.

	Indices	ARCH $\hat{\alpha}$	GARCH $\hat{\beta}$	Q(20)	*p-value*	Q^2(20)	*p-value*	LM	*p-value*
1	AEX (NL)	0.1081 (0.0141)	0.8858 (0.0129)	22.4556	*0.3163*	22.6634	*0.3056*	18.0606	*0.1159*
2	S&P/ASX 200 (AUS)	0.0869 (0.0164)	0.9096 (0.0164)	21.1871	*0.3861*	18.7262	*0.5396*	13.7442	*0.3173*
3	ATX (AT)	0.1284 (0.0211)	0.8578 (0.0249)	28.355	*0.1188*	16.6635	*0.6747*	11.1938	*0.5123*
4	BFX (BE)	0.1444 (0.0216)	0.8466 (0.0208)	22.4823	*0.3149*	16.0483	*0.7136*	8.9599	*0.7063*
5	BVSP (BR)	0.0689 (0.0176)	0.9088 (0.0159)	25.0868	*0.1981*	17.4879	*0.621*	10.4213	*0.579*
6	CAC40 (F)	0.0939 (0.0122)	0.9000 (0.0146)	26.7516	*0.1423*	12.7494	*0.8878*	9.9122	*0.6236*
7	DAX (D)	0.0927 (0.0123)	0.8990 (0.0120)	22.472	*0.3154*	26.3797	*0.1536*	17.3854	*0.1244*
8	EGX30 (ET)	0.0260 (0.0240)	0.9655 (0.0378)	25.0183	*0.1528*	20.174	*0.447*	11.2824	*0.5048*
9	FTSE100 (GB)	0.1053 (0.0135)	0.8898 (0.0131)	22.442	*0.317*	29.8209	*0.1105*	17.9871	*0.1201*
10	FTSEMIB (I)	0.1079 (0.0209)	0.8845 (0.0195)	14.5796	*0.7999*	25.5811	*0.1801*	16.9896	*0.1308*
11	HANG SENG (HK)	0.0664 (0.0095)	0.9286 (0.0091)	23.5587	*0.2621*	24.3376	*0.2279*	17.9232	*0.1259*
12	IBEX 35 (E)	0.1009 (0.0190)	0.8845 (0.0173)	17.2738	*0.6351*	28.1289	*0.1277*	17.2675	*0.1301*
13	IPC (MEX)	0.0789 (0.0157)	0.9089 (0.0187)	30.3476	*0.0998*	9.0994	*0.9817*	7.2364	*0.8415*
14	IPSA (RCH)	0.1763 (0.0304)	0.7962 (0.0291)	31.8239	*0.0812*	18.7324	*0.5392*	12.9544	*0.3723*
15	ISEQ (IRL)	0.1002 (0.0176)	0.8908 (0.0186)	28.6551	*0.1106*	14.695	*0.6797*	9.2692	*0.6797*
16	JKSE (RI)	0.1393 (0.0315)	0.8007 (0.0470)	32.8754	*0.0779*	18.4597	*0.5571*	9.0147	*0.7016*
17	KLSE (MAL)	0.1298 (0.0357)	0.8677 (0.0361)	30.1713	*0.0954*	26.8163	*0.1514*	2.2909	*0.9988*
18	KS11 (ROK)	0.0806 (0.0157)	0.9151 (0.0146)	27.8968	*0.1118*	15.2465	*0.7621*	10.1004	*0.6071*
19	MERV (RA)	0.0969 (0.0145)	0.8764 (0.0174)	29.7804	*0.1034*	14.2712	*0.8164*	10.6137	*0.5622*
20	NIKKEI (J)	0.0948 (0.0132)	0.8947 (0.0126)	18.9275	*0.5265*	27.5483	*0.1205*	17.4932	*0.1319*
21	OMXS30 (S)	0.1240 (0.0204)	0.8487 (0.0243)	16.1155	*0.7094*	19.9271	*0.4624*	11.5688	*0.4808*
22	OSEAX (N)	0.0675 (0.0207)	0.9244 (0.0237)	28.8912	*0.0956*	23.7344	*0.2541*	13.9576	*0.3042*
23	SENSEX (IND)	0.1403 (0.0313)	0.8432 (0.0250)	32.2054	*0.071*	14.5702	*0.8004*	12.2251	*0.4277*
24	SMI (CH)	0.1176 (0.0145)	0.8684 (0.0143)	22.5214	*0.3128*	29.6336	*0.1098*	18.9469	*0.1019*
25	S&P 500 (USA)	0.0801 (0.0108)	0.9124 (0.0108)	13.5258	*0.8537*	23.1422	*0.2818*	18.4981	*0.1093*
26	SSE (CN)	0.0718 (0.0175)	0.9210 (0.0181)	28.1062	*0.1027*	13.0897	*0.8735*	5.9461	*0.9187*
27	STI (SGP)	0.1032 (0.0198)	0.8953 (0.0171)	28.26	*0.1033*	20.9776	*0.3984*	13.437	*0.3381*
28	TA100 (IL)	0.0921 (0.0183)	0.8791 (0.0223)	29.7282	*0.1005*	16.6511	*0.6754*	12.8321	*0.3813*
29	S&P/TSX (CND)	0.0658 (0.0133)	0.9296 (0.0142)	12.5148	*0.8972*	14.0501	*0.8279*	11.6758	*0.4721*
30	TSEC (TW)	0.0672 (0.0129)	0.9281 (0.0130)	12.5148	*0.8972*	29.9133	*0.1027*	17.2473	*0.1283*

model compared with the crisp version of each model. Data are standardized dividing each variable by its maximum value.

The membership degrees are shown in Table 7.3.

By using the Xie-Beni criterion (Xie and Beni, 1991), for all models the optimal number of clusters is equal to 2. The partitions based on the robust fuzzy clustering for the models GARCH-E-FcMdC, GARCH-NC-FcMdC, GARCH-Tr-FcMdC are the following (notice that units 8 and 14 are present only in the partition obtained with GARCH-E-FcMdC):

(1,3,4,9,10,12,14,15,16,17,22,23,24,27) (2,5,6,7,8,9,11,13,18,19,20,21,25, 26,28,29,30).

The partition based on the GARCH-FcMdC model is:

(1,2,3,4,6,7,9,10,12,14,15,16,17,20,21,22,23,24,27) (5,8,11,13,18,19,25,26, 28,29,30).

The analysis of the crisp clustering -i.e, the clustering obtained when each time series is assigned to a cluster according to the maximal membership degree- for all the models shows worse performances with respect to the cluster validity indices.

TABLE 7.3: Membership degrees.

		GARCH-FcMdC			GARCH-NC-FcMdC			GARCH-E-FcMdC			GARCH-Tr-FcMdC		
		membership degrees		crisp	membership degrees		crisp	membership degrees		crisp	membership degrees		crisp
1	AEX	1.000	0.000	1	0.998	0.001	0.001	1	0.999	0.001	1	0.999	0.001	1
2	S&P/ASX 200	0.850	0.150	1	0.008	0.990	0.003	1	0.070	0.930	1	0.059	0.941	2
3	ATX	0.996	0.004	1	0.990	0.003	0.007	1	0.997	0.003	1	0.998	0.002	1
4	BFX	0.975	0.025	1	0.735	0.026	0.239	1	0.943	0.057	1	0.976	0.024	1
5	BVSP	0.057	0.943	2	0.021	0.832	0.147	3	0.020	0.980	2	0.009	0.991	2
6	CAC40	0.958	0.042	1	0.189	0.789	0.022	1	0.474	0.526	1	0.322	0.678	1
7	DAX	0.892	0.108	1	0.072	0.915	0.013	1	0.276	0.724	1	0.265	0.735	2
8	**EGX30**	0.216	0.784	2	0.009	0.038	0.954	3	0.384	0.616	2		outlier	
9	FTSE100	0.999	0.001	1	0.990	0.007	0.003	1	0.995	0.005	1	0.997	0.003	1
10	FTSEMIB	1.000	0.000	1	0.996	0.003	0.001	1	0.998	0.002	1	0.999	0.001	1
11	HANG SENG	0.053	0.947	2	0.013	0.920	0.067	2	0.007	0.993	2	0.003	0.997	2
12	IBEX 35	1.000	0.000	1	0.999	0.000	0.000	1	1.000	0.000	1	1.000	0.000	1
13	IPC	0.021	0.979	2	0.000	0.999	0.001	2	0.000	1.000	2	0.000	1.000	2
14	**IPSA**	0.934	0.066	1	0.289	0.028	0.683	3	0.818	0.182	1		outlier	
15	ISEQ	0.993	0.007	1	0.725	0.250	0.025	1	0.876	0.124	1	0.887	0.113	1
16	JKSE	0.584	0.416	1	0.998	0.001	0.001	3	0.997	0.003	1	0.999	0.001	1
17	KLSE	0.989	0.011	1	0.938	0.011	0.051	1	0.984	0.016	1	0.992	0.008	1
18	KS11	0.159	0.841	2	0.000	1.000	0.000	1	0.001	0.999	2	0.000	1.000	2
19	MERV	0.203	0.797	2	0.030	0.958	0.012	3	0.127	0.873	2	0.101	0.899	2
20	NIKKEI	0.805	0.195	1	0.126	0.857	0.018	1	0.377	0.623	1	0.271	0.729	2
21	OMXS30	0.510	0.490	2	0.001	0.999	0.000	1	0.018	0.982	2	0.015	0.985	2
22	OSEAX	0.979	0.021	1	1.000	0.000	0.000	1	1.000	0.000	1	1.000	0.000	1
23	SENSEX	0.954	0.046	1	0.898	0.015	0.087	1	0.975	0.025	1	0.989	0.011	1
24	SMI	1.000	0.000	1	1.000	0.000	0.000	1	1.000	0.000	1	1.000	0.000	1
25	S&P 500	0.366	0.634	2	0.000	1.000	0.000	1	0.000	1.000	2	0.000	1.000	2
26	SSE	0.000	1.000	2	0.005	0.980	0.015	2	0.001	0.999	2	0.000	1.000	2
27	STI	1.000	0.000	1	0.987	0.010	0.003	1	0.994	0.006	1	0.995	0.005	1
28	TA100	0.029	0.971	2	0.000	1.000	0.000	2	0.007	0.993	2	0.005	0.995	2
29	S&P/TSX	0.131	0.869	2	0.014	0.909	0.077	2	0.008	0.992	2	0.004	0.996	2
30	TSEC	0.039	0.961	2	0.011	0.937	0.052	2	0.005	0.995	2	0.002	0.998	2

The obtained value of w_1 is 0.29 for GARCH-FcMdC, 0.10 for GARCH-E-FcMdC, GARCH-NC-FcMdC, GARCH-Tr-FcMdC showing higher variability for the unconditional volatility component.

Due to the values of w_1, the clusters are identified mainly on the basis of the time-varying volatility. In particular, cluster 1 includes time series with low values of uv and high values of tvv.

In the GARCH-NC-FcMdC model indices 8 (EGX30) and 14 (IPSA) have the highest membership in the noise cluster. In the GARCH-Tr-FcMdC model the indices trimmed are 8 and 14. Then, GARCH-NC-FcMdC and GARCH-Tr-FcMdC identify the Egyptian index EGX30 and the Chilean index IPSA as outliers. The outlier EGX30 shows a strong membership to the noise cluster, while the membership degree of the outlier index IPSA is lighter. Index EGX30 is an outlier as it has very low value for the time-varying volatility, while IPSA has a high value for time-varying volatility.

Indexes 8 and 14 are assigned to clusters 2 and 1 in the models GARCH-FcMdC and GARCH-E-FcMdC, but in GARCH-E-FcMdC with a lower membership, thus not affecting the value of the cluster validity index.

In GARCH-E-FcMdC the medoids are (24, 13) in GARCH-NC-FcMdC, GARCH-Tr-FcMdC (24, 18); in GARCH-FcMdC (12, 26). As for GARCH-FcMdC, the medoids are influenced by the presence of index 8; in fact index 26 has a lower value of tvv with respect to indices 13 or 18. As a consequence indices 2, 6, 7, 20 and 21 move to the other cluster for the reason that they are too far from index 26. Furthermore, beside index 8, also indices 16 and 19 have low membership to the related cluster as the higher value of w_1 leads to considering also the high value of uv as anomalous.

With regards to crisp clustering, the crisp version of GARCH-NC-FcMdC assigns to cluster 3 also indices 5, 16 and 19 beside 8 and 14, due to the higher value of w_1 (higher weight to uv).

7.7 Generalized extreme value distributions

Scotto et al. (2010) proposed a time series clustering approach based on a combination of extreme value theory and Bayesian methodology for the analysis of regional variability of sea-level extremes. The tide gauge records are clustered using hierarchical methods on the basis of predictive distributions of 25-, 50- and 100-year projections. They used Bayesian methods to estimate the parameters of location, scale and shape of generalized extreme value (GEV) distribution.

The generalized extreme value (GEV) distribution is a family of continuous probability distributions developed within extreme value theory to combine the Gumbel, Fréchet and Weibull families, also known as Type I, II and III extreme value distributions, respectively. As a result of the extreme value theorem, the GEV distribution is the limiting distribution of normalized maxima of a sequence of independent and identically distributed random variables. Hence, the GEV distribution is used as an approximation to model the maxima of long finite sequences of random variables. The GEV distribution has the following form:

$$G(x) = \exp\left\{-\left[1 + \xi\left(\frac{x-\mu}{\sigma}\right)\right]^{-\frac{1}{\xi}}\right\}, \qquad (7.39)$$

defined on $\{x : 1 + \xi(\frac{x-\mu}{\sigma}) > 0\}$ where $-\infty < \mu < \infty$, $\sigma > 0$, and $-\infty < \xi < \infty$. The three parameters μ, σ and ξ are the location, scale and shape parameters, respectively. The shape parameter determines the three extreme value types. When $\xi < 0$, $\xi > 0$ or $\xi = 0$, the GEV distribution is the negative Weibull, Fréchet and Gumbel distribution, respectively. This is assumed to be the case by taking the limit of Eq. (7.39) as $\xi \to 0$. For maxima of m years, the log-likelihood function for the annual maxima is given by

$$
\begin{aligned}
\ell(\mu, \sigma, \xi) =\ & -m\log(\sigma) - (1 + 1/\xi)\sum_{i=1}^{m}\log\left[1 + \xi\left(\frac{x_i - \mu}{\sigma}\right)\right] \\
& -\sum_{i=1}^{m}\left[1 + \xi\left(\frac{x_i - \mu}{\sigma}\right)\right]^{-1/\xi},
\end{aligned}
\qquad (7.40)
$$

provided $1 + \xi \left(\frac{x_i - \mu}{\sigma} \right) > 0$ for $i = 1, 2, \ldots, m$. The expression in Eq. (7.40) is valid for $\xi \neq 0$. For $\xi = 0$, the log-likelihood function for the annual maxima is given by

$$\ell(\mu, \sigma) = -m \log(\sigma) - \sum_{i=1}^{m} \left(\frac{x_i - \mu}{\sigma} \right) - \sum_{i=1}^{m} \exp \left[- \left(\frac{x_i - \mu}{\sigma} \right) \right]. \quad (7.41)$$

The above log-likelihood expression presents a difficulty in extreme value analysis when the number of extreme events is small. This is particularly severe when the method of maxima over fixed intervals is used. As mentioned in Coles (2001), a possible solution is to consider the r-largest values over fixed intervals.

The number of largest values per year, r, should be chosen carefully since small values of it will produce likelihood estimators with high variance, whereas large values of r will produce biased estimates. In practice, r is selected as large as possible, subject to adequate model diagnostics. The validity of the models can be checked through the application of graphical methods, in particular, the probability plot, the quantile plot and the return level plot. For further details, see Coles (2001) and the references therein.

The implications of a fitted extreme value model are usually made with reference to extreme quantiles. By inversion of the GEV distribution function, the quantile, x_p, for a specified exceedance probability p is

$$x_p = \mu - \frac{\sigma}{\xi} \left[1 - (-\log(1 - p)^{-\xi}) \right] \text{ for } \xi \neq 0, \quad (7.42)$$

and

$$x_p = \mu - \sigma \log[-\log(1 - p)] \text{ for } \xi = 0. \quad (7.43)$$

x_p is referred to as the return level associated with a return period $1/p$. It is expected to be exceeded by the annual maximum in any particular year with probability p.

Maharaj et al. (2016) conducted a similar study to cluster analyze Spanish temperature time series but using as features the traditional parameter estimates of location, scale and shape, obtained from fitting the generalized extreme value (GEV) distribution to the block maxima and block minima of the series. They used non-hierarchical methods of clustering, namely, the c-means and c-medoids. Validation of the cluster solutions using the k-nearest neighbour approach in the application revealed that the block maxima and minima could be better separation features than the GEV estimates. However, they suggest an advantage of using GEV estimates as clustering features is that return level statements can be made about long-term maxima and minima which, in the case of applying this to real temperature time series may have policy implications in dealing with long-term extreme temperatures. Their simulation studies revealed that the GEV estimates of location, scale and shape as well as the block maxima and minima are good separation features for clustering temperature-type time series in general.

D'Urso et al. (2017a) extended the GEV-approach of Maharaj et al. (2016) to fuzzy clustering of seasonal time series. By considering the time-varying location, scale and slope parameters of the GEV distribution, they proposed new generalized fuzzy clustering procedures taking into account weights, and the derived iterative solutions based on the GEV parameter estimators. Simulation studies conducted to evaluate the methods revealed good performance.

Application 7.3 D'Urso et al. (2017a) applied fuzzy clustering to a set of daily sea-level time series from around the coast of Australia for the period January 1993 to December 2012. Sea levels collected at 17 tide gauge stations have been obtained from the research quality database of the University of Hawaii Sea Level Centre (UHSLC). The measurement of sea levels are with reference to the zero point of the respective tide benchmarks. Refer to the UHSCL database for more details about these sea level series. Table 7.4 lists the tide gauge stations, their coastal directions, latitudes and longitudes.

TABLE 7.4: Tide gauge stations.

Coastal Direction	Tide Gauge Site	Latitude	Longitude
N	Booby Island	-10.600	141.920
SE	Brisbane	-27.367	153.167
NW	Broome	-18.001	122.219
S	Burnie	-41.052	145.907
NE	Cape Fergusen	-19.283	147.067
NW	Carnarvon	-24.900	13.650
NW	Cocos Island	-34.018	151.112
N	Darwin	-12.467	130.850
SW	Esperance	-33.871	121.895
SW	Freemantle	32.050	115.733
SW	Hillarys	-31.798	115.745
S	Portland	38.343	141.613
S	Spring Bay	-42.546	147.933
SE	Sydney	-33.850	151.233
S	Thevenard	-32.149	133.641
NE	Townsville	-19.270	147.060
N	Wyndham	-15.450	128.100

A report by the Department of Climate Change, Commonwealth of Australia (2009) provides findings of the first national assessment of the risks of climate change on Australia's coastal areas. In particular, the report discusses the possible impact of rising sea levels on these coastal areas in the coming decades. The aim of this application is to determine if the fuzzy clustering methods can group together time series of similar sea levels in a meaningful way and if one or more series could belong to more than one group. Figure 7.5 shows sea level series from the tide gauges sites. The seasonal patterns in the

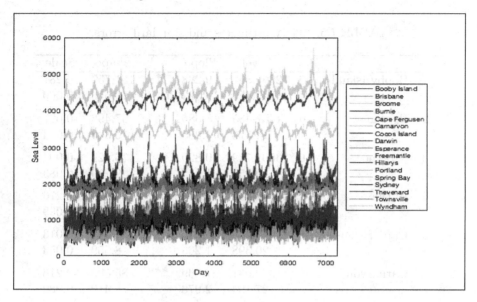

FIGURE 7.5: Daily sea level series.

series are apparent with the Darwin and Wyndham displaying very higher sea levels, and Portland and Freemantle displaying much lower sea levels. Most of these series display gentle slopes.

It should be noted that the GEV distribution with constant location should be fitted to block maxima or the set of r-largest order statistics that are stationary. Since there is a large amount of daily data, fitting the GEV distribution to annual maxima will result in the loss of useful information. Hence, the GEV distribution is fitted to the set of r largest order statistics for each year over the 20 years of data. Since most of the series are not stationary, the trend of each series is also modelled by fitting the GEV distribution with a time-varying location parameter. The appropriate value of r is based on the goodness of fit of the model which is achieved by examining diagnostic plots, namely the residual probability and quantile plots. The fit is considered to be reasonable if the points are close to the diagonal in the plots. Refer to Coles (2001) for more details. Also refer to D'Urso et al. (2017a) for details on how the r-largest observations within each year are extracted.

Table 7.5 shows the estimates of location (made up of level and slope), shape and scale with standard errors (below each estimate), obtained from fitting the GEV distribution to the set of the r-largest order statistics for each of the series.

It can be observed from Table 7.5, with the exception of the series from the tide gauge sites of Sydney and Thevenard, the slopes of the other sea level series are significantly different from zero at either the 5% (**) or 1% (***) levels. All the shape parameter estimates are greater than -0.5 which is

TABLE 7.5: AGEV estimates and standard errors.

		r	Level	Slope		Shape	Scale
1	Booby Island	6	2999.858	9.288	**	151.757	-0.287
			49.450	3.823		10.673	0.060
2	Brisbane	6	1457.435	5.685	***	57.492	-0.027
			14.576	0.985		6.343	0.074
3	Broome	6	3601.749	10.820	***	76.421	-0.004
			19.255	1.245		9.210	0.083
4	Burnie	7	2184.704	3.103	**	50.079	-0.270
			15.155	1.163		3.958	0.059
5	Cape Fergusen	8	1971.479	6.332	***	87.444	-0.013
			20.398	1.269		8.559	0.053
6	Carnarvon	5	1360.031	7.869	***	85.589	-0.216
			27.194	2.076		8.410	0.089
7	Cocos Island	10	1023.560	7.734	***	50.005	-0.401
			15.364	1.205		4.111	0.062
8	Darwin	10	4360.564	11.090	***	71.560	-0.128
			21.287	1.632		7.639	0.088
9	Esperance	7	1145.650	5.839	***	79.500	-0.195
			23.293	1.719		8.826	0.091
10	Freemantle	7	1154.500	7.005	***	84.448	-0.236
			26.046	1.967		6.999	0.064
11	Hillarys	8	1036.351	10.496	***	85.707	-0.212
			24.795	1.847		7.345	0.061
12	Portland	10	919.408	3.706	**	67.175	-0.305
			19.930	1.539		5.072	0.054
13	Spring Bay	7	1424.784	4.039	***	51.359	-0.208
			14.999	1.111		4.535	0.067
14	Sydney	4	1205.972	1.264		44.063	-0.364
			17.343	1.368		3.312	0.080
15	Thevenard	10	1697.502	3.926		95.554	-0.453
			33.716	2.754		9.819	0.078
16	Townsville	8	2225.723	5.558	***	87.471	-0.031
			21.184	1.371		7.838	0.046
17	Wyndham	10	4979.650	8.366	***	141.367	-0.102
			34.633	2.229		13.060	0.054

the range within which the maximum likelihood estimates will have the usual asymptotic properties (Coles, 2001).

Fuzzy c-means and fuzzy c-medoids methods were first applied to the GEV estimates to determine the appropriate number of clusters using a number of optimal fuzzy cluster validity indices which were discussed in Section 4.3. For all of the indices under consideration it was found that a 2-cluster solution appeared to be the most appropriate when m, the parameter of fuzziness, was set to 2 or 1.8. Note that $1.5 < m < 2.5$, is an acceptable range for producing fuzzy clusters (Bezdek , 1981). Table 7.6 shows the values of these indices for 2, 3 and 4 clusters for $m = 2$ for both the fuzzy c-means and fuzzy c-medoids methods.

TABLE 7.6: Indices to determine optimal number of fuzzy clusters.

		#clus = 2	#clus = 3	#clus = 4
Fuzzy c-means : $m = 2$				
Partition Coefficient	PC	**0.914**	0.859	0.860
Partition Entropy	PE	**0.156**	0.261	0.290
Modified Partition Coefficient	MPC	**0.829**	0.789	0.813
Silhouette	SIL	**0.873**	0.787	0.813
Fuzzy Silhouette	SIL.F	**0.904**	0.835	0.845
Fuzzy c-medoids: $m = 2$				
Partition Coefficient	PC	**0.896**	0.859	0.778
Partition Entropy	PE	**0.181**	0.261	0.424
Modified Partition Coefficient	MPC	**0.792**	0.788	0.704
Silhouette	SIL	**0.873**	0.787	0.638
Fuzzy Silhouette	SIL.F	**0.889**	0.832	0.671

Tables 7.7 and 7.8 show the 2-cluster solutions for fuzzy c-means and c-medoids as well as the fuzzy weighed c-means and c-medoids methods for $m = 2$ and the equivalent hard cluster membership. A time series belongs to a particular hard cluster if its membership degrees are the highest for that cluster. Table 7.8 also shows the weights associated with the level, slope, scale and shape which contributed to producing the weighted fuzzy cluster solutions.

All four methods produce the same cluster solution and it is clear, from the weights obtained from the weighted fuzzy cluster methods (as shown in Table 7.8), that the level parameter estimate is the dominating clustering feature. Table 7.9 shows clusters with the estimated location (level and slope), shape and scale parameters. Cluster 1 is associated with high sea levels while Cluster 2 is associated with lower sea levels and this is apparent from Table 7.10 which shows the mean, maximum and minimum location values for each of the clusters.

While most of the series generally have low fuzzy membership in a cluster other than the hard cluster they belong to, for all methods except the fuzzy

TABLE 7.7: Unweighted fuzzy cluster solutions.

	Fuzzy c-means			Fuzzy c-medoids		
	Cluster 1	Cluster 2	Hard Cluster	Cluster 1	Cluster 2	Hard Cluster
Booby Island	*0.671*	*0.329*	1	0.880	0.120	1
Brisbane	0.000	1.000	2	0.002	0.998	2
Broome	0.950	0.050	1	1.000	0.000	1
Burnie	0.135	0.865	2	0.253	0.747	2
Cape Fergusen	0.061	0.939	2	0.123	0.877	2
Carnarvon	0.001	0.999	2	0.000	1.000	2
Cocos Island	0.017	0.983	2	0.017	0.983	2
Darwin	0.992	0.008	1	0.940	0.060	1
Esperance	0.009	0.991	2	0.008	0.992	2
Freemantle	0.009	0.991	2	0.007	0.993	2
Hillarys	0.016	0.984	2	0.016	0.984	2
Portland	0.025	0.975	2	0.026	0.974	2
Spring Bay	0.000	1.000	2	0.001	0.999	2
Sydney	0.006	0.994	2	0.004	0.996	2
Thevenard	0.012	0.988	2	0.030	0.970	2
Townsville	0.153	0.847	2	0.284	0.716	2
Wyndham	0.942	0.058	1	0.873	0.127	1

c-medoids method, the series associated with Booby Island clearly has fuzzy membership in both clusters. It is also evident from its level estimate (in Table 7.8) why this would be the case. Furthermore, it can be observed from the daily sea-level series in Figure 7.4 that the Booby Island series is clearly between the very high and very low sea levels. It should be noted that two of the high sea level series in Cluster 1 (Darwin and Wyndham) as well as the series with fuzzy membership in both clusters (Booby Island) are from tide gauge sites on the north coast of Australia, while the other high sea level series in Cluster 1(Broome) is on the northwest coast.

Figure 7.6 shows the results obtained by means of the weighted fuzzy c-medoids method. In particular the scatterplot (a) depicts the membership degrees of each time series in the two clusters, the bar chart (b) shows the weights obtained for each feature of the GEV distributions in the clustering process and in the violin plot (c) the different structural characteristics of the two clusters are shown with respect to the features of the GEV distributions. The results shown in the violin plot corroborate the choice of the clusters and the fuzzy nature of some of the series.

Figure 7.7 shows the GEV density function for each of the sets of r-largest order statistics under consideration. The broken-line density curves towards the right-hand side of the x-axis are those associated with Cluster 1 (mostly higher sea levels), and the solid line density curves towards the left-hand side are those associated with Cluster 2 (lower sea levels). Both the separation of Clusters 1 and 2 as well as the fuzzy nature of the series associated with

TABLE 7.8: Weighted fuzzy cluster solutions.

	Fuzzy weighted c-means			Fuzzy weighted c-medoids		
	Cluster 1	Cluster 2	Hard Cluster	Cluster 1	Cluster 2	Hard Cluster
Booby Island	*0.697*	*0.303*	1	*0.548*	*0.452*	1
Brisbane	0.026	0.974	2	0.037	0.963	2
Broome	0.935	0.065	1	0.700	0.300	1
Burnie	0.136	0.864	2	0.130	0.870	2
Cape Fergusen	0.102	0.898	2	0.100	0.900	2
Carnarvon	0.016	0.984	2	0.018	0.982	2
Cocos Island	0.041	0.959	2	0.047	0.953	2
Darwin	0.972	0.028	1	0.861	0.139	1
Esperance	0.010	0.990	2	0.000	1.000	2
Freemantle	0.015	0.985	2	0.006	0.994	2
Hillarys	0.062	0.938	2	0.061	0.939	2
Portland	0.031	0.969	2	0.023	0.977	2
Spring Bay	0.013	0.987	2	0.026	0.974	2
Sydney	0.054	0.946	2	0.078	0.922	2
Thevenard	0.058	0.942	2	0.090	0.910	2
Townsville	0.181	0.819	2	0.148	0.852	2
Wyndham	0.925	0.075	1	1.000	0.000	1
	Weights			**Weights**		
	level	0.547		level	0.440	
	slope	0.173		slope	0.226	
	scale	0.157		scale	0.162	
	shape	0.123		shape	0.172	

TABLE 7.9: Parameters estimates according to the cluster solutions.

	Level	Slope	Scale	Shape	Hard Cluster
Booby Island	2999.858	9.288	151.757	-0.287	1
Broome	3601.749	10.820	76.421	-0.004	1
Darwin	4360.564	11.090	71.560	-0.128	1
Wyndham	4979.650	8.366	141.367	-0.102	1
Brisbane	1457.435	5.685	57.492	-0.027	2
Burnie	2184.704	3.103	50.079	-0.270	2
Cape Ferguson	1971.479	6.332	87.444	-0.013	2
Carnarvon	1360.031	7.869	85.589	-0.216	2
Cocos Island	1023.560	7.734	50.005	-0.401	2
Esperance	1145.650	5.839	79.500	-0.195	2
Freemantle	1154.500	7.005	84.448	-0.236	2
Hillarys	1036.351	10.496	85.707	-0.212	2
Portland	919.408	3.706	67.175	-0.305	2
Spring Bay	1424.784	4.039	51.359	-0.208	2
Sydney	1205.972	1.264	44.063	-0.364	2
Thevenard	1697.502	3.926	95.554	-0.453	2
Townsville	2225.723	5.558	87.471	-0.031	2

TABLE 7.10: Means, maxima and minima of the 2-cluster solution.

	Mean	Maximum	Minimum
Cluster 1	4269	5126	3269
Cluster 2	1556	2323	909

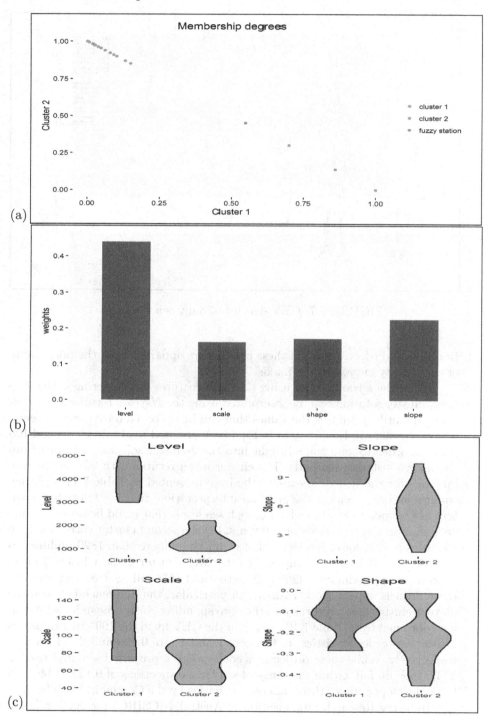

FIGURE 7.6: (a) Scatter plot (b) Bar chart (c) Violin plot.

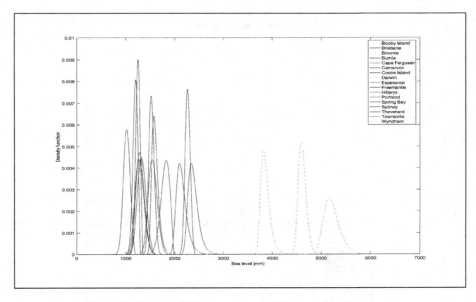

FIGURE 7.7: GEV density of daily sea level series.

Booby Island (dotted line) in these clusters are apparent from the positioning of the density curves on the x-axis.

One of the advantages of using the GEV features for clustering is that the fuzzy cluster solutions can be interpreted using the N-years returns levels (extreme quantiles), that is, the values that can be exceeded once every N-years. The expressions in Eq. (7.42) or in Eq. (7.43) are used to obtain 25, 50 and 100 years in order to gain some insight into the 2-cluster solution obtained from the fuzzy clustering methods. The cluster mean returns with 95% confidence intervals for the fuzzy c-means method are presented in Table 7.11 and they confirm and complement the previous interpretation, that is, (1) the first cluster corresponds to localities having high sea levels that could be no more than 4638 millimetres in periods of 100 years, (2) the second cluster corresponds to localities having lower sea levels that could be no more than 1820 millimetres in periods of 100 years. Compared to the 2012 Cluster 1 and Cluster 2 mean maxima of approximately 4269 millimetres and 1556 millimetres, respectively, these returns appear to be realistic. In particular, the difference between the 25 year cluster mean returns and the corresponding cluster mean location values (obtained from Table 7.10) based on the GEV fit to the 1993 to 2012 series of r-largest order statistics, in Clusters 1 and 2, are 0.198 and 0.171 metres, respectively. While these projections correspond to projected sea level rises in 2037, they do fall within the range of sea level projections of 0.132, 0.146 and 0.200 developed under three different scenarios by the Commonwealth Science and Industry Research Organisation of Australia (CSIRO) for 2030, relative to 1990. Refer to the 2009 Australian Government Department of Climate Change report.

Similar results were obtained for returns using the other fuzzy clustering methods.

TABLE 7.11: Cluster mean maxima and 25, 50 and 100 year mean returns levels.

Cluster	1	2
2012 Cluster Mean Maxima	4268.750	1556.154
25-yr	4466.939	1726.870
95% C.I.	4413.471	1691.560
	4520.407	1762.179
50-yr	4515.189	1752.873
95% C.I.	4451.737	1714.469
	4578.642	1791.278
100-yr	4559.439	1776.148
95% C.I.	4481.181	1732.385
	4637.696	1819.911

7.8 Other model-based approaches

Kalpakis et al. (2001) examined the clustering of time series generated from ARIMA time series using cepstral coefficients derived from AR(k) models fitted to the series as the clustering variables. The cepstrum of a time series is the spectrum of the logarithm of the spectrum. They used the *partition around medoids* (PAM) method with various similarity measures for the purpose of clustering the time series.

Ramoni et al. (2002) proposed a Bayesian algorithm for clustering discrete-valued time series that were clustered in an attempt to discover the most probable set of generating processes. The task of clustering is regarded as a Bayesian model selection problem. The similarity between two estimated Markov chain matrices was measured as an average of the Kullback-Liebler distance between corresponding rows in the matrices. They also presented a Bayesian clustering algorithm for multivariate time series.

Tarpey and Kinateder (2003) examined the clustering of functional curves and derived results for cluster means and distances for functional Gaussian distributions. In applications, they used a Fourier basis to represent the curves and used least squares to estimate the Fourier coefficients. They applied the k-means procedure for clustering the curves.

Boets et al. (2005) proposed a clustering process based on a cepstral distance between stochastic models. Savvides et al. (2008) used cepstral coefficients which were estimated from a semi-parametric model to cluster biological time series. They have shown in simulation studies that clustering time series with cepstral coefficients generally outperforms that with normalized periodogram ordinates and the logarithm of the normalized periodogram ordinates estimated from these semi-parametric models.

Corduas and Piccolo (2008) derived the asymptotic distribution of the squared distance between coefficients of trucated AR models fitted to a pair of stationary time series (AR distance). Then based on the asymptotic distribution of this truncated AR approximation, they proposed a hypothesis test to determine whether two time series originate from processes with the same temporal structure. This was done such that the original matrix of squared AR distances could be transformed into a binary matrix where the (i, j)th entry is one if the squared distance between the i-th and j-th models is significant and zero otherwise. As a result, clusters of time series could be found by reordering this binary matrix into an approximate block diagonal form.

Vilar et al. (2009) proposed a nonparametric method for clustering time series using the trends of time series estimated via local poylnomial regression models. They used a test statistic based on the the Cramer-von-Mises type functional distances between kernel-type estimators of unknown regression functions. For every pair of series, the p-value of the test was obtained and these p-values were used in standard hierarchical clustering procedures. They also proposed a number of other test statistics made up of nonparametric estimators and again the p-values of these tests were used in standard hierarchical clustering procedures.

D'Urso et al. (2013a) proposed a fuzzy c-medoids approach to cluster time series based on autoregressive estimates of models fitted to the time series. They demonstrated that this approach performs well under different simulation scenarios. By means of two applications, they also showed the usefulness of this clustering approach in air pollution monitoring, by considering air pollution time series, namely, CO , CO_2 and NO time series monitored on world and urban scales. In particular, they showed that, by considering in the clustering process the autoregressive representation of these air pollution time series, they were able to detect possible information redundancy in the monitoring networks. This has the capacity of decreasing the number of monitoring stations, to reduce the monitoring costs and then to increase the monitoring efficiency of the networks.

Fruhwirth-Schnatter and Kaufmann (2008) proposed clustering multiple time series using finite-mixture models. They assume that K hidden clusters are present whereby all time series within a certain cluster may be characterized by the same econometric model and information from all time series in a cluster can be used for estimation. Model-based clustering of time series may be based on many different classes of finite mixture models. In the case of a panel of stationary time series, where the main goal is forecasting a few steps ahead, finite mixtures of AR(p) models may be applied to capture the dynamics of each time series. Extensions of this include clustering based on finite mixtures of dynamic regression models or clustering based on finite mixtures of random-effects models, where unobserved heterogeneity is present within each group. Fruhwirth-Schnatter and Kaufmann (2008) estimated the cluster models of time series simultaneously with group-specific Bayesian Markov chain Monte Carlo simulation methods. Using a simulation study, they assessed efficiency gains of their methodology in estimation and forecasting relative to overall pooling of time series, and they applied their methodology to a panel of quarterly industrial production series of 21 OECD countries.

Pamminger and Fruhwirth-Schnatter (2010) discussed two approaches for model-based clustering of categorical time series based on time-homogenous first order Markov chains. One was Markov chain clustering, in which the individual transition probabilities are fixed to a transition matrix specific to a group. The other was a new approach called Dirichlet multinomial clustering, where the rows of the individual transition matrices deviate from the cluster means and follow a Dirichlet distribution with unknown cluster-specific hyperparameters. Estimation was undertaken through Markov chain Monte Carlo and various criteria such as the approximate weight of evidence criteria (AWE) (Banfield and Raftery, 1993) and classical likelihood criteria (CLC) (Biernacki et al., 2000) were applied to select the number of clusters. They applied these methods to a panel of Austrian wage mobility data and found it led to interesting segmentation of the Austrian labour market.

In a panel data modelling context, Sarafidis and Weber (2015) proposed a partially heterogeneous framework for the clustering of multiple time series of the same length based on the assumption that when the population of cross-sectional units is grouped into clusters, the slope homogeneity is maintained only within clusters. Their determination of the number of clusters and corresponding partitions is based on information criteria. The k-means algorithm was adopted to obtain cluster membership. Using a simulation study, they assessed the finite sample properties of their method and applied it to a random sample of 551 US banks.

Some other model-based clustering techniques have been proposed by Longford and D'Urso (2012) on mixtures of autoregressions with an improper component for panel data, D'Urso et al. (2013c) on fuzzy clustering of noisy time series by the autoregressive metric, D'Urso et al. (2015) on the use of a robust autoregressive metric, and Disegna et al. (2017), on copula-based fuzzy clustering of spatial time series.

8

Other time series clustering approaches

CONTENTS

8.1 Introduction

There is a vast array of various other methods that have been proposed for time series clustering over the past three decades. Many of them have been used in data mining and several are machine learning approaches. We discuss some of these methods in this chapter.

8.2 Hidden Markov Models

A Markov model is a probabilistic process over a finite set, $S_1, ..., S_k$, usually called its states. Each state-transition generates a character from the alphabet of the process. Of interest are matters such as the probability of a given state coming up next, $P(X_t = S_i)$, and this may depend on the prior history of t-1. A hidden Markov model (HMM) is simply a Markov model in which the states are hidden.

Oates et al. (1999) proposed a hybrid time series clustering algorithm that uses dynamic time warping and hidden Markov model induction. The two methods complement each other in that DTW produces a rough initial clustering solution and HMM removes from these clusters time series that do not belong to them. However, one downside of HMM is that it can sometimes remove series that should belong to a cluster along with series that do not belong to the clusters. Their algorithm appeared to work well with artificial data.

Jebara et al. (2007) proposed a method to cluster time series that couples non-parametric spectral clustering with parametric hidden Markov models. They indicate that HMMs add some beneficial structural and parametric assumptions such as Markov properties and hidden state variables which are useful for clustering. They showed that using probabilistic pairwise kernel estimates between parametric models provided improved experimental results for clustering and visualization of real and synthetic data sets.

Ghassempour et al. (2014) proposed an approach to cluster time series based on hidden Markov models where they first map each time series into an HMM and then proceed to cluster the HMMs with a method based on the distance matrix. They tested their approach on a simulated, but realistic, data set of 1,255 trajectories of individuals of age 45 and over, on a synthetic validation set with known clustering structure, and on a smaller set of 268 trajectories extracted from a longitudinal Health and Retirement Survey.

8.3   Support vector clustering

Support vectoring clustering (SVC) algorithms have arisen from support vector machines which are supervised learning models with learning algorithms used to analyse data used for classification. Refer to Vapnik (1995) for details on support vector machines. Support vector clustering was introduced by Ben-Hur et al. (2001). It is closely related to classification and density estimation where a set of hyperplanes contain data points with similar underlying distributions. SVC is carried out in two stages. The first stage involves describing the clusters, namely, where the minimal enclosing hypersphere of the data is computed by finding the support vectors which define the cluster boundaries and it uses a similar constraint optimisation approach as that of support vector machines. During the second stage, clusters are labelled such that patterns are assigned to clusters. The two stages are carried out iteratively in order to tune the hyper-parameters of SVC.

Boeking et al. (2015) discussed two ways through which SVC can be used for time series data. The first approach involves pre-processing of the raw time series before using a standard kernel function with SVC, while the second approach uses similarity measures such as dynamic time warping (DTW) which recognise distinctive traits of the time series. Based on their experimentation, using global alignment and triangular global alignment kernels introduced by Cuturi et al. (2007) for time series, they concluded that SVC with these kernels are capable of distinguishing differences between cyclic patterns and normal patterns as well as differences between upward and downward trends, hence enabling useful cluster identification.

However, designing the clustering method with specific kernels involves the use of a similarity measure, with the condition that kernels are positive semi-definite (PSD). Hence, Gudmundsson et al. (2008) proposed an alternative approach which places no restrictions on the similarity measure used to construct a set of inputs. It allows each case to be represented by its similarity to all cases in the set. The conventional SVM is then applied to the transformed data. They investigate the feasibility of the similarity based approach for DTW by applying the method to a large set of time-series classification problems.

8.4 Self-Organising Maps

In the literature different Self-Organzing Maps (SOMs) for classifying time series have been proposed. For instance, D'Urso and De Giovanni (2008) suggested classifying time series by adopting a SOM with a variant of the distance measures in Eq. (5.1) and Eq. (5.2) in Chapter 5.

D'Urso et al. (2014) proposed a SOM for clustering time series. The SOM takes into account a composite wavelet-based information of the multivariate time series by adding to the information connected to the wavelet variance, namely, the influence of variability of individual univariate components of the multivariate time series across scales, the information associated with wavelet correlation, represented by the interaction between pairs of univariate components of the multivariate time series at each scale, and then suitably tuning the combination of these pieces of information (D'Urso et al., 2014). SOM has also been used by Wang et al. (2006) for clustering time series. We now present the Wavelet-based SOM proposed by D'Urso et al. (2014).

8.4.1 Wavelet-based Self-Organizing Map (W-SOM)

The SOM is a lattice of L neurons (units). Each neuron l is characterized by a location in the lattice (coordinate) r_l dependent on the configuration (linear or rectangular) and an initial P-dimensional reference vector $\mathbf{m}_l = (m_{l1}, m_{l2}, \ldots, m_{lP})$. The SOM produces a mapping of a set of I P-dimensional input vectors $\boldsymbol{\xi}_i = (\xi_{i1}, \xi_{i2}, \ldots, \xi_{iP})$ onto the neurons of the lattice. In Figure 8.1 a linear (left) and rectangular (right) lattice of neurons is displayed.

The mapping is realized as follows. At ordering step s the reference vector m_c of neuron c (winner or best matching unit, *bmu*) that matches best in any metric (Kohonen 2001) the input vector $\xi_i(s)$ is selected. The reference vectors of the winning neuron and of its neighbour units adapt to represent the input vector according to the following updating rule (Kohonen 1995):

$$\boldsymbol{\mu}_l(s+1) = \alpha(s)\boldsymbol{\xi}_i(s) + (1 - \alpha(s))\boldsymbol{\mu}_l(s) \quad \text{if } l \in N_c$$

$$\boldsymbol{\mu}_l(s+1) = \boldsymbol{\mu}_l(s) \qquad \text{otherwise}$$

(8.1)

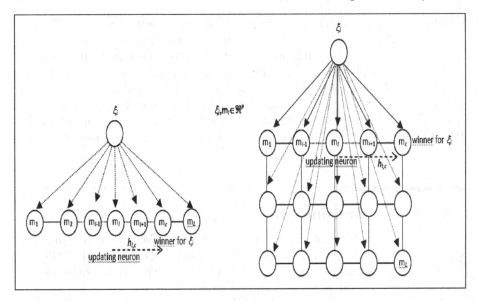

FIGURE 8.1: A P-dimensional input vector mapped to a linear (left) and rectangular (right) lattice of neurons.

where $\alpha(s)$ is the learning rate and $N_c = N_c(s)$ is the topological neighbourhood of $\mathbf{m}_c$. The number of the units learned can be expressed in terms of a neighbourhood function h which is a decreasing function of the distance of the units from the winning neuron on the map lattice. In this case the reference vectors are changed according to the following updating rule:

$$\mathbf{m}_c(s+1) = h_{l,c}(s)\,\boldsymbol{\xi}_i(s) + (1 - h_{l,c})\,\mathbf{m}_c(s) \tag{8.2}$$

where $h_{l,c}(s) = \alpha(s)h'_{l,c}(s)$ and $h'_{l,c}(s)$ measures the distance between the locations of neuron l and winner neuron c for the input vector $\boldsymbol{\xi}_i(s)$.

The neighbourhood function can be written in terms of a Gaussian function $h'_{l,c}(s) = \exp\frac{\|r_l - r_c\|^2}{2\sigma(s)^2}$ where r_l and r_c identify the locations (coordinates) of neurons l and c in the lattice and $\sigma(s)$ is the (decreasing) width of the neighbourhood. During the learning of the SOM the neurons that are topologically close in the lattice up to a certain geometric distance activate to learn something from the same input $\boldsymbol{\xi}$.

The SOMs produce a mapping of high-dimensional input data onto the units of a low-dimensional lattice that is *ordered* and *descriptive of the distribution* of the input. In fact, Kohonen (1995) claims that the randomly chosen initial values for the $\mathbf{m}_l$ gradually change to new values in a process specified by Eq. (8.1) and Eq. (8.2) such that, as $s \to \infty$, the reference vectors of the neurons $\mathbf{m}_1, \ldots, \mathbf{m}_l, \ldots, \mathbf{m}_L$ become ordered (neurons with nearest location exhibit smaller distance with respect to reference vectors), and that the probability density function of the reference vectors finally approximates some monotonic function of the probability density function $p(\boldsymbol{\xi})$ of the P-dimensional continuous random variable $\boldsymbol{\xi}$. For more detail on ordering ability, topology of the SOMs and on the probability density function of the reference vectors see D'Urso et al. (2014). The quality of learning in the SOMs is measured through the *average expected quantization error* and the *average expected distortion measure*. They are defined as:

$$\int_{R^P} d_g\left(\mathbf{m}_c, \boldsymbol{\xi}\right) p\left(\boldsymbol{\xi}\right) \qquad (8.3)$$

$$\int_{R^P} \sum_{l=1}^{L} h_{l,c}(s) d_g^2\left(\mathbf{m}_c, \boldsymbol{\xi}\right) p\left(\boldsymbol{\xi}\right) \qquad (8.4)$$

respectively, where d_g is a generalized distance function (Kohonen, 1995), $\boldsymbol{\xi} \in \mathbb{R}^p$ is the input vector, $\mathbf{m}_c$ is the reference vector closest to the input vector $\boldsymbol{\xi}$ according to d_g. The average quantization error and the average distortion measure are the sample counterpart of Eq. (8.3) and Eq. (8.4) and are defined as:

$$I^{-1} \sum_{i=1}^{I} d_g\left(\mathbf{m}_c, \boldsymbol{\xi_i}\right) \qquad (8.5)$$

$$\sum_{l=1}^{L} \sum_{i=1}^{I} h_{l,c}(s) d_g^2\left(\mathbf{m}_c, \boldsymbol{\xi_i}\right). \qquad (8.6)$$

D'Urso et al. (2014) used the SOMs for clustering time series. In order to use the SOMs for clustering and vector quantization of multivariate time series based on their wavelet representation, the winner is selected on the basis of a suitable distance measure for multivariate time series based on a wavelet representation of the time series, that is, the wavelet variance and the wavelet correlation. The proposed distance between the reference vector $\mathbf{m}_l(s)$ and the generic input vector $\mathbf{X}_i$ sorted for updating the SOM at ordering step s, $\boldsymbol{\xi}_i(s) = \mathbf{X}_i$, is the following:

$$d_W\left(\mathbf{m}_l, \mathbf{X}_i\right) = \{[a_{WV} \, d_{WV}\left(\mathbf{m}_l, \mathbf{X}_i\right)]^2 + [a_{WC} \, d_{WC}\left(\mathbf{m}_l, \mathbf{X}_i\right)]^2\}^{\frac{1}{2}} \qquad (8.7)$$

where $d_{WV}\left(\mathbf{m}_l, \mathbf{X}_i\right)$, called the *wavelet variance-based distance measure*, indicates the Euclidean distance between the multivariate time series $\mathbf{m}_l$ and $\mathbf{X}_i$ ($l = 1, \ldots, L$; $i = 1, \ldots, I$) based on the wavelet variances; $d_{WC}\left(\mathbf{m}_l, \mathbf{X}_i\right)$, called the *wavelet correlation-based distance measure*, represents the Euclidean distance between the multivariate time series $\mathbf{m}_l$ and $\mathbf{X}_i$ ($l = 1, \ldots, L$; $i = 1, \ldots, I$) based on the wavelet correlations; a_{WV}, and a_{WC} are the weights for the wavelet variance-based distance and the wavelet correlation-based distance. The average quantization error and the average distortion measure with the considered distance Eq. (8.7) turn into:

$$I^{-1} \sum_{i=1}^{I} d_W \left(\mathbf{m}_c, \boldsymbol{\xi}_i \right) \tag{8.8}$$

$$\sum_{l=1}^{L} \sum_{i=1}^{I} h_{l,c}(s) \, d_W^2 \left(\mathbf{m}_c, \boldsymbol{\xi}_i \right). \tag{8.9}$$

In order to improve the quality of learning, the value of α_{WV} and α_{WC} is determined to minimize the average distortion measure Eq. (8.9). By computing the derivative of Eq. (8.9) with respect to α_{WC} the optimum value of α_{WC} results are

$$\alpha_{WC} = \frac{\sum_{i=1}^{I} \sum_{l=1}^{L} h_{i,c}(s) \, d_{WV}^2 \left(\mathbf{m}_i, \mathbf{X}_i \right)}{\sum_{i=1}^{I} \sum_{l=1}^{L} h_{i,c} \left[d_{WC}^2 \left(\mathbf{m}_i, \mathbf{X}_i \right) + d_{WV}^2 \left(\mathbf{m}_i, \mathbf{X}_i \right) \right]}. \tag{8.10}$$

The updating rule for the reference vector $\mathbf{m}_l(s)$ when the generic input vector $\mathbf{X}_i$ is sorted for updating the SOM at ordering step s, $\boldsymbol{\xi}_i(s) = \mathbf{X}_i$, is:

$$\mathbf{m}_l(s+1) = h_{l,c}(s) \, \boldsymbol{\xi}_i(s) + (1 - h_{l,c}) \, \mathbf{m}_l(s).$$

The ordering ability of the W-SOM is measured by D'Urso et al. (2014) through analysis of the distances between the reference vectors with respect to the topology. The topology preservation ability of the W-SOMs (closest input vectors should have closest reference vectors in the W-SOMs) is measured through the Spearman correlation coefficient between the ranks of the $I(I-1)/2$ distances between the input vectors and the ranks of the distances of the reference vectors of the related closest neurons.

Application 8.1 D'Urso et al. (2014) applied the W-SOM for clustering pollutant time series collected in Rome where air quality is assessed by a monitoring network made up of 12 stations at various locations under the control of the municipality of Rome. In Italy, according to a Decree of the Ministry of the Environment, four classes of stations have been defined for monitoring urban air quality. The two classes denoted B and C could be considered as the urban classes. They are distinguished according to the traffic density of the areas involved. In particular, Class B (Arenula, Cinecittá, Magnagrecia, Preneste) refers to residential areas and Class C (Francia, Fermi, Libia, Montezemolo, Tiburtina) refers to high traffic areas and low air ventilation. One monitoring station (Ada) belongs to Class A. This station is located in an area not directly affected by urban emission sources; in particular, it is located near a park.

Therefore it will have low pollution; it should provide information about the lowest level of pollution in Rome. However, we can observe that meteorological phenomena can lead to air pollution also in this area. Finally, two monitoring stations, Castel di Guido and Tenuta del Cavaliere belong to Class

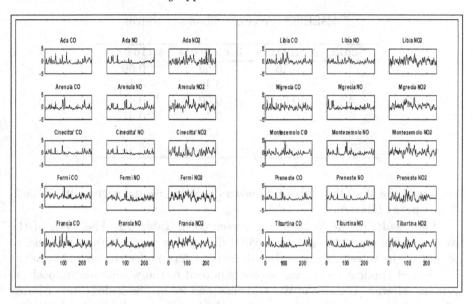

FIGURE 8.2: Standardized hourly levels of CO, NO and NO2 over a 10-day period.

D. They are areas indirectly exposed to vehicular pollution. Their utilization aims at understanding the complex photochemical phenomena that usually occur in Rome and in the suburban areas around Rome. The stations detect the following pollutant concentrations: CO, SO2, O3, NO, NO2, NOX, PM10 (amount of inhalable dust, that is, atmospheric particles, the aerodynamic diameter of which is lower than 10 mm). In the considered application hourly levels of air pollution in Rome over a three month (October to December 2000) period are considered. Ten stations over twelve are considered due to the lack of data related to the stations Castel di Guido and Tenuta del Cavaliere. Three indicators of pollution - carbon monoxide CO, nitrogen oxide NO and nitrogen dioxide NO2 - over ten have been considered due to the large amounts of missing data records for the other pollutants. The standardized hourly levels of CO, NO and NO2 over a 10-day period for all the locations are presented in Figure 8.2. The time series consist of T=1976 time points. The wavelet variances and correlations have been generated using the SYM8 filter for 7 scales down to 2 scales giving rise for each station to a multivariate variance/correlation vector of the wavelet coefficients with dimension (number of scales*3+ number of scales*3). The highest number of scales has been selected according to Percival and Walden (2000).

The aim of the application is to determine the characteristics of air pollution of the locations on the basis of the data recorded by the monitoring network. The W-SOM with linear topology has been run considering 2, 3, 4 neurons. The clustering is obtained assigning each station to the best matching

TABLE 8.1: Average silhouette widths.

Scale	2 clusters	3 clusters	4 clusters
2	0.56	0.56	0.50
3	0.50	0.46	0.40
4	0.56	0.50	0.48
5	0.56	0.56	0.45
6	0.55	0.55	0.44
7	0.55	0.48	0.46

neuron of the W-SOM. Table 8.1 shows the average silhouette width S for 2, 3, 4 neurons (clusters).

The results of the W-SOM are presented in Table 8.2. The value of the weight of the wavelet correlation-based distance is very low (and the related weight of the wavelet variance-based distance very high), showing that in the considered application the variance component of the wavelet decomposition is more relevant. For all the W-SOM sizes and for all the scales total ordering of the reference vectors with respect to the topology is observed. The Spearman correlation coefficient shows a good level of topology preservation. The quantization error and the average distortion measure show a good level of quality of learning. The quality of learning increases at lowering the number of scales due to the reduced dimension of the data.

The classification obtained by the W-SOM and the d_W distance between the reference vectors of the topological neighbour neurons are presented in Table 8.2. To show the topological ability of the SOM the classifications into 2, 3 and 4 clusters are considered.

The classification results in terms of cluster separation and cohesion are interpreted considering the distance between the reference vectors of topological neighbour neurons and the individual silhouette values. The results are shown for 5 scales as the classifications are stable for 5, 6 and 7 scales.

In order to achieve cluster separation and cohesion the number of clusters is selected on the basis of the value of the average width S and of the analysis of the distances among reference vectors of adjacent neurons. The average silhouette widths for 2 clusters outperform the average silhouette widths for 3 and 4 clusters for all the scales. Figure 8.3 presents the clustering results and the silhouette S widths for 5 scales and 2 neurons (and related 2) W-SOM.

Considering the classification into 2 clusters and taking into account the classes A, B, C it can be concluded that, with the exception of Stations 10 and 7 that show a low individual silhouette to the related clusters, the areas monitored by the stations in Cluster 1 can be interpreted as low pollution areas, the areas monitored by the stations in Cluster 2 as high pollution areas. It should be noticed that the availability of the time series of the other pollutants could lead to a different clustering.

TABLE 8.2: Average silhouette widths.

Scale	α_{WC}		
	2 clusters	3 clusters	4 clusters
2	0.01	0.01	0.01
3	0.04	0.04	0.03
4	0.06	0.06	0.06
5	0.05	0.04	0.04
6	0.04	0.04	0.03
7	0.04	0.03	0.03

Scale	Spearman correlation coefficient		
	2 clusters	3 clusters	4 clusters
2	0.63	0.80	0.90
3	0.60	0.73	0.60
4	0.66	0.65	0.67
5	0.66	0.68	0.77
6	0.65	0.67	0.73
7	0.68	0.67	0.80

Scale	Quantization error		
	2 clusters	3 clusters	4 clusters
2	0.02	0.02	0.02
3	0.05	0.04	0.04
4	0.08	0.07	0.06
5	0.08	0.07	0.06
6	0.08	0.07	0.06
7	0.09	0.08	0.06

Scale	Average distortion measure		
	2 clusters	3 clusters	4 clusters
2	0.58	0.66	0.61
3	1.08	1.36	1.25
4	1.58	1.79	1.81
5	1.61	1.92	1.86
6	1.77	1.96	1.97
7	1.86	1.95	2.04

8.5 Other data mining algorithms

Severals algorithms based on comparing the levels of complexity of time series, i.e., measuring the level of shared information by two time series, have been

TABLE 8.3: Cluster versus SOM size (left) and d_W distance between adjacent neurons (right).

SOM size	neuron				neuron pairs		
	1	2	3	4	1,2	2,3	3,4
2	1,3,9,10	2,4,5,6,7,8			0.15		
3	1,3,9	7,10	2,4,5,6,8		0.16	0.14	
4	1,3,9	10	5,7	2,4,6,8	0.16	0.16	0.10

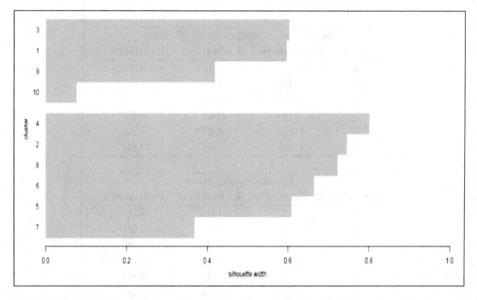

FIGURE 8.3: Clustering results and silhouette S widths for 5 scales and 2 neurons (and related 2) W-SOM.

proposed, and used to cluster time series. Compression-based dissimilarity measures (Li et al., 2004; Cilibrasi and Vitányi, 2005; Keogh et al., 2007), and permutation distribution (PDC) proposed by Brandmaier (2011) are two well-known approaches.

Part II

Supervised Approaches: Classification Techniques for Time Series

9

Feature-based approaches

CONTENTS

9.1 Introduction

Several authors have investigated ways of classifying time series using the features of the time series. Kakizawa et al. (1998) proposed spectral analysis methods which rely on the assumption that the time series under consideration are stationary; Shumway (2003) proposed methods based on time-varying spectra that are also applicable to the class of locally stationary processes introduced by Dahlhaus (1997); Sakiyama and Taniguchi (2004) have also proposed methods based on time-varying spectra for locally stationary processes. Huang et al. (2004) proposed the smooth locals exponential methodology (SLEX) methods based on Fourier-type bases using local spectral features of the time series. Maharaj and Alonso (2007, 2014) proposed classifying time series using wavelet features with discriminant analysis. In their 2007 paper, they developed a scheme for locally stationary univariate time series while in their 2014 paper, they extended this to multivariate time series.

We first provide a brief description of discriminant analysis which is used in some of the above-mentioned classification approaches.

9.2   Discriminant Analysis

In practice, a time series is known to belong to one of g populations denoted by $\Pi_1, \Pi_2, \ldots, \Pi_g$. The task is to classify the time series into one of these g populations in an optimal manner. The problem can be formulated by assuming the observed series $\mathbf{x}$ has a probability density function $f_i(\mathbf{x})$ when the observed series is from population Π_i. The space spanned by the process $\mathbf{X}$ from which $\mathbf{x}$ has been generated can be partitioned into g mutually exclusive regions $R_1, R_2, \ldots, R_g$ such that if $\mathbf{x}$ falls in to R_i, $\mathbf{x}$ is assigned to population Π_i.

The misclassification probability is the probability of classifying the observation into population Π_j when it belongs to Π_i, for $j \neq i$

$$P(j/i) = \int_{R_j} f_i(\mathbf{x})$$

Given the prior probabilities, $\pi_1, \pi_2, \ldots, \pi_g$ of belonging to one of the g groups, the total error probability is

$$P_e = \sum_{i=1}^{g} \pi_i \sum_{j \neq i} P(j/i).$$

The overall error P_e is minimized by classifying $\mathbf{x}$ into Π_i if

$$\frac{f_i(\mathbf{x})}{f_j(\mathbf{x})} > \frac{\pi_j}{\pi_i}.$$

If it is assumed that the vector $\mathbf{x}$ has a p-dimensional normal distribution with mean vector μ_j and covariance matrix Σ_j under Π_j , $j = 1, 2, \ldots, g$. Then the density is

$$f_j(\mathbf{x}) = (2\pi)^{-p/2} |\Sigma_j|^{-1/2} \exp\left\{ -\frac{1}{2}(\mathbf{x} - \mu_j)' \Sigma_j^{-1}(\mathbf{x} - \mu_j) \right\}.$$

The classifications functions can be conveniently expressed by quantities that are proportional to the logarithms of the densities

$$g_j(\mathbf{x}) = -\frac{1}{2} \ln |\Sigma_j| - \frac{1}{2}\mathbf{x}' \Sigma_j^{-1} \mathbf{x} + \mu_j' \Sigma_j^{-1} \mathbf{x} - \frac{1}{2}\mu' \Sigma_j^{-1} \mu + \ln \pi_j. \qquad (9.1)$$

Then the series $\mathbf{x}$ can be assigned to population Π_i whenever

$$g_i(\mathbf{x}) > g_j(\mathbf{x}) \qquad\qquad j \neq i, \qquad\qquad j = 1, 2, \ldots, g. \qquad (9.2)$$

If there are two groups and they have equal covariance matrices, and hence vary only in respect to their means, the discriminant function is linear, and Eq. (9.2) can be expressed in terms of the linear discriminant function.

$$D_L = g_1(\mathbf{x}) - g_2(\mathbf{x})$$
$$= (\mu_1 - \mu_2)^T \Sigma^{-1} \mathbf{x} - \tfrac{1}{2}(\mu_1 - \mu_2)^T \Sigma^{-1}(\mu_1 + \mu_2) + ln\tfrac{\pi_1}{\pi_2} \qquad (9.3)$$

If the groups have unequal covariance matrices the discriminant function is quadratic and can be expressed in terms of the quadratic discriminant function:

$$D_Q = g_1(\mathbf{x}) - g_2(\mathbf{x})$$
$$= -\tfrac{1}{2}ln\tfrac{\Sigma_1}{\Sigma_2} - \tfrac{1}{2}\mathbf{x}^T(\Sigma_1^{-1} - \Sigma_2^{-1})\mathbf{x} + (\mu_1^T\Sigma_1^{-1} - \mu_2^T\Sigma_2^{-1})\mathbf{x} + ln\tfrac{\pi_1}{\pi_2}. \qquad (9.4)$$

The performance of the sample discriminant functions can be evaluated in several ways, one of which is to calculate the apparent error rates using the results of applying the classification procedure to training samples. If n_{ij} denotes the number of observations from population Π_j classified into Π_i, the apparent error rate for group j is given by

$$\widehat{e(j)} = n_j^{-1}\sum_{i \neq j} n_{ij}, \qquad (9.5)$$

where n_j is the number of observations from population Π_j in the sample. The apparent overall error rate is given by

$$\widehat{OER} = \sum_{j=1}^{g} \hat{\pi}_j \widehat{e(j)} = n^{-1}\sum_{j=1}^{g}\sum_{i \neq j} n_{ij}, \qquad (9.6)$$

where $\hat{\pi}_j$ denotes the proportion of observations from population Π_j in the sample and $n = \sum_{j=1}^{g} n_j$.

If the training samples are not large, this procedure is biased and a resampling option such as cross-validation or the bootstrap can be employed (see, e.g., Chapter 10 of McLachlan, 1992). A simple version of cross validation is the hold-out-one technique as described by Lachenbruch and Mickey (1968). This technique holds out the observation to be classified, deriving the classification function from the remaining observations. Repeating this procedure for each member of the population Π_j in the training sample allows us to calculate the number, $n_{ij,-1}$, of observations from population Π_j classified into Π_i when this observation is left out and not used in deriving the classification rule. Then, computing Eq. (9.5) to Eq. (9.6) with $n_{ij,-1}$ instead of n_{ij} leads to better estimators of the classification error rates.

9.3 Frequency domain approaches

Many authors have adopted different versions of classifying time series by means of discriminant analysis in the frequency domain. Optimal methods have been developed for time series classification that make use of differences between multivariate means and covariance matrices. By developing a log likelihood function similar to Eq. (9.1), the log likelihood function can be expressed as

$$g_j(\mathbf{X}) = \ln \pi_j - \sum_{0 < \nu_k < \frac{1}{2}} \left[ln|f_j(\nu_k)| + \mathbf{X}^T(\nu_k)f_j^{-1}(\nu_k)\mathbf{X}(\nu_k) \right. \\ \left. - 2\mathbf{M}^T(\nu_k)f_j^{-1}(\nu_k)\mathbf{X}(\nu_k) + \mathbf{M}^T(\nu_k)f_j^{-1}(\nu_k)\mathbf{M}(\nu_k) \right] \tag{9.7}$$

where the vector discreet Fourier transforms DFTs, $\mathbf{X}(\nu_k)$, are assumed to be approximately normal with means $\mathbf{M}_j(\nu_k)$ and spectral matrices $f_j(\nu_k)$ for population Π_j at frequencies $\nu_k = \frac{k}{n}$, $k = 0, 1, ...\frac{n}{2}$ and are approximately uncorrelated at different frequencies. The periodicity of the spectral density matrix and the DFT allows for adding over $k = 0$ and $k = 1/2$. The classification rule is as in Eq. (9.2). Since in many situations it is more likely that the covariance matrices are different and the means are equal, it will be useful to use the Whittle approximation of the log likelikhood of the form

$$ln\, p_j(\mathbf{X}) = \sum_{0 < \nu_k < \frac{1}{2}} \left[-ln|f_j(\nu_k)| - \mathbf{X}^T(\nu_k)f_j^{-1}(\nu_k)\mathbf{X}(\nu_k). \right] \tag{9.8}$$

The quadratic discriminant in this case can be expressed as

$$ln\, p_j(\mathbf{X}) = \sum_{0 < \nu_k < \frac{1}{2}} \left[-ln|f_j(\nu_k)| - trace\{I(\nu_k)f_j^{-1}(\nu_k)\} \right] \tag{9.9}$$

where
$$I(\nu_k) = \mathbf{X}(\nu_k)\mathbf{X}^T(\nu_k)$$

denotes the periodogram matrix.

Then the series $\mathbf{x}$ can be assigned to population Π_i whenever

$$ln\, p_i(\mathbf{x}) > ln\, p_j(\mathbf{x}) \qquad j \neq i, \qquad j = 1, 2, \dots, g$$

Many authors have considered various versions of discriminant analysis to classify time series in the frequency domain. By considering Eq. (9.7), Shumway and Unger (1974) applied the criterion to discriminate between earthquakes and explosions using teleseismic P data in which the means over the two groups was considered to be fixed. Alagon(1989) and Dargahi-Nubary and Laycock (1981) also considered discriminant functions of the form of Eq. (9.7) in the univariate case when the means are zero and the spectra for the two groups are different. Taniguchi (1991) adopted Eq. (9.9) as a criterion and discussed its non-Gaussian robustness.

Now since the periodogram is asymptotically an unbiased estimator of the spectral density function

$$E_j[I(\nu_k)] = f_j(\nu_k),$$

under the assumption that the series is from population Π_j, the discrimination information which is the Kullback-Leibler (KL) measure of disparity between two spectral densities $f_1(\mathbf{X})$ and $f_1(\mathbf{X})$ (Kullback and Leibler, 1951) is

$$
\begin{aligned}
I(f_1; f_2) &= \tfrac{1}{n} E_1\left[ln\frac{p_1(\mathbf{X})}{p_2(\mathbf{X})} \right] \\
&= \tfrac{1}{n} \sum_{0<\nu_k<\frac{1}{2}} \left[trace\{f_1(\nu_k)f_2^{-1}(\nu_k)\} - ln\frac{|f_1(\nu_k)|}{|f_2(\nu_k)|} - p \right]
\end{aligned}
\tag{9.10}
$$

Kakizawa et al. (1998) developed approaches for classifying stationary time series using Eq. (9.10) and also proposed using the Chernoff discrepancy measure (Chernoff, 1952, Rényi, 1961) defined as

$$B_\alpha(1; 2) = -lnE_2\left[\left(\frac{p_1(\mathbf{x})}{p_2(\mathbf{x})} \right)^\alpha \right]$$

where the measure is indexed by the parameter α, for $0 < \alpha < 1$.

The large sample spectral approximation to the Chernoff information measure is analogous to that for discrimination information measure.

$$B_\alpha(f_1; f_2) = \frac{1}{2n} \sum_{0<\nu_k<\frac{1}{2}} \left[ln\frac{|\alpha f_1(\nu_k) + (1-\alpha)f_2(\nu_k)|}{|f_2(\nu_k)|} - \alpha\, ln\frac{|f_1(\nu_k)|}{|f_2(\nu_k)|} \right]$$

Using the Kullback-Leibler (KL) discrepancy, Shumway (2003) extended classification of stationary time series to locally stationary time series based on time-varying spectra that are also applicable to the class of locally stationary processes introduced by Dahlhaus (1997). In this case, frequency bandwidths and window lengths have to be determined.

Sakiyama and Tanigushi (2004) have also proposed methods based on time-varying spectra for locally stationary processes based on an approximation of the Kullback-Leibler divergences. Their approach required the specification of a parametric model for the time-varying spectral density function of such a process. Huang et al. (2004) proposed the smooth local exponential methodology (SLEX) methods based on Fourier-type bases using local spectral features of the time series. Frequency bandwidths and blocks of time with relation to the degree of overlap in frequency and time, for the bases, have to be selected. However, they did not provide a systematic way of selecting the parameters of their discriminant procedure.

Vilar and Pertega (2004) proposed an approach for classifying stationary time series where non-parametric estimators of unknown spectra are obtained by local polynomial regression techniques. They used these estimates in the general spectral discrimination procedure proposed by Kakizawa et al. (1998).

9.4   Wavelet feature approaches

A motivation for using the wavelets rather than spectral features of time series is that when using the frequency domain methods, it is not easy to make the connection to specific time points in the time domain. On the other hand, the wavelets approach enables discrimination between time series patterns using available information from both the time and frequency domains simultaneously. Furthermore, the wavelets method is advantageous over the frequency domain methods because it is straightforward to estimate the wavelet coefficients and this is all that is required in a wavelet analysis, whereas the frequency domain methods may require de-trending, windowing, data tapers or averaging procedures prior to estimating the spectral coefficients.

9.4.1   Classification using wavelet variances

Maharaj and Alonso (2007) have developed a discriminant scheme for locally stationary time series using modified discrete wavelet transform (MODWT) time-dependent variances as discriminating features in Eq. (9.1) and Eq. (9.2). They show that the time-dependent MODWT variance is consistently estimated for a class of locally stationary processes introduced by Dahlhaus (1997). While Serroukh et al. (2000) have shown that the MODWT variances are asymptotically normally distributed, the assumption of multivariate normality may not necessarily be met. However many authors have conducted studies on the robustness of discriminant functions and have found that some of them are fairly robust to departures from assumed models with little or no modification (e.g, refer to Chinganda and Subrahaniam, 1979; Fatti et al., 1982).

Maharaj and Alonso (2007) implemented their procedure by dividing each time series into blocks, each of which is of a length that is compatible with the condition that the series therein can be regarded as stationary. To enable easy implementation, the block sizes were taken to be equal. Thus a stationary series comprised a single block, while a locally stationary series can be approximated by a piecewise stationary series with two or more blocks. If the time series at hand display trends, this method can still be used. This is because the trend, which is a low-frequency motion, will be captured by the highly dilated wavelets within the bands corresponding to the highest values of the index j. Unless the trend is itself an object of interest, which it may be if it displays interesting variations, these bands can be disregarded, and attention can be confined to the remaining bands.

Wavelet filters of lengths 2, 4, 6 and 8 of the Daubechies family (db2, db4, db6, db8), of length 8 from the Symmletts (least asymmetric) family (sym8), and of length 6 from the Coiflets family (cf6) were used to generate the MODWT coefficients, and hence the MODWT variances of the signal. For more details on the wavelet filters refer to Chapter 4 of Percival and Walden

(2000). In order to ensure that the boundary coefficients which have an effect on the estimated scale by scale wavelet variance and correlation coefficients are excluded, only a specific number of scales must be used for each filter, depending on the sample size. Suppose that $W_{j,t}$ is a Gaussian stationary process with zero mean and spectral density function, (SDF) $S_j(\cdot)$. If S_j is finitely square integrable and strictly positive almost everywhere, then the estimator $\widehat{\nu}_X^2(\tau_j)$ is asymptotically normal with mean $\nu_X^2(\tau_j)$ and large sample variance $2A_j/M_j$ (see Serroukh et al., 2000), where

$$A_j = \int_{-1/2}^{1/2} S_j^2(f) df.$$

Hence, given a number of time series which belong to one of g groups, with the number of blocks of equal size previously decided upon, the MODWT is obtained for each block for the frequency bands corresponding to values of the index running from the lowest, that is, $j = 1$ to the highest $j = J$. The MODWT wavelet variances, $\widehat{\nu}_{X_i}^2(\tau_j)$ for $i = 1, 2, \ldots, k$ and for $j = 1, 2, \ldots, J$, are then estimated for each wavelet time series and used as inputs in a discriminant procedure using (10.1) and (10.2). Since the wavelet variance estimators are asymptotically normal (see Serroukh et al., 2000), the normal linear or normal quadratic discriminants are asymptotically optimal for homoscedastic or heteroscedastic MODWT wavelet variances, respectively (see, e.g., Chapter 5 of McLachlan, 1992).

The procedure based on MODWT variances will work reasonably well when the wavelet variance is a good characterization of the spectral density function (e.g. in the power law SDF). It is known that

$$\nu_X^2(\tau_j) \approx \int_{1/2^{j+1}}^{1/2^j} S_X(f) df.$$

Therefore, assuming that S_X is continuous, there exists a frequency $f^* \in (1/2^{j+1}, 1/2^j)$ such that $\nu_X^2(\tau_j) \approx 2^{-1} S_Y(f^*)$. Therefore, the wavelet variances provide information similar to the other spectral estimation procedures if the SDF can be approximated by a piecewise constant function in the dyadic intervals. As mentioned in Cornish et al. (2004), the wavelet and multitaper methods for spectral estimation yield the same information for time series that are well modeled locally in frequency or scale by a power law. On the other hand, if the SDF exhibits structure (e.g. narrow peaks) in the dyadic intervals, then Fourier-based methods are preferable to the wavelet method.

If the number of time series is such that it is too small to permit the estimation of the complete variance-covariance matrices, diagonal linear or diagonal quadratic discriminant procedures are used. These diagonal discriminant procedures have been considered by Dudoit et al. (2002) in gene expression data where the number of variables is greater than the number of individuals in the samples. The hold-out-one cross validation method was used to evaluate our procedure.

Application 9.1 One of the applications in Maharaj and Alonso (2007) involved differentiation between the patterns of control charts. This dataset contains 600 control charts synthetically generated by the process in Alcock and Manolopoulos (1999) and is available from the UCI KDD Archive, see Hettich and Bay (1999). This data contains six different classes of control charts:

1. Normal patterns (N): $X_t = \mu + \sigma Y_t$,
2. Cyclic patterns (C): $X_t = \mu + \sigma Y_t + a \sin(2\pi t/T)$,
3. Increasing trend patterns (IT): $X_t = \mu + \sigma Y_t + gt$,
4. Decreasing trend patterns (DT): $X_t = \mu + \sigma Y_t - gt$,
5. Upward shift patterns (US): $X_t = \mu + \sigma Y_t + ks$,
6. Downward shift patterns (DS): $X_t = \mu + \sigma Y_t - ks$,

where μ is the mean of the process (set to 80), σ is the standard deviation of the process (set to 5), Y_t is a standard Gaussian white noise, a is the amplitude of cyclic variation (set in the range $0 < a < 15$), T is the period of a cycle (set between 4 and 12), g is the gradient of the trend (set in the range $0.2 < g < 0.5$), k is the shift position function ($k = 0$ before the shift and $k = 1$ at the shift and thereafter), and s is the magnitude of the shift (set between 7.5 and 20). These control chart time series were sampled within $t = 0$ to $t = 59$.

Pham and Chan (1998) used self-organizing neural networks to discriminate among the different patterns. They presented the results for ten different networks. Their training and hold-out classification rates ranged between 62.6% and 95.4% and between 62.1% and 93.2%, respectively. Table 9.1 shows our classification results for a hold-out-one procedure. For the single-block approach (TI), two zeroes each were padded at the beginning and the end of each time series and the wavelet variances were obtained in $J = 6$ frequency bands. For the multi-block approach with two (TD2) blocks, one zero each was padded at the beginning and the end of each block and the wavelet variances were obtained in $J = 5$ frequency bands. Here, the Haar wavelet (db(2)) produced the best results when all the frequency bands corresponding to values of the index j running from the lowest to the highest were considered. The hold-out-one classification error rates were 3.2% and 5.2%, respectively. A notable improvement was observed when the number of frequency bands increased for both approaches. In this case, the single-block approach, provides the lowest classification error rate and it improves the best network results of Pham and Chan (1998). Moreover, the main misclassifications can be explained since they are IT classified as US, DT classified as DS and vice versa.

9.4.2 Classification using wavelet variances and correlations

Maharaj and Alonso (2014) extended the classification of univariate time series to that of multivariate series. In this case wavelet variance and correlations were used as features to classify 12-lead Electrocardiogram (ECG) data using Eq. (9.1) and Eq. (9.2) for the linear and quadratic cases. Serroukh et al. (2000)

TABLE 9.1: Classification results for a hold-out-one procedure in control charts dataset (six patterns).

Real patterns	Predicted (TI)						Predicted (TD2)					
	N	C	IT	DT	US	DS	N	C	IT	DT	US	DS
N	100	0	0	0	0	0	96	0	0	0	0	4
C	0	100	0	0	0	0	0	98	0	0	2	0
IT	0	0	95	0	5	0	0	0	96	0	4	0
DT	0	0	0	96	0	4	0	0	0	97	0	3
US	0	0	5	0	95	0	0	2	7	0	91	0
DS	1	0	0	4	0	95	4	0	0	4	1	91

(TI) corresponds to the time independent approach.
(TD2) corresponds to the time dependent approach with two blocks.

have shown that MODWT wavelet variance estimators are asymptotically normal for linear processes, while Serroukh and Walden (2000) have shown that for bivariate linear processes, the MODWT wavelet covariance estimators are asymptotically normal. It follows that the MODWT wavelet correlation estimators are also asymptotically normal. While a situation in which all variables under consideration are shown to exhibit univariate normality may help achieve multivariate normality, it will not guarantee it. Thus, the group feature variables of the combined MODWT wavelet variances and wavelet correlations may not necessarily be asymptotically multivariate normal.

Many authors have proposed methods to classify ECG signals with varying degrees of accuracy. In particular, Al-Naima and Al-Timemy (2009), De Chazal and Reilly (2000), Heden et al. (1997) and Bozzola et al. (1996) have proposed methods that have been applied to 12-lead ECG signals.

Al-Naima and Al-Timemy (2009) used discrete Fourier transform (DFT) coefficients and discrete wavelet transform (DWT) coefficients as the discriminating features with neural network classifiers. Using 12-lead ECG data with a training set of 45 records (26 controls and 19 with myocardial infarction) and a test set of 20 records (12 controls and eight with myocardial infarction), the sensitivities achieved for the test set were between 80% and 90%, while the specificity was 90%. Sensitivity is the percentage of cases correctly classified as being in the class of a particular condition, e.g., myocardial infarction, while specificity is the percentage of cases correctly classified in the control group, that is, being of the normal class. De Chazal and Reilly (2000) used linear and quadratic discriminants with five features sets, including DWT coefficients, standard cardiology features and time domain features. Using a database of 500 12-lead ECG signals from 345 patients with different cardiac diseases, and from 155 controls, and multiple runs of tenfold cross-validation, they obtained sensitivities of 69% to 73%, 78% to 83% and 25% to 38% when they classified anterior, inferior or combined myocardial infarction, while the specificity of their best classifier was 90%. Heden et al. (1997) conducted a study using 12-lead ECG records of a group of 1120 individuals with acute myocardial infarction and a control group consisting of 10 352 cases. They used six time domain measurements from each of the 12 leads as inputs into artificial neural networks. Using a threefold cross-validation procedure, their method achieved sensitivities of 46.2% to 65.9% and specificities of 86.3% to 95.4%. Bozzola et al. (1996) extracted a set of eight time domain parameters from each of the 12-lead ECG records and input these into a hybrid neuro-fuzzy system for the classification of myocardial infarction. They used a training set of ECG records of 179 controls and 404 with myocardial infarction, and a test set of ECG records of 60 controls and 135 with myocardial infarction. Their method achieved test set sensitivities of 72%, 80% to 88% and 52% to 60% when they classified anterior, inferior or combined myocardial infarction and specificities of 92% to 93%.

In all of the techniques employed by the above-mentioned authors, the components of the 12-lead ECG signal are treated as if they were independent of each other. In practice, each 12-lead ECG signal can be regarded as a 12-component multivariate time series. An important consideration in the analysis of multivariate time series is the relationship between the individual components of each series. Hence, given the absence of this consideration in ECG classification literature, Maharaj and Alonso (2014) were motivated to examine the inclusion of these interrelationship features to assess whether they provide useful information, and thus lead to perhaps more accurate classification results. Hence, they proposed the discriminant analysis of the multivariate time series, namely, the 12-lead ECG signals, based on wavelet features of variances and correlations. In using these features, their goal was to distinguish between the patterns of multivariate ECG signals based on the variability of the individual components of each ECG signal, and the relationships between these components. Taking into account the relationships between every pair of components is a novel approach, and to their knowledge has not been considered before in multiple-lead ECG classification. Since an ECG signal is of high frequency, time domain analyses of such signals, using summary statistics misses out on useful information in the intricacies of the signal. Hence a frequency representation of the signal would be more useful. This can be achieved by using the fast Fourier transform (FFT) technique. However, the limitation of the FFT is that it is unable to provide that information regarding the exact location of the frequency components in time. Wavelet transformation of the time series overcomes this limitation in that the signal is decomposed into coefficients at a number of frequency bands referred to as scales. The coefficients at each scale have a time location and represent the ECG signal in a particular frequency band. Furthermore, an advantage of using wavelet features is that the time series under consideration do not necessarily have to be mean stationary or variance stationary as indeed most ECG data are not.

Because Maharaj and Alonso (2014) are interested in the variability of each of the 12-lead ECG components more useful information can be obtained from the variances of the wavelet coefficients at each of the frequency bands than by simply obtaining the single variance of each lead in the time domain. Since they are also interested in the relationship between every pair of leads, more useful information can be obtained from the correlation between every pair of leads at each of the frequency bands, instead of a single correlation coefficient between a pair of leads in the time domain. All of this therefore provides a motivation for the use of these wavelet based features.

Application 9.2 The ECG data used by Maharaj and Alonso (2014) comes from the PTB Diagnostic ECG Database (Goldberger et al. (2000)). This freely available data is a small subset of the database used by *cardioPATTERN - Telemedical ECG-Evaluation and Follow up* (2009) that has a patented procedure for ECG classification. In this application, the interest was in distinguishing between ECG signals of individuals with myocardial infarction and those of healthy controls.

A typical waveform from a single heart beat is shown in Figure 9.1. Any ECG signal imparts two pieces of information. The first is the duration of the electrical wave crossing the heart which in turn works out whether the electrical activity is normal, slow, or irregular , and the second is the amount of electrical activity passing through the heart muscle which determines whether parts of the heart are too large or overworked. Normally, the frequency range of an ECG signal is of 0.05-100 Hz and its dynamic range is of 1 - 10 mV. The ECG is characterized by five peaks and valleys labeled by the letters P, Q, R, S, T. In some cases another peak, the one to the extreme right in Figure 9.1. and referred to U is also present. The performance of an ECG analysing system depends mainly on the accurate and reliable detection of the QRS complex, as well as the T- and P-waves. The P-wave represents the activation of the upper chambers of the heart, the atria, while the QRS complex and the T-wave represent the excitation of the lower chambers of the heart, the ventricles. The QRS complex is the most prominent part of the waveform within the ECG signal. Since it reflects the electrical activity within the heart during ventricular contraction, the time of its occurrence as well as its shape provide some information about the current state of the heart.

The available dataset consists of 200 records of the conventional 12 leads (i, ii, iii, avr, avl, avf, v1, v2, v3, v4, v5, v6) for 148 patients with myocardial infarction and 52 healthy controls. Relevant information from the PTB Diagnostic ECG Database in Goldberger et al. (2000) and in Bousseljot et al. (1995) about how the ECG data in this collection were obtained, is as follows: Each signal is digitized at 1000 samples per second (sampling frequency of 1kHz)), with 16 bit resolution over a range of 16.384 mV. The signal bandwidth is 0Hz - 1kHz. and the noise level is $< 0.3 \ \mu \text{V}/ \sqrt{\text{Hz}}$. The anti-aliasing filter used to counteract information loss is an 8-th order 1kHz Bessel Filter of 3dB frequency. (mV represents a milli-volt and μ V a micro-volt; a volt is the

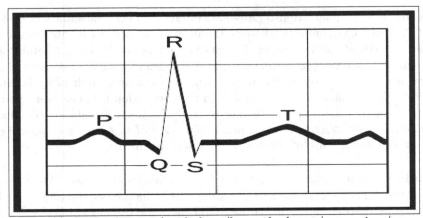

FIGURE 9.1: A typical ECG waveform.

unit for electric potential (voltage); Hz represents a hertz which is the inverse of a second, kHz represents a kilohertz and dB represents a decibel which is a logarithmic unit that indicates the ratio of a physical quantity (power of intensity) relative to a specified or implied reference level.)

For each record, the first $2^{12} + 2^{13}$ observations were read and the first 2^{12} observations were dicarded since they could have some exogenous anomalies. The remaining $2^{13} = 8192$ observations correspond to around eleven heart beats. In this case the number of scales $J = 13$ and the maximum allowable number of scales when the different wavelet filters are used can be determined from Table 9.2. Figure 9.2 and Figure 9.3 present the 12-lead ECG signals of a subject with myocardial infarction and of a healthy control, respectively. Examination of finer resolutions of these signals reveal that for all leads the time of occurrence of the QRS complex as well as the P- and T-waves in the signals of a subject with myocardial infarction is about 250 ms before that in the signals of a healthy control. The shapes of the QRS complex and the P- and T-waves in the ECG signals of a subject with myocardial infarction compared to those in the ECG signals of a healthy control are described below.

- Lead i: Slightly wider QRS, slightly flatter T-wave.
- Lead ii: More peaked P- and T-waves, slightly narrower QRS, lower R-wave but deeper S-wave.
- Lead iii: QRS is noticeably inverted and slightly wider compared to the upright QRS in the healthy control signal; the T-wave is a trough compared to the healthy control signal which has a slight peak.
- Lead avr: Deeper P-wave, QRS is wider with a higher R-wave and a deeper S-wave

- Lead avl: QRS is upright and wider compared to that of the healthy control signal which is inverted; T-wave is more peaked.
- Lead avf: P-wave is more peaked, QRS inverted and wider compared to that of the healthy control signal which is upright.
- Lead v1: P-wave is distinctly peaked compared to a flattened P-wave in the healthy control signal, QRS is wider and upright compared to that of the healthy control signal which is inverted.
- Lead v2: QRS is upright compared to that of the healthy control signal which is inverted; T-wave is more peaked.
- Lead v3: No apparent difference in shapes in any of the waves compared to those of the healthy control signal.
- Lead v4: No apparent difference in shapes in any of the waves compared to those of the healthy control signal.
- Lead v5: QRS is inverted and wider compared to that of the healthy control signal which is upright; T-wave is flatter.
- Lead v6: QRS is inverted and wider compared to that of the healthy control signal which is upright; T-wave is more peaked.

So, clearly there are differences in the patterns of the ECG signals of subjects with myocardial infarction and healthy controls. Figure 9.4 shows boxplots of wavelet variances and correlations generated using the **sym8** filter of the corresponding 12-lead ECG signals from Figure 9.2 and Figure 9.3 at each of 9 scales. We make the following observations: there is a distinct difference in the spread of the wavelet variances of the 12 leads from Scales 5 to 9 between the myocardial infarction subject and the healthy control; there is a larger number of outlying wavelet correlation values for the myocardial infarction subject than for the healthy control.

Figure 9.5 shows the classification rates for patients with myocardial infarction, for healthy controls and the overall classification rates using linear and quadratic discriminant analyses, with the wavelet variances (var), wavelet variances and wavelet correlations (var-cor) and wavelet correlations (cor). Wavelet filters of lengths 2, 4, 6 and 8 of the Daubechies family (db2, db4, db6, db8), of length 8 from the Symmletts family (sym8), and of length 6 from the Coiflets family (cf6) will be used to generate the MODWT coefficients, and hence the MODWT variances and correlations of the signal. Table 9.2 shows the maximum allowable scales for each wavelet filter and the number of wavelet features used in what follows.

The results are shown using each of the six wavelet filters. In most cases, the best results were obtained when the wavelet variances and correlations were both the input variables. When only wavelet variances were the input variables, the classification rates were much lower. When only wavelet correlations were the input variables, in some cases the misclassification rates were similar to, or sometimes slightly larger than when both wavelet variance and correlations were input together. It is clear that the wavelet correlations provide useful information about the relationships between the leads of each ECG signal and hence make an important contribution to distinguishing between

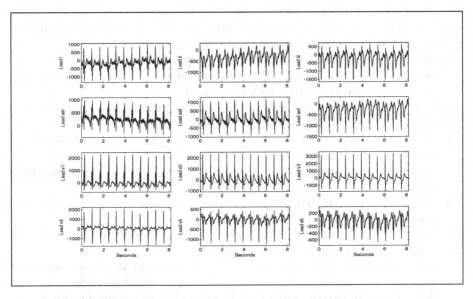

FIGURE 9.2: ECG of a patient with myocardial infarction.

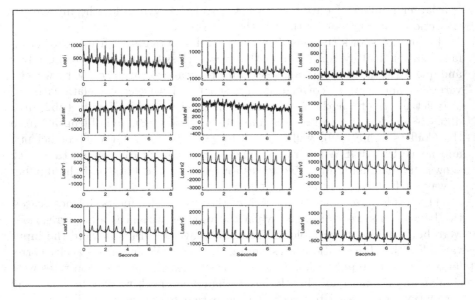

FIGURE 9.3: ECG of a healthy control.

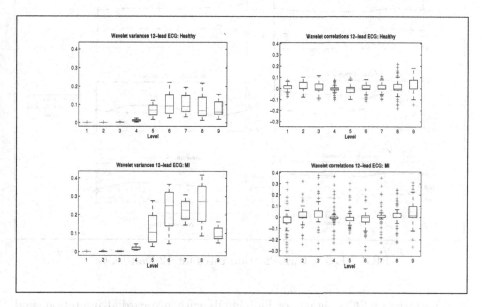

FIGURE 9.4: Boxplots of wavelet variances and correlations of the 12-lead ECGs.

TABLE 9.2: Maximum allowable number of scales for $T = 2^{13}$ and number of wavelet features.

Wavelet filter	db2	db4	db6	db8	sym8	cf6
	J	J-2	J-3	J-3	J-3	J-3
Scales	13	11	10	10	10	10
Wavelet variances	156	132	120	120	120	120
Wavelet correlations	858	726	660	660	660	660

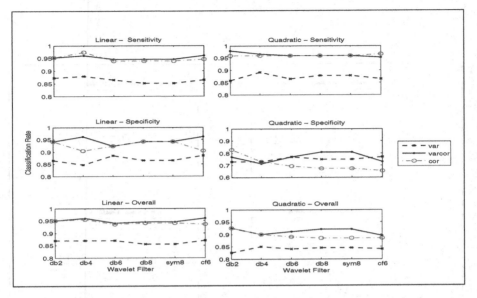

FIGURE 9.5: Classification rates for 12-lead ECGs.

the patterns of ECG signals of individuals with myocardial infarction, and those of healthy controls. These classification results imply sensitivities of 95% to 96% (95% to 98%) and specificities of 92% to 96% (73% to 81%) when using the linear (quadratic) procedure with wavelets variances and correlations together. Regarding the overall classification rates, the linear procedure generally outperforms the quadratic procedure. Only in a few cases did the quadratic procedure outperform the linear procedure when classifying myocardial infarction ECGs. In general, for the linear procedure, the error rates were fairly similar for the different wavelet filters. This was also the case for the quadratic procedure.

In order to test how sensitive their proposed procedure was under different conditions, Maharaj and Alonso (2014) conducted several experiments., namely, with, pre-processed signals, varying the sampling frequency, varying the signal lengths and measuring the repeatability of the classification, and found that similar results were obtained.

Figure 9.6 compares the classification rates using the Kullback-Leibler (KL) discrimination information and the Chernoff(CH) information measures with the average classification rates across the six wavelet filters. Note that on the horizontal axis, L1, L2, L3 refer to results from the linear discriminant using the features, wavelet variances, combined wavelet variance and correlations and wavelet correlation, respectively. Likewise the results pertaining to the quadratic discriminant are labelled accordingly.

On average, all wavelet-based discriminant procedures outperformed the Kullback-Leibler information and Chernoff information procedures. For the

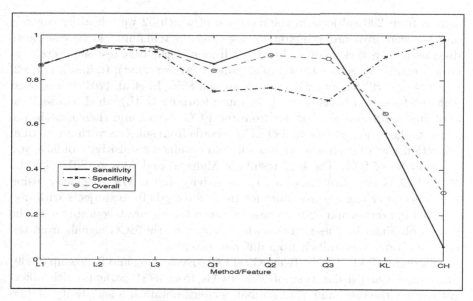

FIGURE 9.6: Comparison of classification rates for 12-lead ECGs.

Kullback-Leibler information and Chernoff information procedures, we consider different values for the bandwidth used to estimate the spectral densities. The considered bandwidths were in the range [0.001, 0.01] that corresponds to from 9 to 81 contiguous fundamental frequencies that are close to the frequency of interest (refer to Shumway and Stoffer (2016) for more details).

These classification results imply sensitivities of 94.6-95.9% (95.3-98.0%) and specificities of 92.3-96.2% (73.1-80.8%) when using the linear (quadratic) procedure with wavelets variances and correlations together. The procedures based on the Kullback-Leibler information and Chernoff information have good sensitivities (90.4% and 98.1%, respectively) but very poor specificities (56.1% and 6.1%, respectively).

Many researchers have analysed the samples of ECG data for the PTB database. In particular, Banerjee and Mitra (2010), Kopiec and Martyna (2011), and Li et al. (2012) proposed pattern recognition approaches to classifying the ECG signals between subjects with myocardial infarction and healthy controls from this database. Banerjee and Mitra (2010) developed an algorithm based on the discrete wavelet transform (DWT), which extracts features such as the QRS complex and computes the QRS vector of the 12-lead ECG signals. They applied it to 12-lead signals from 25 subjects with myocardial infarction and 25 healthy controls. They obtained a sensitivity of 100% and a specificity of 92% but they did not use test data or any cross-validation technique to validate the accuracy of their results. Kopiec and Martyna (2011) used a combination of support vector machine (SVM) and particle swarm optimization (PSO) to extract significant features for each of the 12-lead ECG

signals from 290 subjects in the database of which 52 were healthy controls
and 148 were myocardial infarction cases and the remaining 90 were subjects
diagnosed with various other heart conditions. Their best test set overall accuracy results for sets of three leads, namely, (avl, avr, avf); (i, ii, iii); (v1, v2,
v3); (v4, v5, v6); (i, avf, v3) were all around 80%. Li et al. (2012) developed
a method referred to as multiple instance learning (MIL) which is based on
extracted QRS and ST features from the ECG signals and their heartbeats.
They applied the methods to 389 ECG records from subjects with myocardial
infarction and 79 from healthy controls and obtained a sensitivity of 93% and
a specificity of 90%. The best results of Maharaj and Alonso (2014) for the
12-lead ECG classification of a 96% sensitivity and a 96% specificity, using
the linear discriminant procedure for the 148 records from subjects with myocardial infarction and 52 from healthy controls compare favourably with the
results obtained by these other authors who used the ECG signals from the
same PTB database, albeit from different samples.

The cardioPATTERN - Telemedical ECG-Evaluation and Follow up (2009)
procedure, using a database of 8500 ECGs from 3781 patients with different cardiac diseases, and 4719 normal persons, obtained a sensitivity of 72%
and a specificity of 80% when classifying myocardial infarction. Although
this database as well as those used by Al-Naima and Al-Timemy (2009), De
Chazal and Reilly (2000), Heden et al. (1997) and Bozzola et al. (1996) are
not comparable with the PTB database, their sensitivity and specificity results can be used as reference values; the procedure of Maharaj and Alonso
(2014) with the 12-lead ECG signals, compares quite favourably. Furthermore,
given that for most of the time, their best results were achieved when both
wavelet variances and correlations were input together in the discriminant
procedures, it does appear that the relationships between the components
of the multi-lead ECG signals provide more useful information for classification.

9.4.3   Classification using evolutionary wavelet spectra

Fryzlewicz and Ombao (2012) proposed a procedure for classifying non-
stationary time series using the evolutionary wavelet spectrum which is the
time scale decomposition of the variance. Refer to Percival and Walden (2000)
for details of the evolutionary wavelet spectrum. They view the observed time
series as realizations of locally stationary wavelet (LSW) processes and they
use the modified discrete wavelet transform (MODWT) in estimating the
wavelet spectrum.

Their proposed classification rules that assign an LSW process $\mathbf{X}_{t,T}$ to
$G \geq 2$ groups $\Pi_1, \Pi_2, \ldots, \Pi_g$ with evolutionary spectra $S_j^1(z), S_j^2(z), \ldots, S_j^G(z)$,
are as follows:

For a suitable subset M of wavelet scales and location indices (j, k), they
compute the empirical wavelet spectrum $L_{t,T}^j$ of $\mathbf{X}_{t,T}$ Then they compute the

squared distance between the empirical wavelet spectrum and the evolutionary wavelet spectrum of each group.

$$D_g = \sum_{(j,k)\epsilon M} [L_{t,T}^j - S_j^g(k/T)]^2$$

for $j = 1, 2, \ldots, g$, and if $D_i < D_j$, $\mathbf{X}_{t,T}$ is classified into Π_j, and show the consistency of their classification procedure.

Their method was demonstrated to work well in simulation studies and to an application to distinguish between earthquakes and explosions signals.

9.5 Time-domain approaches

While there are numerous methods for classifying time series in the frequency domain and a few methods that use wavelets features, there are relatively few methods in the time domain. In this section we discuss two such methods.

9.5.1 Classification using shapes

Chandler and Polonik (2006) proposed a discrimination procedure for locally stationary time series by using a time-varying autoregressive process. A rescaled version of the time varying autoregressive model (Dahlhaus, 1997) is of the form:

$$\mathbf{X}_t^c = \sum_{k=1}^{p} \phi_k(t/T)\mathbf{X}_{t-k}^c + \varepsilon_t \sigma(\frac{t}{T}) \tag{9.11}$$

where $\mathbf{X}_t^c = \mathbf{X}_t - \mu_t$ and where the errors are assumed to be iid with mean 0.

Their discrimination method is based on Eq. (9.11) and on measures of concentration of the variance function $\sigma(.)$, namely, the excess mass functional of a distribution F with probability density function f which is defined as

$$E_F(\lambda) = \sup_C \left(\int_C dF(x) - \lambda|C| \right) = \int_{-\infty}^{\infty} (f(x) - \lambda)^+ dx$$

where $a^+ = max(a, 0)$, the supremum of which is extended over all measurable sets C and $|C|$ denoted the Lebesgue measure of C. Note that the Lebesgue measure is the standard way of assigning a measure to subsets of a n-dimensional Euclidean space. Sets that can be assigned a Lebesgue measure are called Lebesgue measurable and the measure of the Lebesgue measurable set C is denoted by $\lambda(C)$.

In this case the role of the density f is taken over by the normalized variance function

$$\overline{\sigma}^2(\alpha) = \frac{\sigma^2(\alpha)}{\int_0^1 \sigma^2(u)du}.$$

$\overline{\sigma}^2(.)$ does not depend on the magnitude of the series. The excess mass function of the normalized variance function is then

$$E_F(\lambda) = E_{\overline{\sigma}}(\lambda) = \int_0^1 (\overline{\sigma}^2(u) - \lambda)^+ du \tag{9.12}$$

Chandler and Polonik (2006) use (9.12) as a basis to define two different types of measures that they use for discrimination, namely, the integrated excess mass

$$IE(\beta) = \int_0^\infty \lambda^\beta E(\lambda)d\lambda, \qquad \beta > 0 \tag{9.13}$$

and the quantile of the excess mass functional

$$\lambda(q) = E^{-1}(q) = \sup[\lambda : E(\lambda) \geq g] \qquad 0 < q < 1. \tag{9.14}$$

Empirical versions of Eq. (9.13) and Eq.(9.14) are obtained by using the estimator of $\overline{\sigma}^2(.)$. Refer to Chandler and Polonik (2006) for details about the construction of this estimator. They derive the asymptotic normality of their estimated discrimination measures and hence use optimal normality-based discrimination rules that were discussed in Section 10.2. Their method was demonstrated to work well in simulation studies and in an application to distinguish between earthquakes and explosions signals.

9.5.2   Classification using complex demodulation

Maharaj (2014) proposed the classification of cyclical time series using complex demodulation which is a local version of harmonic analysis. This involved investigating the time varying nature of the amplitude of the dominant cyclical component of each time series under consideration and using the time varying amplitude of the dominant cycle to discriminate between patterns of cyclical time series. In order to distinguish between the patterns of these cyclical time series, the time varying amplitudes, estimated using complex demodulation will be the input features variables in classical discriminant analysis. Since complex demodulation is a local version of harmonic analysis, a brief discussion on some aspects of harmonic analysis is provided before a brief description of complex demodulation in provided.

Harmonic Analysis Harmonic regression models are useful in describing time series with one or more cycles (refer to Bloomfield, 2000) for more details). A harmonic regression model with a single cycle is defined as

$$x_t = \mu + A\cos\omega t + B\sin\omega t + \varepsilon_t \tag{9.15}$$

where x_t is the time series, μ is the mean of the underlying time series, $A = R\cos\phi$ and $B = -R\sin\phi$. R is the amplitude or height of the cycle peaks, ϕ is the phase or the location of the peaks relative to time zero, $\omega = \frac{2\pi}{\tau}$ is the frequency and τ is the cycle length, i. e., the distance from one peak to the next. ε_t is the random error term which is white noise and the errors are uncorrelated with the sine and cosine terms.

By varying the A and B parameters that indicate how much weight is given to the sine and cosine components, it is possible to generate a sinusoid waveform of period τ with any particular amplitude and phase. Sine and cosine functions have the same waveform shape but differ in phase, that is, the cosine function has a peak value of one at $t = 0$, whereas the sine function has a peak value of one at a quarter of a cycle later. The sine and cosine functions of period τ are orthogonal, that is they are uncorrelated. Therefore by varying the relative size of the A and B coefficients, it is possible to generate all possible sinusoids of period τ; sinusoids with any mean μ, amplitude R, and phase ϕ. Given an assumed value of τ, the period or cycle length, the remaining three parameters, i. e., the mean, amplitude and phase of the cycle can be estimated using least squares regression to obtain the best possible fit to an observed time series. The estimated amplitude and phase are obtained from $\widehat{R} = \sqrt{\widehat{A}^2 + \widehat{B}^2}$ and $\tan 2\pi\hat\phi = -\hat{B}/\hat{A}$, respectively.

Now if a time series displays multiple cycles, these can be incorporated into the harmonic model as follows:

$$x_t = \mu + \sum_{i=1}^{k}(A_i \cos\omega_i t + B_i \sin\omega_i t) + \varepsilon_t, \qquad (9.16)$$

where k is the number of cycles.

While harmonic regression models can capture multiple cycles that may be present in a time series, they are unable to capture the time varying nature of the cycles. The dynamic harmonic regression (DHR) model developed by Young et al. (1999) is better able to do so. The DHR model can be considered as an extension of the harmonic regression model defined in Eq. (9.15) in which the amplitude and phase of the harmonic components can vary as a result of estimated temporal changes in the parameters A_i and B_i which now become A_{it} and B_{it}. The estimation of the time varying parameters is obtained through state space and frequency domain formulation. Young et al. (1999) who state that their DHR model which is asymptotically equivalent to other time varying approaches, but is more computationally attractive, give details of this estimation process. However, the estimation of the time varying parameters is quite complex and involves several steps. In contrast to this the estimation of the time varying amplitude of a particular cycle, that is, $\widehat{R}_t = \sqrt{\widehat{A}_t^2 + \widehat{B}_t^2}$ can be much more easily achieved using complex demodulation.

Complex demodulation: Suppose that the deterministic part of a zero mean stationary time series with a single cycle or periodic component can be represented by

$$x_t = R_t e^{2\pi i(\omega_0 t + \phi_t)} \tag{9.17}$$

where R_t is the slowly changing amplitude, ϕ_t is the slowly changing phase and ω_0 is the known frequency. Hence, the cycle length $\pi_0 = 2\pi/\omega_0$ is known. In practice, this frequency will be identified as that corresponding to the dominant peak of the periodogram of the time series under consideration.

The aim of complex demodulation is to extract approximations to the series R_t and ϕ_t . Hence, complex demodulation is regarded as a local version of harmonic analysis because its aim is to describe the amplitude and phase of an oscillation as they change over time. Constructing a new series from Eq. (9.17) gives

$$y_t = x_t e^{-2\pi i \omega_0 t} = R_t e^{2\pi i \phi_t} \tag{9.18}$$

This new series y_t is said to be obtained from x_t by complex demodulation. Then, the estimated time varying amplitude is $\widehat{R}_t = |y_t|$, and the estimated time varying phase is obtained from $e^{2\pi i \hat{\phi}_t} = y_t/|y_t|$. In practice, a plot of the time varying amplitude obtained by complex demodulation is useful to determine if constant amplitude which is so often assumed for seasonal and other cyclical time series is in fact justified. If it is, then the time series under consideration can be modeled by means of Eq. (9.16) instead of Eq. (9.15).

In practice a series that is analysed does not consist solely of a single periodic component and furthermore there is also the noise component. Hence, in general the series would be represented by

$$x_t = R_t e^{2\pi i(\omega_0 t + \phi_t)} + \varepsilon_t \tag{9.19}$$

Hence $\widehat{R}_t$ will tend to be noisy and to extract a smooth version of the time varying amplitude, it must be filtered. Bloomfield (2000) suggests using various types of linear filters with a simple moving average filter being one of them. Refer to Bloomfield (2000) for illustrations of this concept of the time varying amplitude and its usefulness in practice.

Implementation and Considerations: The implementation of the discrimination procedure using time varying amplitudes consists of the following three steps.

1. For each time series under consideration, identify the frequency and hence the cycle length corresponding to the dominant peak in the periodogram.
2. The time-dependent amplitude R_t corresponding to the cycle length obtained in Step 1, is estimated by complex demodulation and this estimator is smoothed by a moving average filter of order that is equal to the cycle length. This filter uses equal weights.

3. The smoothed time varying amplitude ordinates are the input variables in the classical discriminant procedure.

Considerations that need to be taken into account include the following:
1. The method proposed here applies to time series that are mean stationary but are not necessarily variance stationary. However, if all the time series under consideration are not mean stationary, the trend can be filtered out by one of the trend filtering methods that are available and Steps 1 to 3 will be applied to the filtered time series.
2. If the periodogram of a series shows up a number of dominant cycles close to each other and there is difficulty identifying the frequency at which the most dominant cycle appears, a smoothed periodogram which will reduce the noise can be generated and hence, the dominant cycle identified.
3. While for a given time series, the number of smoothed time varying amplitudes ordinates is equal to the length of the time series, the use of these ordinates as the discriminating variables is preferable to using the actual time series observations. This is because the noise in the actual time series would have an impact on the discrimination process. Furthermore, if we were to use the periodogram ordinates of the time series as the discriminating features, this would reduce the number of discriminating features by half, but the noise present in the periodogram would also have an impact on the discrimination process. While Shumway (2003) uses smoothed periodograms in discriminating between patterns of time series signals, and it reduces the number of discriminating variables even further and removes the noise present in the periodogram, decisions still have to be made regarding the bandwidth of the smoothing window. In contrast, no decisions have to be made in smoothing the time varying amplitude because the smoothing order is the cycle length identified at the first step of the process for obtaining the time varying amplitude.
4. To address the potential computational problems that may exist with the input of a large number of variables, namely, the time varying amplitude ordinates into the discriminant procedure, diagonal discriminant procedures if necessary can be used (see Dudoit, 2002).

Application 9.3 Several authors including Kakizawa et al. (1998), Shumway (2003), Huang et al. (2004), Chinipardaz and Cox (2004) and Maharaj and Alonso (2007) have evaluated their time series classification procedures using the suite of eight earthquakes and eight mining explosions originating in the Scandinavian Peninsula as well as an unknown event that originated in Novaya-Zemmlya, Russia. See Shumway and Stoffer (2016) for more details about the data. Figure 9.7 shows the waveforms of an earthquake, an explosion and the unknown event.

The general problem is discriminating between the waveforms generated from earthquakes and explosions. Each waveform has two phases of arrival; the primary (P-phase) which accounts for approximately the first half of the

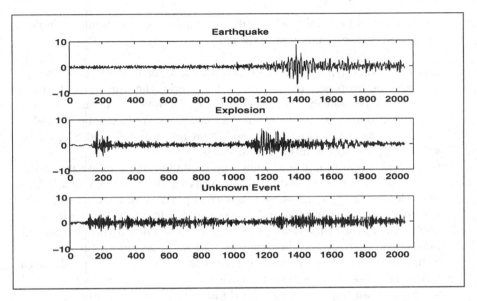

FIGURE 9.7: Waveforms of an earthquake, an explosion and the unknown event.

waveform, and the secondary (S-phase), which accounts for approximately the second half. Maharaj (2014) used the ratio of filtered time varying amplitude of the S-phase to the P-phase as the feature variables. Shumway and Stoffer (2016) discuss the rationale for using the S-phase to P-phase ratio for discriminating between earthquakes and explosions.

Figure 9.8 shows the ratios of the time varying amplitude of the S-phase to the P-phase of an earthquake, an explosion and the unknown event. It can be observed that the patterns associated with the earthquake and explosion can be clearly distinguished. The pattern associated with the unknown event appears to be closer to that associated with the explosion. The classification results are given in Table 9.3.

Using the stepwise method with the linear discriminant function, all earthquakes and explosions were correctly classified, and the unknown event was classified as an explosion. This is consistent with results obtained by Kakizawa (1998), Shumway (2003), Huang (2004), Chinipardaz and Cox (2004) and Maharaj and Alonso (2007). From Table 9.3, it can be observed that the other three combinations of method and discriminant functions gave classification error rates of 2/16, 4/16 and 4/16.

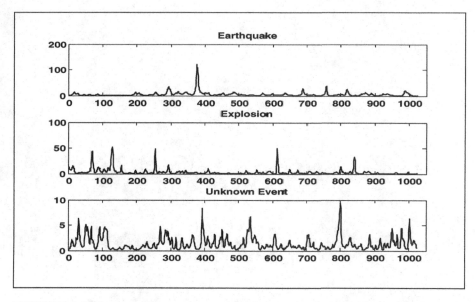

FIGURE 9.8: Ratios of time varying amplitudes S-phase/P-phase of an earthquake, an explosion and the unknown event.

TABLE 9.3: Classification results for a hold-out-one procedure for earthquakes and explosions.

	Real Pattern	Predicted Pattern	
		Earthquake	Explosion
Standard Linear	Earthquake	6	0
	Explosion	2	8
Stepwise Linear	Earthquake	8	0
	Explosion	0	8
Standard Quadratic	Earthquake	7	3
	Explosion	1	5
Stepwise Quadratic	Earthquake	6	2
	Explosion	2	6

10

Other time series classification approaches

CONTENTS

10.1 Introduction

There is a vast literature on time series classification where the time series under consideration must be aligned in a particular way. The discrimination methods here find certain features in the time series such as structural breaks and then discrimination is based on the presence or absence of these features. Many of these methods are machine learning approaches, some of which are used in data mining and others in signal processing. In what follows, we will discuss a few these methods.

10.2 Classification trees

A decision tree is a combination of mathematical and computational techniques to assist in the description and classification of a given set of data associated with variables $\mathbf{X}$ and $\mathbf{Y}$, where $\mathbf{Y}$ is the dependent variable which is the target variable and where $\mathbf{X} = (X_1, X_2, ..., X_k)$ is composed of input variables that are used for the task of classification. Decision trees used in data mining are of two types:

- Classification trees where the predicted outcome is a class to which the data belongs; that is, the target variable is a label.
- Regression trees where the predicted outcome is a real number; that is, the target variable is numeric.

Decision trees have nodes and edges; there are two types of nodes:
- Intermediate nodes - each such node is labelled by a single attribute, with edges extending from the intermediate being the attribute type or value.
- Leaf nodes - each such node is labelled by the class which contains the label or numeric value of the prediction.

The attributes that appear near the top of the tree typically indicate they are more important in making classifications. Creating a binary decision tree is a process of dividing up the input space by some sort of splitting.

Douzal-Chouakria and Amblard (2012) proposed an extension of classification trees to time series input variables and introduced new split criteria which are characterized by two additive values. The first is the use of an adaptive metric that may change from one internode to another and bisect the set of time series effectively. The second involves the automatic extraction of the most discriminating subsequences of the time series. They developed an algorithm called *TsTree* which they applied to a number of well-known publicly available datasets and to some new synthetic data sets.

They assessed the performance of their algorithm using adaptive metrics-based on temporal correlations and metrics based on several variants of dynamic time warping (DTW) and on the Euclidean distance using 10-fold cross-validation and applied it to datasets from the URC Archive, the details of which are provided in their paper. They also compared the performance of their *TsTree* algorithm using adaptive metrics-based temporal correlations to other machine learning approaches to time series classification and they reported that their *TsTree* classifier is competitive with that of these other methods. For more details about these other methods, see the relevant references in Dousal-Chouakria and Amblard (2012).

10.3 Gaussian mixture models

A Gaussian mixture model (GMM) is a parametric density function represented as a weighted sum of Gaussian component densities. GMM parameters are estimated from training data using the iterative expectation-maximisation (EM) algorithm. GMM models are commonly used to classify cross-sectional data but have also been used in the classification of time series, in particular signals, especially in the areas of electrical and biomedical engineering and speech recognition, where the dynamics of a system are captured in a reconstructed phase space. For example, the dynamics of a time series can be captured by its autocorrelation function; hence, when there are multiple time series making up a system, the reconstructed phase space of the system is the space of autocorrelation functions.

Povinelli et al. (2004) proposed a new signal classification approach based upon modelling the dynamics of a system (consisting of multiple signals) as they are captured in a reconstructed phase space. The modelling is done using the full covariance Gaussian mixture models in the time domain. The proposed approach has strong theoretical foundations based on dynamical systems resulting in signal reconstruction which asymptotically provides a complete reconstruction of the system with properly chosen parameters. Their algorithm automatically estimates these parameters from an appropriate reconstructed phase space, requiring only the number of mixtures, the signals and their class labels as input.

They use three separate data sets, namely, motor current simulations, ECG signals and speech waveforms, for validation. Their results reveal that their proposed method is robust for the data sets from these diverse domains and it outperforms time delay neutral networks. See the reference in their paper for more more details on the time delay neural network.

10.4   Bayesian approach

Sykacek and Roberts (2002) propose a Bayesian approach to classify adjacent segments of a time series into one of K classes. They use a two-stage approach with a hierarchical model consisting of extracted features and then build a classifier on top of these features.

The classifier is implemented as a hidden Markov model with Gaussian and multinomial distributions defined on specific autoregressive models and inference is undertaken with Markov chain Monte Carlo (MCMC) techniques. They apply their approach to the classification of synthetic data and EEGs that were measured while the subjects performed different cognitive tasks and they report improved classification accuracy.

10.5   Nearest neighbours methods

The k-nearest neighbours classification algorithm, k-NN, is a non-parametric method that predicts class memberships of observations based on the k closest training samples in the feature space. The k-NN is a simple algorithm that stores all available cases based on a similarity measure such as the Euclidean distance. An observation is assigned to the class most common amongst its k nearest neighbours, where k is a positive integer and is typically small. If $k = 1$, then the observation is simply assigned to the class of that single nearest neighbour. In general, a large k value is probably more precise since it reduces the overall noise. Cross-validation is one way of determining a good k value by using an independent dataset to validate the k value. Historically, the optimal

k for most datasets has been between 3 and 10. Refer to Hastie et al. (2009) for more details.

Kotsifakos and Panagiotis (2014) proposed a model-based time series nearest neighbours classification approach within a filtered and refined framework. They first model training time series belonging to certain classes through Hidden Markov Models (HMM). Given a particular time series whose class membership is unknown, they identify the top K models that have most likely produced this time series. This is the filter step. At the refine step, a distance measure is applied between this time series and all the training time series of the top K models, This time series is then assigned within the class of the nearest neighbour. They evaluated the k-NN classification error rate for the HMMs on 45 time series data sets from the UCR archive and compared their performance to that of three variations of the Dynamic Time Warping (DTW) algorithms. They observed that their approach is fairly competitive with these other methods.

Do et al. (2017) proposed a new approach to classifying time series using the nearest neighbours method. They first segment each time series, and then transform each segment into their Fourier representation. They describe a time series which is represented by these transformed segments as multimodal and multiscale, the mode being the frequency domain property and the scale referring to the local segments. To compare two series, they use the Euclidean distances between their respective complex number modules in a pair-wise space. For classifying the time series in this pairwise space into known groupings, they apply the k-nearest neighbour method. They evaluate the efficiency of their method on a large number of public datasets, from the URC archive. Refer to Chen et al. (2015) for details of the URC archive.

10.6   Support vector machines

A Support Vector Machine (SVM) is a classifier defined by a separating hyperplane. Given training data of known groupings, the algorithm outputs an optimal hyperplane which categorizes new observations into one of the groupings. The SVM algorithm is based on finding the hyperplane that gives the largest minimum distance to the training data so that the optimal separating hyperplane maximizes the margin of the training data. Refer to Hastie et al. (2009) for more details about SVMs and hyperplanes in general.

SVMs have been extensively used to classify time series in the area of data mining. A problem-specific kernel function is designed to be the dissimilarity measure of the objects under consideration. In that standard setting, the kernel is required to be symmetric and positive definite (PDS). Since this requirement is difficult to meet in practice, Gudmundsson et al. (2008) suggest an arbitrary kernel SVM which involves the use of general pairwise dissimilarity measures . In particular, they suggest using dynamic time warping (DTW) to obtain the distance between two time series instead of the Euclidean distance because DTW alleviates the alignment problems inherent in the Euclidean distance. Given two time series of the same length, they define what they describe as the the negated dynamic time warping (NDWT) kernel

$$k_{NDWT}(\mathbf{x}, \mathbf{y}) = -d_{DTW}(\mathbf{x}, \mathbf{y})$$

where $\mathbf{x}$ and $\mathbf{y}$ are the time series at hand. The NDWT kernel can be shown to be indefinite. They also refer to a Gaussian dynamic time warping kernel proposed by Bahlmann et al. (2002) which they apply to hand-writing recognition and achieved superior recognition rates compared to conventional hidden Markov model (HMM) based methods.

Zhang et al. (2010) discuss the use of the Gaussian DWT kernel (GDTW) and the Guassian radial basis function (RBF) kernel in SVMs which is one of the most commonly used kernels with SVMs and propose extending the RBF kernel to a Gaussian elastic metric kernel (GEMK). Given two time series of the same length, the RBF kernel is defined as

$$k_{GRBF}(\mathbf{x}, \mathbf{y}) = exp\Big(\frac{||(\mathbf{x} - \mathbf{y}||^2}{2\sigma^2}\Big) \tag{10.1}$$

where σ is the common standard deviation of these series which are assumed to be the same. The GRBF kernel is a PDS kernel and can be regarded as embedding the Euclidean distance in the form of a Gaussian function. However, because resampling is required in the use of this kernel if the time series are not of the same length, Zhang et al. (2010) suggests that the GRBF kernel is not suitable for time series classification and hence propose the Gaussian elastic metric kernel (GEMK) where the numerator of Eq. 10.1 is replaced by a combination elastic metrics as discussed in the paper. Experimental results from the application of SVMs to the series from the URC data archive reveal that their proposed GEMK kernel displays superior performance to that of the GDTW and GRBF kernels.

Part III

Software and Data Sets

11

Software and data sets

CONTENTS

11.1 Introduction

In this chapter, we first provide information about the data sets and software used in the applications. For most of the the data sets, links are provided to the website of this book, as well as to other relevant public websites. Both MATLAB and R software were used to obtain the results for the applications. We also provide links to the website of this book and to other relevant websites where specific scripts to functions can be accessed.

In addition, we provide links to R packages that may be useful for many of the methods discussed in the book.

11.2   Chapter 5 Application

11.2.1   Application 5.1

Software: **R**
Data Set: **Climatic Time Series**
Software and data set available from Pierpaolo D'Urso (pierpaolo.durso@uni roma1.it) on request.

11.3   Chapter 6 Applications

11.3.1   Application 6.1

Software: **MATLAB**
Available from: **http://www.tsclustering.homepage.pt/**
Data Set: **DJIA Stocks**
Source of Data: **https://www.globalfinancialdata.com/**
Prepared data set: **DJIA Stocks.xlsx**
Available from: **http://www.tsclustering.homepage.pt/**

11.3.2   Application 6.2

Software: **R**
Data Set: **Daily Stock Returns**
Source of Data: **IBEX-35** – **https://www.stockmaster.in/ibex-35-components-2.html**
Software and data set available from Pierpaolo D'Urso (pierpaolo.durso@uni roma1.it) on request.

11.3.3   Application 6.3

Software: **MATLAB**
Available from: **http://www.tsclustering.homepage.pt/**
Data Set: **EEG Time Series**
Source of Data: **http://www.meb.unibonn.de/epileptologie/science/physik/eegdata.html**
Prepared data set: **EEGdataset.mat**
Available from: **http://www.tsclustering.homepage.pt/**

11.3.4   Application 6.4

Software: **MATLAB**
Available from: **http://www.tsclustering.homepage.pt/**
Data Sets: **Simulated Time Series**

11.3.5   Application 6.5

Software: **MATLAB**
Available from: **http://www.tsclustering.homepage.pt/**
Data Sets: **Simulated Time Series**

11.3.6   Application 6.6

Software: **MATLAB**
Available from: **http://www.tsclustering.homepage.pt/**
Data Set: **Emerging and Developing Market Returns**
Source of Data: **Morgan Stanley Capital Indices (MSCI)** – **https://www.msci.com**
Prepared data set: **dev–emg–returns.xlsx**
Available from: **http://www.tsclustering.homepage.pt/**

11.3.7   Application 6.7

Software: **MATLAB**
Available from: **http://www.tsclustering.homepage.pt/**
Data Sets: **Simulated Time Series**

11.3.8   Application 6.8

Software: **MATLAB**
Available from: **http://www.tsclustering.homepage.pt/**
Data Sets: **Simulated Time Series**

11.4   Chapter 7 Applications

11.4.1   Application 7.1

Software: **MATLAB**
Available from: **http://www.tsclustering.homepage.pt/**
Data Set: **Temperature Time Series**
Source of Data: **Australian Government Bureau of Meteorology** – **http://www.bom.gov.au/climate/data-services**

Prepared data set: **AusTemp15.xlsx**
Available from: **http://www.tsclustering.homepage.pt/**

11.4.2   Application 7.2

Software: **R**
Data Set: **Daily Index Returns**
Source of Data: **http://finance.yahoo.com**
Software and data set available from Pierpaolo D'Urso (pierpaolo.durso@uni roma1.it) on request.

11.4.3   Application 7.3

Software: **MATLAB and R**
Available from: **http://www.tsclustering.homepage.pt/**
Data Set: **Sea Level Time Series**
Source of Data: **University of Hawaii Sea Level Centre (UHSLC)** –
http://uhslc.soest.hawaii.edu/data/download/rq
Prepared data set: **Aus Sea Levels 17.xlsx**
Available from: **http://www.tsclustering.homepage.pt/**

11.5   Chapter 8 Application

11.5.1   Application 8.1

Software: **R**
Available from: *Pierpaolo D'Urso (pierpaolo.durso@uniroma1.it) on request.*
Data Set: **Air Quality Time Series**
Source of Data: **Italian National Institute for Environmental Protection and Research (ISPRA)**– http://eurogoos.eu/member/ispra-institute-for-environmental-protection-and-research-ispra/
Prepared data set: **Pollutants.xlsx**
Available from: **http://www.tsclustering.homepage.pt/**

11.6   Chapter 9 Applications

11.6.1   Application 9.1

Software: **MATLAB**
Available from: **http://www.est.uc3m.es/amalonso/esp/addenda.html**

MATLAB routines used in Maharaj, E.A. and Alonso, A.M. (2007) Discrimination of locally stationary time series using wavelets: Courtesy of Andres Alonso.
Data Set: **Synthetic Control Chart Time Series**
Source of Data: **IUCI KDD Archive – https://kdd.ics.uci.edu**
Prepared data set: **Control Charts.xlsx**
Available from: **http://www.tsclustering.homepage.pt/**

11.6.2 Application 9.2

Software: **MATLAB**
Available from: **http://www.est.uc3m.es/amalonso/esp/addenda.html**
MATLAB routines used in Maharaj, E.A. and Alonso, A.M. (2012) Discriminant analysis of multivariate time series using wavelets: Courtesy of Andres Alonso.
Data Set: **ECG Time Series**
Source of Data: **cardioPATTERN–Telemedical ECG-Evaluation and Follow up 2009 – http://radib.dyndns.org**
Prepared data set: **PTBecg.mat**
Available from: **http://www.tsclustering.homepage.pt/**

11.6.3 Application 9.3

Software: **MATLAB**
Available from: **http://www.tsclustering.homepage.pt/**
Data Set: **Earthquake and Explosions Time Series**
Source of Data: **Blandford (1993)**
Prepared data set: **EqEx.mat**
Available from: **http://www.tsclustering.homepage.pt/**

11.7   Software packages

Time series analysis
There are many libraries in R for time series analysis. A list of software in R for time series analysis is shown:
`https://cran.r-project.org/web/views/TimeSeries.html`

Cluster analysis and finite mixture models
A list of software in R for cluster analysis and finite mixture models is shown:
`https://cran.r-project.org/web/views/Cluster.html`

Fuzzy clustering

Fuzzy clustering methods are implemented, for examples, in the following libraries in R:

- "cluster" (http://cran.r-project.org/web/packages/cluster/),
- "vegclust" (http://cran.r-project.org/web/packages/vegclust/),
- "kml" (http://cran.r-project.org/web/packages/kml/),
- "skmeans" (http://cran.r-project.org/web/packages/skmeans/),
- "clustrd" (http://cran.univ-lyon1.fr/web/packages/clustrd/),
- "clue" (http://cran.r-project.org/web/packages/clue/)

Time series clustering

Examples of libraries in R for time series clustering are:

- "TSclust" (https://cran.r-project.org/web/packages/TSclust/),
- "TSdist" (https://cran.r-project.org/web/packages/TSdist/),
- "dtwclust" (https://cran.r-project.org/web/packages/dtwclust/),
- "kml3d" (https://cran.r-project.org/web/packages/kml3d/).

Hidden Markov Models

- "HMM" (https://cran.r-project.org/web/packages/HMM/),
- "HiddenMarkov" (https://cran.r-project.org/web/packages/HiddenMarkov/).

Support Vector Machine

- "SwarmSVM" (https://cran.r-project.org/web/packages/SwarmSVM/).

Self-Organizing Maps

- "som" (https://cran.r-project.org/web/packages/som/),
- "kohonen" (https://cran.r-project.org/web/packages/kohonen/).

Classification trees

- "tree" (https://cran.r-project.org/web/packages/tree/).

Bibliography

[1] Alagon, J. (1989). Spectral discrimination for two groups of time series, *Journal of Time Series Analysis* 10:3, 203-214.

[2] Alcock, R.J., Manolopoulos, Y. (1999). Time-series similarity queries employing a feature-based approach. In: *Seventh Hellenic Conference on Informatics,* Ioannina, Greece.

[3] Al-Naima, F., Al-Timemy, A. (2009). In: Peng-Yeng, Y. (Ed.), Neural Network based Classification of Myocardial Infraction: A Comparative Study of Wavelet and Fourier Transforms in Pattern Recognition. In-Tech, 338-352.

[4] Alonso, A.M., Maharaj, E.A. (2006). Comparison of time series using subsampling, *Computational Statistics & Data Analysis* 50, 2589-2599.

[5] Alonso, A.M., Berrendero, J.R., Hernandez, A. and Justel, A. (2006). Time series clustering based on forecast densities. *Computational Statistics & Data Analysis* 51, 762-776.

[6] Anderson, G.J., Linton, O.B. and Whang, Y.-J. (2012). Nonparametric estimation and inference about the overlap of two distributions. *Journal of Econometrics* 171, 1-23.

[7] Andrzejak, R.G., Lehnertz, K., Rieke, C., Mormann, F., David, P. and Elger, C.E. (2001). Indications of nonlinear deterministic and finite dimensional structures in time series of brain electrical activity: dependence on recording region and brain state. *Phys. Rev. E* 64, 061907.

[8] Aach, J., Church, G. (2001). Aligning gene expression time series with time warping algorithms. *Bioinformatics* 17, 495-508.

[9] Ausloos, M.A., Lambiotte, R. (2007). Clusters or networks of economies? A macroeconomy study through Gross Domestic Product, *Physica A* 382, 16-21.

[10] Australian Bureau of Statistics (2009). http://www.abs.gov.au/Retail-and-Wholesale-Trade.

[11] Bahlmann, C., Hassdonk, B. and Burkhardt. (2002). Online handwriting recognition with support vector machines - a kernel approach. *Proceedings. 8th International Workshop on Frontiers in Handwriting Recognition (IWFHR)*, 49-54.

[12] Banerjee, S., Mitra, M. (2010). ECG feature extraction and classification of anteroseptal myocardial infarction and normal subjects using discrete wavelet transform. In: *Proceedings of 2001 International Conference on Systems in Medicine and Biology*, 16-18 December 2010, IIT, Kharagpur, India.

[13] Banfield, J.D., Raftery, A.E. (1993). Model-based Gaussian and non-Gaussian clustering, *Biometrics*, 49:803-821. 345, 354.

[14] Bastos, J.A., Caiado J. (2014). Clustering financial time series with variance ratio statistics. *Quantitative Finance* 12, 2121-2133.

[15] Basalto, N., Bellotti, R., De Carlo, F., Facchi, P., Pantaleo, E. and Pascazio, S. (2007). Hausdorff clustering of financial time series, *Physica A*, 379, 635-644.

[16] Ben-Hur, D., Horn, H.T., Siegelmann, V. and Vapnik, V. (2001). Support vector clustering. *J. Mach. Learn. Res.*, 2,125-137.

[17] Berndt, D., Clifford, J. (1994). Using dynamic time series warping to find patterns in time series, *AAA1-94 Workshop on Knowledge Discovery in Databases*, 229-248.

[18] Beyen, K., Goldstein, J., Ramakrishnan, R. and Shaft, U. (1999). When is the nearest neighbour meaningful?, *Proceedings of the 7th International Conference on Database Theory*, 217-235.

[19] Bezdek, J.C. (1981). *Pattern Recognition with Fuzzy Objective Function Algorithms*, Kluwer Academic Publishers,Plenum Press, New York.

[20] Bezdek, J.C. (2001). *Pattern Recognition with Fuzzy Objective Function Algorithms*, Kluwer Academic Publishers, Plenum Press, New York.

[21] Biernacki, C., Celeux, G. and Govaert, G. (2000). Assessing a mixture model for clustering with integrated completed likelihood, *IEEE Transactions on Pattern Analysis and Machine Intelligence*, 22: 719-725. 353.

[22] Blandford, R.R. (1993). Discrimination of earthquakes and explosions at regional distances using complexity, *AFTAC–TR–93–044 HQ, Air Force Technical Applications Centre*, Patrick Air Force Base, FL.

[23] Bloomfield, P. (2000). *Fourier Analysis of Time Series: An Introduction*. Wiley, New York.

[24] Boeking, B., Stephan, K.C., Detlef, S. and Wong, A.S.W. (2015). Support vector clustering of time series data with alignment kernels. *Pattern Recognition Letters*, 2,125-137.

[25] Boets, J., De Cock, K., Espinoza, M. and De Moor, B. (2005). Clustering time series, subspace identification and cepstral distances, *Commun. Info. Syst.* 5, 1, 69-96.

[26] Bollerslev, T., Chou, R.Y. and Kroner, K.F. (1992). ARCH modeling in finance. *Journal of Econometrics* 1-2, 5-59.

[27] Bousseljot, R., Kreiseler, D. and Schnabel, A. (1995). *Nutzung der EKG-signaldatenbank CARDIODAT der PTB ber das internet. Biomedizinische Technik.* 40 (S1), S317.

[28] Bozzola, G., Bortolan, G., Combi, C., Pinciroli, F. and Brohet, C. (1996). A hybrid neuro-fuzzy system for ECG classification of myocardial infraction. *Computers in Cardiology*, 241-244.

[29] Brandmaier, A.M. (2011). *Permutation distribution clustering and structural equation model trees.* Ph.D. Thesis Universitat des Saarlandes, Saarbrucken, Germany.

[30] Brockwell, P.J., Davis, R.A. (1991). *Time Series: Theory and Methods.* 2nd ed., Springer, New York.

[31] Box, G.E.P., Jenkins, G.M. and Reinsel, G.C. (1994). *Time Series Analysis. Forecasting and Control*, 3rd Edition, Prentice Hall, New Jersey.

[32] Coles, S. (2001). *An Introduction to Statistical Modeling of Extreme Values*, Springer-Verlag: London.

[33] Caiado, J., Crato, N. (2010). Identifying common dynamic features in stock returns, *Quantitative Finance* 10, 797-807.

[34] Caiado, J. (2006). *Distance-Based Methods for Classification and Clustering of Time Series.* PhD Thesis, ISEG, University of Lisbon, Portugal.

[35] Caiado, J., Crato, N. and Peña, D. (2006). A periodogram-based metric for time series classification, *Computational Statistics & Data Analysis* 50, 2668-2684.

[36] Caiado, J., Crato, N. and Peña, D. (2009). Comparison of time series with unequal length in the frequency domain, *Communications in Statistics-Simulation and Computation* 38, 527-540.

[37] Caiado, J., Crato, N. and Peña, D. (2012). Tests for comparing time series of unequal lengths, *Journal of Statistical Computing and Simulation* 12. 1715-1725.

[38] Caiani, E.G., Porta, A., Baselli, G., Turiel, M., Muzzupappa, S., Pieruzzi, F., Crema, C., Malliani, A. and Cerutti, S. (1998). Warped-average template technique to track on a cycle-by-cycle basis the cardiac filling phases on left ventricular volume.*IEEE Computers in Cardiology*. 73-76.

[39] Calinski, T., Harabasz, J. (1974). A dendrite method for cluster analysis. *Communications in Statistics*, 3(1):1-27.

[40] Campello, R.J.G.B., Hruschka, E.R. (2006). A fuzzy extension of the silhouette width criterion for cluster analysis. *Fuzzy Sets and Systems*, 157(21):2858-2875.

[41] cardioPATTERN, Telemedical ECG-Evaluation and Follow up (2009). http://radib.dyndns.org.

[42] Chandler, G., Polonik, W. (2006). Discrimination of locally stationary time series based on the excess mass functional. *Journal of the American Statistical Association*, 101:473, 240-253.

[43] Chatfield, C. (2004). *The Analysis of Time Series, An Introduction*, 3rd Edition. Chapman and Hall/CRC, New York.

[44] Chernoff, H. (1952). A measure of asymptotic efficiency for tests of a hypothesis based on the sum of observations. *The Annals of Mathematical Statistics* 23:4, 493-507.

[45] Chen, Y., Keogh, E., Hu, B., Begum, N., Bagnall, A., Mueen, A. and Batista, G. (2015). The UCR time series classification archive. URL www.cs.ucr.edu/~eamonn/time_series_data.

[46] Chinganda, E.F., Subrahaniam, K. (1979). Robustness of the linear discriminant function to nonnormality: Johnson's system. *Journal of Statistical Planning and Inference* 3, 69-77.

[47] Chinipardaz, R., Cox, T.F. (2004). Nonparametric discrimination of time series, *Metrika* 59:1, 13-20.

[48] Chow, K., Denning, K.C. (1993). A simple multiple variance ratio test, *Journal of Econometrics* 58:3, 385-401.

[49] Chu, S., Keogh, E., Hart, D. and Pazzani, M. (2002). Iterative deepening dynamic time warping for time series. *Proc 2nd SIAM International Conference on Data Mining*.

[50] Cilibrasi, R., Vitányi, P.M.B. (2005). Clustering by compression. *IEEE Tranactions on Information Theory*. 51, 1523-1545.

[51] Clifford, G., Nemati, S. and Sameni, R. (2010). An artificial vector model for generating abnormal electrocardiographic rhythms, *Journal of Physiological Measurements* 31 (5), 595-609.

[52] Coates, D.S., Diggle, P.J. (1986). Test for comparing two estimated spectral densities. *J. TimeSer. Anal.* 7, 7-20.

[53] Cochrane, J. (1991). A critique of the application of unit root tests, *Journal of Economic Dynamics and Control* 15:2, 275-284.

[54] Coles, S. (2001). *An Introduction to Statistical Modeling of Extreme Values.* Springer-Verlag: London (2001).

[55] Coppi, R., D'Urso, P. (2000). Fuzzy time arrays and dissimilarity measures for fuzzy time trajectories, in *Data Analysis, Classification, and Related Methods* (eds. H.A.L Kiers, J.P. Rasson, P.J.F. Groenen, M. Schader), 273-278, Springer-Verlag, Berlin.

[56] Coppi, R., D'Urso, P. (2001). The geometric approach to the comparison of multivariate time trajectories, in *Advances in Data Science and Classification* (eds. S. Borra, R. Rocci, M. Vichi, M. Schader), 93-100, Springer-Verlag, Heidelberg.

[57] Coppi, R., D'Urso, P. (2002). Fuzzy K-Means Clustering models for triangular fuzzy time trajectories, *Statistical Methods and Applications*, 11, 21-40.

[58] Coppi, R., D'Urso, P. (2003). Three-Way Fuzzy Clustering models for LR fuzzy time trajectories, *Computational Statistics & Data Analysis*, 43, 149-177.

[59] Coppi, R., D'Urso, P. (2006). Fuzzy unsupervised classification of multivariate time trajectories with the Shannon Entropy Regularization, *Computational Statistics & Data Analysis*, 50 (6), 1452-1477.

[60] Coppi, R., D'Urso, P. and Giordani, P. (2006). Fuzzy c-medoids clustering models for time-varying data. In Bouchon-Meunier, B., Coletti, G. and Yager, R.R. (eds), Modern Information Processing: From Theory to Applications, Elsevier, Perugia.

[61] Coppi, R., D'Urso, P. and Giordani, P. (2010). A Fuzzy clustering model for multivariate spatial time series, *Journal of Classification*, 27, 54-88.

[62] Corduas, M., Piccolo, D. (2008). Time series clustering and classification by the autoregressive metric, *Computational Statistics & Data Analysis* 52, 1860-1872.

[63] Cornish, C.R., Bretherton, C.S. and Percival, D.B. (2004). Maximal overlap wavelet statistical analysis with applications to atmospheric turbulence, *Boundary-Layer Meteorology*, 119 (2), 339-374.

[64] Crato, N., Taylor, H. (1996). Stationary persistent time series misspecified as nonstationary ARIMA. *Statistische Hefte/Statistical Papers* 37, 215-223.

[65] Cuturi, M., Vert, J.-P., Birkenes, O. and Matsui, T. (2007). A kernel for time series based on global alignments. *Proceedings of ICASSP*, volume II, 413-416.

[66] Dahlhaus, R. (1997). Fitting time series models to nonstationary processes, *The Annals of Statistics* 25:1 1-37.

[67] Dargahi-Noubary, G.R. and Laycock, P.J. (1981). Spectral ratio discriminants and information theory. *Journal of Time Series Analysis* 2:2 71-86.

[68] Davé, R.N. (1991). Characterization and detection of noise in clustering. *Pattern Recognition Letters*, 12(11):657-664.

[69] Davé, R.N., Sen, S. (1997). Noise clustering algorithm revisited. In 1997 Annual Meeting of the North American Fuzzy Information Processing Society. NAFIPS-97, pages 199-204. IEEE.

[70] Davé, R.N., Sen, S. (2002). Robust fuzzy clustering of relational data. *IEEE Transactions on Fuzzy Systems*, 10(6):713-727.

[71] Davies, R.B., Harte, D.S. (1987). Tests for Hurst effect, *Biometrika* 74: 1, 95-101.

[72] Davis R.A., Mikosch, T. (2009). The extremeogram: a correlogram for extreme events, *Bernoulli*, 15(4), 977-1009.

[73] Dahlhaus, R. (1997). Fitting time series models to nonstationary processes, *The Annals of Statistics* 25:1 1-37.

[74] De Chazal, P., Reilly, R.B. (2000). A comparison of the ECG classification performance of different feature sets. *Computers in Cardiology* 27, 327-330.

[75] Department of Climate Change, Commonwealth of Australia (2009). www.climatechange.gov.au , ISBN: 978-1-921298-71-4 .

[76] DeJong, D.N., Nankervis, J.C., Savin, N.E. and Whiteman, C.H. (1992). Integration versus trend stationary in time series, *Econometrica* 60:2, 423-433.

[77] Dette, H., Hallin, M., Kley, T. and Volgushev, S. (2014). Of copulas, quantiles, ranks and spectra: an l_1-approach to spectral analysis, ArXiv e-prints, arXiv:1111.7205v2.

[78] Diebold, F.X., Rudebusch, G.D. (1991). On the power of Dickey-Fuller tests against fractional alternatives, *Economics Letters* 25:2, 155-160.

[79] Diggle, P.J., Fisher, N.I. (1991). Nonparametric comparison of cumulative periodograms, *Appl. Statist.* 40, 423-434.

[80] Disegna, M., D'Urso, P. and Durante, F. (2017). Copula-based fuzzy clustering of spatial time series, *Spatial Statistics* 21, 209-225.

[81] Do, C., Douzal-Chouakria, A., Marié, S. and Rombaut, M. (2017). Multi-modal and multi-scale temporal metric learning for a robust time series nearest neighbours classification. *Information Sciences* 418-419, 272-285.

[82] Dose, C., Cincotti, S. (2005). Clustering of financial time series with application to index and enhanced-index tracking portfolio, *Physica A*, 355, 145-151.

[83] Dunn, C. (1974). Well separated clusters and optimal fuzzy partitions *J.Cybern* 4, 1, 95-104.

[84] Dunn, C. (1977). Indices of partition fuzziness and detection of clusters in large data sets, in: *Fuzzy Automata and Decision Processes*, M. Gupta, G. Saridis (eds.) Elsevier, New York.

[85] Douzal-Chouakria, A., Amblard, C. (2012). Classification trees for time series. *Pattern Recognition* 45, 1076-1091.

[86] D'Urso, P., Vichi, M. (1998). Dissimilarities between trajectories of a three-way longitudinal data set, in *Advances in Data Science and Classification*, (eds. A. Rizzi, M. Vichi, H.H. Bock), 585-592, Springer-Verlag, Berlin.

[87] D'Urso, P. (2000). Dissimilarity measures for time trajectories, *Statistical Methods and Applications*, 1-3, 53-83.

[88] D'Urso, P. (2004). Fuzzy C-Means Clustering models for multivariate time-varying data: different approaches, *International Journal of Uncertainty, Fuzziness and Knowledge-Based Systems*, 12 (3), 287-326.

[89] D'Urso, P. (2005). Fuzzy clustering for data time arrays with inlier and outlier time trajectories, *IEEE Transactions on Fuzzy Systems*, 13, 5, 583-604.

[90] D'Urso, P., De Giovanni, L. (2008). Temporal self-organizing maps for telecommunications market segmentation, *Neurocomputing*, 71, 2880-2892.

[91] D'Urso, P., Maharaj, E.A. (2009). Autocorrelation-based fuzzy clustering of time series, *Fuzzy Sets and Systems* 160, 3565-3589.

[92] D'Urso, P., Maharaj, E.A. (2012). Wavelets-based clustering of multivariate time series, *Fuzzy Sets and Systems* 196, 33-61.

[93] D'Urso, P., Di Lallo, D. and Maharaj, E.A. (2013a). Autoregressive model-based fuzzy clustering and its application for detecting information redundancy in air pollution monitoring networks, *Soft Computing* 17, 83-131.

[94] D'Urso, P., Cappelli, C., Di Lallo, D. and Massari, R. (2013b). Clustering of financial time series, *Physica A: Statistical Mechanics and its Applications*, 392(9): 2114-2129.

[95] D'Urso, P., De Giovanni, L., Massari, R. and Di Lallo, D. (2013c). Noise fuzzy clustering of time series by the autoregressive metric, *Metron* 71, 217-243.

[96] D'Urso, P., De Giovanni, L., Maharaj, E.A. and Massari, R. (2014). Wavelet-based Self-Organizing Maps for classifying multivariate time series, *Journal of Chemometrics* 28, 1, 28-51.

[97] D'Urso, P. (2015). Fuzzy Clustering. In Hennig, C., Meila, M., Murtagh, F. and Rocci, R., editors, *Handbook of Cluster Analysis*, 545-573. Chapman and Hall.

[98] D'Urso, P., De Giovanni, L. and Massari, R. (2015). Time series clustering by a robust autoregressive metric with application to air pollution, *Chemometrics and Intelligent Laboratory Systems* 141(15), 107-124.

[99] D'Urso, P., De Giovanni, L. and Massari, R. (2016). GARCH-based robust clustering of time series, *Fuzzy Sets and System*, 305: 1-28.

[100] D'Urso, P., Maharaj, E.A. and Alonso, A.M. (2017a). Fuzzy clustering of time series using extremes, *Fuzzy Sets and Systems* 318, 56-79.

[101] D'Urso, P., Massari, R., Cappelli, C. and De Giovanni, L. (2017b). Autoregressive metric-based trimmed fuzzy clustering with an application to P M10 time series. *Chemometrics and Intelligent Laboratory Systems*, 161:15-26.

[102] D'Urso, P., De Giovanni, L. and Massari, R. (2018). Robust fuzzy clustering of multivariate time trajectories, *International Journal of Approximate Reasoning*, 99, 12-38.

[103] Dudoit, S., Fridlyand, J. and Speed, T.P. (2002). Comparison of discrimination methods for the classification of tumors using gene expression data. *Journal of the American Statistical Association* 97:457, 77-87.

[104] Enders, W. (1995). *Applied Econometric Time Series*, John Wiley & Sons, New York.

[105] Everitt, B.S., Landau, S., Leese, M. and Stahl, D. (2011). *Cluster Analysis*, 5th Edition. Wiley, United Kingdom.

[106] Fatti, L.P., Hawkins, D.M. and Raath, E.L. (1982). Discriminant analysis. In: Hawkins, D.M. (Ed.), *Topics in Applied Multivariate Analysis*. Cambridge University Press, Cambridge, pp. 1-71.

[107] Fruhwirth-Schnatter, S., Kaufmann, S. (2008). Model-based clustering of multiple time series, *Journal of Business and Economic Statistics*, 26: 1, 78-89.

[108] Fryzlewicz, P., Ombao, H. (2012). Consistent classification of non-stationary time series using stochastic wavelet representations, *Journal of the American Statistical Association* 104:485, 299-312.

[109] Fu, K.S. (1982). *Syntactic Pattern Recognition and Applications*. Academic Press, San Diego.

[110] Galeano, P., Peña, D. (2000). Multivariate analysis in vector time series, *Resenhas* 4, 383-404.

[111] Gan, G., Wu, J. (2008). A convergence theorem for the fuzzy subspace clustering (FSC) algorithm. *Pattern Recognition*, 41(6):1939-1947.

[112] García-Escudero, L.A., Gordaliza, A. (1999). Robustness properties of k-means and trimmed k-means. *Journal of the American Statistical Association*, 94(447):956-969.

[113] García-Escudero, L.A., Gordaliza, A. (2005). A proposal for robust curve clustering. *Journal of Classification*, 22(2):185-201.

[114] García-Escudero, L.A., Gordaliza, A. and Matrán, C. (2003). Trimming tools in exploratory data analysis. *Journal of Computational and Graphical Statistics*, 12:434-449.

[115] García-Escudero, L.A., Gordaliza, A., Matrán, C. and Mayo-Iscar, A. (2010). A review of robust clustering methods. *Advances in Data Analysis and Classification*, 4:89-109.

[116] Ghassempour, S., Girosi, F. and Maeder A. (2014). Clustering multivariate time series using hidden Markov models. *Int. J. Environ. Res. Public Health.* 11:3 2741-2763.

[117] Goldberger, A.L., Amaral, L.A.N., Glass, L., Hausdorff, J.M., Ivanov, P.Ch., Mark, R.G., Mietus, J.E., Moody, G.B., Peng, C.-K. and Stanley, H.E. (2000). PhysioBank, physiotoolkit, and physionet: components of a new research resource for complex physiologic signals. Circulation 101 (23), e215-e220. Circulation Electronic Pages: http://circ.ahajournals.org/cgi/content/full/101/23/e215. The PTB Diagnostic ECG Database: http://www.physionet.org/ physiobank/database/ptbd.

[118] Glosten, L.R., Jagannathan, R. and Runkle, D.E. (1993). On the relation between the expected value and the volatility of the nominal excess return on stocks, *Journal of Finance* 48:5, 1779-1801.

[119] Goutte, C., Toft, P., Rostrup, E., Nielsen, F. and Hansen, L.K. (1999). On clustering fMRI time series, *NeoroImage* 9 (3), 298-310.

[120] Granger, C.W.J., Joyeux, R. (1980). An introduction to long memory time series and fractional differencing, *Journal of Time Series Analysis* 1:1, 15-29.

[121] Guedes Soares, C., Scotto, M.G. (2004). Application of the r-order statistics for long-term predictions of significant wave heights. *Coast. Eng.* 51, 387-394.

[122] Gudmundsson, S., Runarsson, T.P. and Sigurdsson, S. (2008). Support vector machines and dynamic time warping for time series, *Neural Networks, 2008. IJCNN 2008. (IEEE World Congress on Computational Intelligence). IEEE International Joint Conference*, 2772-2776.

[123] Hagemann, A. (2013). Robust spectral analysis, ArXiv and e-prints, arXiv:1111.1965v1.

[124] Hassler, U., Wolters, J. (1994). On the power of unit root tests against fractional alternatives, *Economics Letters* 45:1, 1-5.

[125] Hastie, T., Tibshirani, R., Friedman. J. (2009). *The Elements of Statistical Learning.* Springer, New York.

[126] Heden, B., Ohlin, H., Rittner, R. and Edenbrandt, L. (1997). Acute myocardial infarction detected in 12-lead ECG by artificial neural networks. *Circulation: American Heart Association Inc.* 96, 1798-1802.

[127] Heiser, W.J., Groenen, P.J.F. (1997). Cluster differences scaling with a within-clusters loss component and a fuzzy successive approximation strategy to avoid local minima. *Psychometrika*, 62(1):63-83.

[128] Hettich, S., Bay, S.D. (1999). The UCI KDD Archive. Irvine, CA: University of California, Department of Information and Computer Science, Available from: *http : //kdd.ics.uci.edu.*

[129] Hosking, J.R.M. (1981). Fractional differencing, *Biometrika* 68:1, 165-176.

[130] Huang, H., Ombao, H. and Stoffer, D.S. (2004). Discrimination and classification of nonstationary time series using the SLEX model, *Journal of the American Statistical Association* 99:467, 763-774.

[131] Huang, X., Ye, Y., Xiong, L., Lau, R.Y.K., Jiang, N. and Wang, S. (2016). Time series k-means: a new k-means type smooth subspace clustering for time series data, *Information Sciences*, 367-368, 1-13.

[132] Izakian, H., Pedrycz, W. and Jamal, I. (2015). Fuzzy clustering of time series data using dynamic time warping distance, *Engineering Applications of Artificial Intelligence*, 39, 235-244.

[133] Jebara, T., Song, Y. and Thadani, K. (2007). Spectral clustering and embedding with hidden Markov models. *ECML*, 164-175.

[134] Jeong, Y.-S., Jeong, M.K. and Omitaomu, O.A. (2011). Weighted dynamic time warping for time series classification, *Pattern Recognition*, 44, 2231-2240.

[135] Johnson, R.A., Wichern, D.W. (1992). *Applied Multivariate Statistical Analysis*. 3rd edition., Englewood Cliffs, Prentice-Hall.

[136] Kakizawa, Y., Shumway, R.H. and Taniguchi, M. (1998). Discrimination and clustering for multivariate time series, *Journal of the American Statistical Association* 93, 328-340.

[137] Kalpakis, K., Gada, D. and Puttagunta, V. (2001). Distance measures for the effective clustering of ARIMA time-series, *Proceedings of the IEEE International Conference on Data Mining, San Jose*, 273-280.

[138] Kamdar, T., Joshi, A. (2000). On Creating Adaptive Web Servers using Weblog Mining. Technical report TR-CS- 00-05, Department of Computer Science and Electrical Engineering, University of Maryland, Baltimore County.

[139] Kannathal, N., Choo, M.L., Acharya, U.R. and Sadasivan, P.K. (2005). Entropies in the detection of epilepsy in EEG. *Comput. Methods Programs Biomedicine* 80:3, 187-194.

[140] Kaufman, L., Rousseeuw, P.J. (1987). Clustering by Means of Medoids, *Statistics Data Analysis based on the L1-Norm and Related Methods* (Ed. Y. Dodge). Elsevier, North-Holland, Amsterdam.

[141] Kaufman, L., Rousseeuw, P.J. (1990). *Finding Groups in Data: An Introduction to Cluster Analysis*. New York: J. Wiley and Sons.

[142] Kaufman, L., Rousseeuw, P.J. (2009). *Finding Groups in Data: an Introduction to Cluster Analysis*, Volume 344. John Wiley & Sons.

[143] Keogh, E., Lonardi, S., Ratanamahatana, C.A., Wei, L., Lee, S.H. and Handley, J. (2007). Compression-based data mining of sequential data. *Data Mining and Knowledge Discovery*, 14, 1, 99-129.

[144] Keogh, E., Pazzani, S. (2000). Scaling up dynamic time warping for data mining applications, *6th ACM SIGKDD International Conference on Knowledge Discovery and Data Mining*. Boston, 16-22.

[145] Keogh, E., Pazzani, S. (2001). Derivative dynamic time warping, *Proceedings of the 2001 SIAM International Conference on Data Mining*.

[146] Kiefer, J. (1959). K-Sample analogues of the Kolmogorov-Smirnov and Cramer-V. misses tests, *The Annals of Mathematical Statistics* 30: 2 420-447.

[147] Kannathal, N., Choo, M.L., Acharya, U.R. and Sadasivan, P.K. (2005). Entropies in the detection of epilepsy in EEG. *Computer Methods and Programs in Biomedicine* 80, 3, 187-194.

[148] Kopiec, D., Martyna, J. (2011). A hybrid approach for ECG classification based on particle swarm optimization and support vector machine. In: Corchado, E., Kurzynski, M., Wozniak, M. (Eds.), *HAIS2011, Part 1, LNAI*, vol. 6678. pp. 329-337.

[149] Kotsifakos, A., Panagiotis, P. (2014). Model-based time series classification. *Advances in Intelligent Data Analysis XIII* in *Lecture Notes in Computer Science, Springer International Publishing*, 8819, 179-191.

[150] Košmelj, K., Batagelj, V. (1990). Cross-sectional approach for clustering time varying data, *Journal of Classification*, 7, 99-109.

[151] Krishnapuram, R., Joshi, A., Nasraoui, O. and Yi, L. (2001). Low-complexity fuzzy relational clustering algorithms for web mining. *IEEE Transactions on Fuzzy Systems*, 9(4):595-607.

[152] Krishnapuram, R., Joshi, A. and Yi, L. (1999). A fuzzy relative of the k-medoids algorithm with application to web document and snippet clustering. In Fuzzy Systems Conference Proceedings, 1999. FUZZ-IEEE-99. 1999 IEEE International, volume 3, pages 1281-1286. IEEE.

[153] Kruse, R., Doring, C. and Lesot, M.-J. (2007). Fundamentals of fuzzy clustering. In De Oliveira, J.V., Pedrycz, W., editors, *Advances in Fuzzy Clustering and its Applications*, pages 3-30. Wiley.

[154] Kullback, S., Leibler, R.A. (1951). On information and sufficiency, *The Annals of Mathematical Statistics* 22:1 79-86.

[155] Lachenbruch, P.A., Mickey, M.R. (1968). Estimation of error rates in discriminant analysis. *Technometrics* 10, 1-10.

[156] Lafuente-Rego, B., D'Urso, P. and Vilar, J.A. (2017). Robust fuzzy clustering of time series based on the quantile autocovariances, *submitted.*

[157] Lafuente-Rego, B., Vilar, J.A. (2015). Clustering of time series using quantile autocovariances, *Advances in Data Analysis and Classification*, 10, 391-415.

[158] Lee, J., Rao, S. (2012). The quantile spectral density and comparison based tests for nonlinear time series, *Unpublished manuscript*, Department of Statistics, Texas A&M University, College Station, USA, arXiv:1112.2759v2,

[159] Liao, T.W. (2005). Clustering of time series data - a survey. *Pattern Recognition* 38, 1857-1874.

[160] Li, M., Chen, X., Li, X., Ma, B. and Vitányi, P.M.B. (2004). The similarity metric. *IEEE Tranactions on Information Theory.* 50, 12, 3250-3264.

[161] Li, R.P., Mukaidono, M. (1995). A maximum-entropy approach to fuzzy clustering. In *Proceedings of the 4th IEEE Conference on Fuzzy Systems* (FUZZ-IEEE/IFES-95), volume 4, pages 2227-2232, Yokohama. IEEE.

[162] Li, R.P., Mukaidono, M. (1999). Gaussian clustering method based on maximum-fuzzy-entropy interpretation. *Fuzzy Sets and Systems,* 102(2):253-258.

[163] Li, S., Lu, Y.L., Yang, K. and Li, S. (2012). ECG Analysis using multiple instance learning for myocardial infarction detection. *IEEE Transactions on Biomedical Engineering* 59 (12), 3348-3356.

[164] Liu, S., Maharaj, E.A. (2013). A hypothesis test using bias-adjusted AR estimators for classifying time series, *Computational Statistics and Data Analysis* 60, 32-49.

[165] Liu, S., Maharaj, E.A. and Inder, B.A. (2014). Polarization of forecast densities: a new approach to time series classification, *Computational Statistics & Data Analysis* 70, 245-361.

[166] Lo, A.W., MacKinlay, A.C. (1988). Stock market prices do not follow random walks: evidence from a simple specification test, *Review of Financial Studies* 1:1, 41-66.

[167] Longford, N.T., D'Urso, P. (2012). Mixtures of autoregressions with an improper component for panel data, *Journal of Classification* 29, 341-362.

[168] MacQueen, J. (1967). Some methods for classification and analysis of multivariate observations. In *Proceedings of the Fifth Berkeley Symposium on Mathematical Statistics and Probability,* volume 1, pages 281-297. California, USA.

[169] Maharaj, E.A. (1996). A significance test for classifying ARMA models, *Journal of Statistical Computation & Simulation* 54, 305-331.

[170] Maharaj, E.A. (1997). Pattern recognition techniques for time series, PhD Thesis, Monash University, Australia.

[171] Maharaj, E.A. (1999). The comparison and classification of stationary multivariate time series, *Pattern Recognition* 32, 7, 1129-1138.

[172] Maharaj, E.A. (2000). Clusters of time series, *Journal of Classification* 17, 297-314.

[173] Maharaj, E.A. (2002). Comparison of non-stationary time series in the frequency domain, *Computational Statistics & Data Analysis* 40, 131-141.

[174] Maharaj, E.A. (2005). Using wavelets to compare time series patterns, *International Journal of Wavelets, Multiresolution & Information Processing* 3, 4, 511-521.

[175] Maharaj, E.A., Alonso, A.M. (2014). Discrimination of multivariate time series: application to diagnosis based on ECG signals,*Computational Statistics & Data Analysis* 70, 67-87.

[176] Maharaj, E.A., D'Urso, P. (2010). A coherence-based approach for the pattern recognition of time series, *Physica A: Statistical Mechanics* 389, 17, 3516-3537.

[177] Maharaj, E.A., D'Urso, P. and Galagedera, D.U.A. (2010). Wavelets-based fuzzy clustering of time series, *Journal of Classification* 27, 2, 231-275.

[178] Maharaj, E.A., D'Urso, P. (2011). Fuzzy clustering of time series in the frequency domain, *Information Sciences*, 181, 1187-1211.

[179] Maharaj, E.A. (2014). Classification of cyclical time series using complex demodulation, *Statistics and Computing* 24,6,1031-1046.

[180] Maharaj, E.A., Alonso, A.M. (2007). Discriminant analysis of locally stationary time series using wavelets,*Computational Statistics & Data Analysis* 52, 879-895.

[181] Maharaj, E.A., Alonso, A.M. and D'Urso, P. (2016). Clustering seasonal time series using extreme value analysis: an application to Spanish temperature time series, *Communications in Statistics: Case Studies and Data Analysis*, 1, 175-191.

[182] Makridakis, S., Wheelwright, C., Hyndman, R.J. (1998). *Forecasting: Methods and Applications*, 3rd Edition. Wiley, New York.

[183] Montero, P., Villar, J. (2014). TClust: an R package for time series clustering, *Journal of Statistical Software* 62, 1, 1-43.

[184] McLachlan, G.J. (1992). *Discriminant Analysis and Statistical Pattern Recognition*. Wiley, New York.

[185] McBratney, A.B., Moore, A.W. (1985). Application of fuzzy sets to climatic classification. *Agricultural and Forest Meteorology*, 35(1):165-185.

[186] Mikosch, T., Stărică, C. (2000). Limit theory of the sample autocorrelation and extreme of a GARCH(1,1) process, *Annals of Statistics*, 28(5), 1427-1451.

[187] Milligan, G.W., Cooper, M.C. (1985). An examination of procedures for determining the number of clusters in a data set. *Psychometrika*, 50, 159-179.

[188] Miskiewicz, J., Ausloos, M. (2008). Correlation measure to detect time series distances, whence economy globalization, *Physica A* 387, 6584-6594.

[189] Miyamoto, S., Mukaidono, M. (1997). Fuzzy c-means as a regularization and maximum entropy approach. In *IFSA 97 Prague: Proceedings of the Seventh International Fuzzy Systems Association World Congress*, pages 86-92.

[190] Nasraoui, O., Krishnapuram, R., Joshi, A. and Kamdar, T. (2002). Automatic web user profiling and personalization using robust fuzzy relational clustering. In *E-commerce and Intelligent Methods*, 233-261. Springer.

[191] Nigam, V.P., Graupe, D. (2004). A neural-network-based detection of epilepsy. *Neurological Research* 26, 1, 55-60.

[192] Oates, T., Firoiu, L., Cohen, P.R. (1999). Clustering time series with Hidden Markov Models and Dynamic Time Warping. *Proceedings of the IJCAI*

[193] Ohashi, Y. (1984). Fuzzy clustering and robust estimation. In *Ninth Meeting of SAS Users Group Int.*

[194] Otranto, E. (2008). Clustering heteroskedastic time series by model-based procedures, *Computational Statistics & Data Analysis* 52, 4685-4698.

[195] Otranto, E. (2010). Identifying financial time series with similar dynamic conditional correlation, *Computational Statistics & Data Analysis* 54, 1, 1-15.

[196] Ord, K., Fildes, F. (2013). *Principles of Business Forecasting*. Southwestern Cenage Learning.

[197] Pamminger, C., Fruhwirth-Schnatter, S. (2010). Model-based clustering of categorical time series, *Bayesian Analysis*, 2, 345-368.

[198] Percival, D.B., Walden, A.T. (2000). *Wavelet Methods for Time Series Analysis*. Cambridge University Press, Cambridge.

[199] Pham, D.T., Chan, A.B. (1998). Control chart pattern recognition using a new type of self organizing neural network. *Proc. Inst. Mech. Eng.* 212: 2, 115-127.

[200] Piccolo, D. (1990). A distance measure for classifying ARIMA models, *Journal of Time Series Analysis* 11, 2, 153-164.

[201] Povinelli, R.J., Johnson, M.T. and Lindgren, A.C. (2004). Time series classification using Gaussian mixture models of reconstructed phase spaces. *IEEE Tranactions on Knowledge and Data Engineering* 16: 6, 779-783.

[202] Ramoni, M., Sebastiani, P. and Cohen, P. (2002). Bayesian clustering by dynamics, *Mach. Learning* 47, 1, 91-121.

[203] Rényi, A. (1961). On measures of entropy and information. *Proceedings of the Fourth Berkeley Symposium on Mathematical Statistics and Probability*, 1, Berkeley: University of California Press, 547-561.

[204] Rousseeuw, P.J. (1987). Silhouettes: a graphical aid to the interpretation and validation of cluster analysis. *Journal of Computational and Applied Mathematics*, 20, 53-65.

[205] Runkler, T.A., Bezdek, J.C. (1999). Alternating cluster estimation: a new tool for clustering and function approximation. *IEEE Transactions on Fuzzy Systems*, 7(4):377-393.

[206] Sakiyama, K., Taniguchi, M. (2004). Discriminant analysis for locally stationary processes, *Journal of Multivariate Analysis*, 90:2, 282-300.

[207] Sameni, R., Clifford, G.D., Jutten, C. and Shamsollahi, M.B. (2007). Multi-channel ECG and noise modeling: application to maternal and fetal ECG signals. *IEURASIP Journal on Advances in Signal Processing*, 14 pages. http://dx.doi.org/10.1155/2007/43407. Article ID 43407.

[208] Sarafidis, V., Weber, N. (2015). A partially heterogeneous framework for analyzing panel data, *Oxford Bulletin of Economics and Statistics*, 77, 2, 274-296.

[209] Savvides, A., Promponas, V.J. and Fokianos, K. (2008). Clustering of biological time series by cepstral coefficients based distances, *Pattern Recognition* 41, 2398-2412.

[210] Serroukh, A., Walden, A.T. and Percival, D.B. (2000). Statistical properties and uses of the wavelet variance estimator for the scale analysis of time series. *Journal of the American Statistical Association* 95: 450, 184-196.

[211] Serroukh, A., Walden, A.T. (2000). Wavelet scale analysis of bivariate time series II: statistical properties for linear processes. *Journal of Nonparametric Statistics* 13, 37-56.

[212] Scotto, M.G., Barbosa, S.M. and Alonso, A.M. (2010). Clustering time series of sea levels: extreme value approach, *J. Waterway, Port, Coastal, Ocean Eng.* 136, 2793-2804.

[213] Shumway, R.H. (2003). Time-frequency clustering and discriminant analysis. *Statist. Probab. Let.* 63, 3, 307-314.

[214] Shumway, H., Stoffer, D.S. (2016). *Time Series Analysis and Its Applications*, Springer, New York.

[215] Shumway, H., Unger, A.N. (1974). Linear discriminant functions for stationary time series, *Journal of the American Statistical Association* 69:348 948-956.

[216] Singhal, A., Seborg, D. (2005). Clustering multivariate time series data, *J. Chemometrics* 19, 427-438.

[217] Silverman, B.W. (1986). *Density Estimation for Statistics and Data Analysis.* Chapman & Hall, London.

[218] Sykacek, P., Roberts, S. (2002). Bayesian time series classification. *Advances in Neural Information Processing Systems* 14, T. G. Dietterich, S. Becker and Z. Ghahramani (eds.), 937-944, MIT Press, Boston.

[219] Takayuki, M., Takayasu, H. and Takayasu, M. (2006). Correlation networks among currencies, *Physica A.* 364, 336-342.

[220] Taniguchi, M. (1991). Third-order asymptomic properties of a class of test statistics under a local alternative, *Journal of Multivariate Analysis* 37:2, 223-238.

[221] Tarpey, T., Kinateder, K.K.J. (2003). Clustering functional data, Tarpey, Thaddeus; Kinateder, Kimberly K J., eds. *Journal of Classification*, 20.1 93-114.

[222] Taylor (2007). *Modelling Financial Time Series.* World Scientific Publishing, London.

[223] Tong, H., Dabas, P. (1990). Clusters of time series models: An example, *Journal of Applied Statistics* 17, 187-198.

[224] Tsay, R.S. (2010). *Analysis of Financial Time Series*, 3rd Edition, South-western Cenage Learning. John Wiley and Sons, Canada.

[225] University of Hawaii Sea Level Centre UHSLC, http://uhslc.soest. hawaii.edu/data/download/rq

[226] Vapnik, V.N. (1995). *The Nature of Statistical Learning Theory*, Springer-Verlag, New York, Inc., New York, NY, USA.

[227] Vilar, J.A., Pertega, S. (2004). Discriminant and cluster analysis for Gaussian stationary processes: local linear fitting approach, *Nonparametric Statistics* 16:3-4, 443-462.

[228] Vilar, J.A., Alonso, A.M., Vilar, J.M. (2010). Non-linear time series clustering based on non-parametric forecast densities. *Computational Statistics & Data Analysis.* 54, 2850-2865.

[229] Vilar, J.A., Lafuente-Rego, B., D'Urso, P. (2018). Quantile autocovariances: a powerful tool for hard and soft partitional clustering of time series, *Fuzzy Sets and Systems*, 340, 38-72.

[230] Vilar, J.A., Vilar J.M. (2013). Time series clustering based on nonparametric multidimensional forecast densities. *Electronic Journal of Statistics*, 7, 1019-1046.

[231] Vullings, H.J.L.M., Verhaegen, M.H.G., Verbruggen, H.B. (1998). Automated ECG segmentation with dynamic time warping. *Proceedings of the 20th Annual International Conference of the IEEE.*

[232] University of Hawaii Sea Level Centre UHSLC, http://uhslc.soest.hawaii.edu/data/download/rq.

[233] Wang, N., Bolstein, S. (2004). Adaptive zero-padding OFDM over frequency-selective multipath channels, *Journal of Applied Signal Processing*, 10, 1478-1488.

[234] Wang, X., Smith, R. and Hyndman, R. (2006). Characteristic-based clustering of time series data. *Data Mining and Knowledge Discovery*, 13, 335-364.

[235] Wang X., Wirth, A. and Wang, L. (2007). Structure-based statistical features and multivariate time series clustering. *Seventh IEEE International Conference on Data Mining*, 351-360.

[236] Wang, W., Zhang, Y. (2007). On fuzzy cluster validity indices. *Fuzzy Sets and Systems*, 158(19):2095-2117.

[237] Wedel, M., Kamakura, W.A. (2012). *Market Segmentation: Conceptual and Methodological Foundations*, Volume 8. Springer Science & Business Media.

[238] Wichern, D.W. (1973). The behaviour of the sample autocorrelation function for an integrated moving average process, *Biometrika* 60:2, 235-239.

[239] Wright, J.H. (2000). Alternative variance-ratio tests using ranks and signs, *Journal of Business and Economic Statistics* 18:1, 1-9.

[240] Wu, K.-L., Yang, M.-S. (2002). Alternative c-means clustering algorithms. *Pattern Recognition*, 35(10):2267-2278.

[241] Xie, X.L., Beni, G. (1991). A validity measure for fuzzy clustering. *IEEE Transactions on Pattern Analysis and Machine Intelligence*, 13(8):841-847.

[242] Xiong, Y., Yeung, D.Y. (2002). Mixtures of ARMA models for model-based time series clustering, *Proceedings of the IEEE International Conference on Data Mining*, Maebaghi City, Japan, 9-12 December, 2002.

[243] Xu, Y., Brereton, R.G. (2005). A comparative study of cluster validation indices applied to genotyping data. *Chemometrics and Intelligent Laboratory Systems*, 78(1):30-40.

[244] Xu, R., Wunsch, D.C. (2009). *Clustering*. Hoboken, New Jersey: IEEE Press, Wiley & Sons, Inc.

[245] Yang, M.-S., Wu, K.-L. (2006). Unsupervised possibilistic clustering. *Pattern Recognition*, 39(1):5-21.

[246] Young, P.C., Pedregal, D.J. and Tych, W. (1999). Dynamic harmonic regression, *Journal of Forecasting*, 18, 369-394.

[247] Zellner, A. (1962). Estimators for seemly unrelated regression equations and test of aggregation bias. *Journal of the American Statistical Association*, 57, 500-509.

[248] Zhang, D.Q., Chen, S.-C. (2004). A comment on "Alternative c-means clustering algorithms", *Pattern Recognition*, 37(2): 173-174.

[249] Zhang, D., Zuo, W. and Zhang. D. (2010). Time series classification using support vector machine with Gaussian elastic metric kernel. *Proceedings 2010 International Conference on Pattern Recognition* 29-32.

[250] Zhang, H., Ho, T.B., Zhang, Y. and Lin, M. (2005). Unsupervised feature extraction for time series clustering using orthogonal wavelet transform, *Informatica* 30, 305-319.

[251] Zakoian, J. (1994). Threshold heteroskedastic models, *Journal of Economic Dynamics and Control* 18:5, 931-955.

Subject Index

ACF, 12, 68
ACF-based metrics, 69
Agglomerative clustering, 29
Akaike's information criterion
    (AIC), 114, 119
AR, 16, 114
AR coefficients-based distance,
    114
ARCH, 17, 70
ARIMA, 16, 113
ARMA, 16, 113
ARMA mixture model, 123
Autocorrelation function (ACF),
    12
Autocorrelation-based Fuzzy
    c-means clustering model
    (A-FcM), 71
Autocovariance function, 10
Autoregressive (AR) model, 15
Autoregressive conditionally
    heteroscedastic (ARCH)
    model, 17
Autoregressive expansions, 113
Autoregressive, integrated moving
    average (ARIMA)
    model, 16
Autoregressive, moving average
    (ARMA) model, 15

Bayesian approach, 193
Bayesian information criterion
    (BIC), 114, 120
Bias-adjusted AR estimators, 119

c-Means clustering method, 33
c-Medoids clustering method, 34
Calinski and Harabasz criterion,
    35

Centroid linkage method, 32
Cepstral coefficients, 83
Cepstral-based fuzzy clustering
    model, 84
Cepstrum, 83
Chernoff discrepancy measure,
    169
Chernoff information, 96, 180
Classification, 2
Classification trees, 191
Classification using complex
    demodulation, 184
Classification using evolutionary
    wavelet spectra, 182
Classification using shapes, 183
Classification using wavelet
    variances and
    correlations, 172
Classification using wavelets
    variances, 170
Cluster validity criteria, 39
Clustering, 1
Clustering based on forecast
    densities, 121
Clustering based on the
    polarization of forecast
    densities, 122
Coiflets family of filters $CF(N)$,
    22
Complete linkage method, 32
Compression-based dissimilarity
    measures, 162
Cross validation, 167

Data mining, 153, 191
Daubechies family of filters
    $DB(N)$, 22

225

Printed in the United States
by Baker & Taylor Publisher Services